MODERN LEGAL STUDIES

THE FAMILY HOME

AUSTRALIA
The Law Book Company Ltd.
Sydney : Melbourne : Perth

CANADA AND U.S.A.
The Carswell Company Ltd.
Agincourt, Ontario

INDIA
N.M. Tripathi Private Ltd.
Bombay
and
Eastern Law House Private Ltd.
Calcutta and Delhi
M.P.P. House
Bangalore

ISRAEL
Steimatzky's Agency Ltd.
Jerusalem : Tel Aviv : Haifa

MALAYSIA : SINGAPORE : BRUNEI
Malayan Law Journal (Pte.) Ltd.
Singapore

PAKISTAN
Pakistan Law House
Karachi

MODERN LEGAL STUDIES

THE FAMILY HOME

by

W. T. MURPHY, M.A. (Cantab.)
*Lecturer in Law at the London School of
Economics and Political Science*

and

HILARY CLARK, LL.B. (Hull), LL.B. (Cantab.)
*Formerly Lecturer in Law at the
University of Hull*

LONDON
SWEET & MAXWELL
1983

Published in 1983 by
Sweet & Maxwell Limited of
11 New Fetter Lane, London.
Computerset by Promenade Graphics Limited, Cheltenham.
Printed in Great Britain by
J. W. Arrowsmith Limited,
London and Bristol.

British Library Cataloguing in Publication Data

Murphy, W.T.
    The family home.—(Modern Legal Studies)
    1. Real property—England
    I. Title   II. Clark, Hilary   III. Series
    344.2064'3   KD829

    ISBN 0-421-28740-3
    ISBN 0-421-28750-0 Pbk

PREFACE

This book is concerned with the law relating to ownership
and occupation of owner-occupied housing, and thus with
the legislative framework governing, and the judicial
approach towards resolving, disputes arising in this
context between home-owners, occupants, home-buyers
and mortgagees. It has become increasingly evident that
this is an area best understood as a zone of intersection
between property law and family law. Each has evolved
along distinct lines, each bearing the traces of its point of
origin and the marks of its successes and failures, each
compelled to reconcile any divergences which surface
between its fundamental goals and its operational difficulties. "The family home"—for want of a better term—
denotes, however uneasily and who knows for how long, a
"temporary" point of convergence between these two
"movements," each of which possesses its own logic,
momentum and objectives.

This uneasy, "convergent," status of "the family home"
as an object of legal or policy analysis creates obvious
difficulties, though most of these are common to any book
of this kind. Most obviously, any such book, even an
encyclopaedia (which this is not), presents problems of
selection. What place, for example, is there in a "law
book" for "old," now moribund, law? Must relevance—so
often equated with "current law"—serve as the only
guide? Should writers confine themselves to questions
which have already been asked—to issues on which there
is authority—or venture, sometimes, in uncharted waters?
And what kind of understanding should inform such
travels, if they are to be undertaken at all? The writers'
apprehension of their potential importance? Their "intrin-
sic" conceptual interest?

There is also a problem of perspective. How can one judge, at any particular time, which decisions will prove to be important, which will last and which will be forgotten, politely or otherwise? No doubt only time tells, but even time, for the law, is a somewhat uncontrollable matter. Some decisions are later devalued—doubted, distinguished, even overruled—but others, which may, for a while, be ignored, not spoken about, may suddenly become intensely interesting, the *fons et origo* or expression of an important principle.

This problem of perspective is nowhere more acute than in areas of rapid doctrinal or practical "shift" where the dust rarely seems to settle. Conceptual clarity is most readily achieved, by judge or commentator, in circumstances of indifference to outcome or values, or where no practical relevance is discernible. Where, however, an issue combines conceptual intricacy, value-preference and practical significance, problems of emphasis or priority inevitably result. The law relating to the family home involves just such a combination. The most perhaps that can be said is that these complexities render any form of reductionism—to values, conceptualism or pragmatism—inherently suspect. An adequate understanding requires all these elements to be kept in play.

If the allure of the present can sometimes cloud our vision, it can also lead us to disregard or be impatient with the past. Yet we work in its shadow, and it shapes our conceptual horizons, however much we may like to suppose that our values float freely, endlessly renegotiated, forged anew.

A less modest venture than the present work would tackle these problems directly; here, for the most part, we have simply endeavoured to bear them in mind.

Many people have helped, in one way or another, in the production of this book. We take this opportunity to thank, in particular, Stuart Anderson, Michael Bentley, Jane Bradford, Jane Clemetson, Bill Cornish, Fiona Crawley, Paul Fairest, Kim Gayle, Rick Rawlings and

Simon Roberts. A very special debt is owed to Alison Real, who prepared the index, for her advice and encouragement throughout. Without Pam Hodges's patience and enthusiasm, this book would never have appeared. We are deeply indebted to her for her perseverance in the face of constant authorial vacillation. The questions of our students past and present—whose insatiable thirst for clear answers is somehow never quenched—provided the stimulus to write this book. We hope we have answered some of them, or explained why no answer is available.

March 15, 1983   W.T.M.
                                                                       H.C.

NOTE

In the 1983 Budget, the Chancellor has proposed to raise the mortgage interest tax relief limit to £30,000 (see p.9) and the C.T.T. threshold to £60,000 (see p.135).

CONTENTS

Preface v
Table of Cases xi
Table of Statutes xvii
Table of Statutory Instruments xxi
Table of Rules of the Supreme Court xxi

1 The Rise of Owner-Occupation 1
2 The Origins of the Modern Legal Framework 14
3 A Share of the Equity 26
4 Protecting Occupation 80
5 Death 129
6 Priorities: Trusts 152
7 Priorities: Licences and Estoppel 181
8 Bankruptcy, Debt and Mortgage Arrears 194

Index 221

OTHER BOOKS IN THE SERIES

Anatomy of International Law (Second Edition), by J. G. Merrills

Compensation and Government Torts, by C. Harlow

Constructive Trusts, by A. J. Oakley

Council Housing (Second Edition), by David C. Hoath

Court of Justice of the European Communities (Second Edition), by L. N. Brown and F. G. Jacobs

Development Control, by J. Alder

Drugs and Intoxication, by David Farrier

Economic Torts (Second Edition), by J. D. Heydon

Exclusion Clauses in Contracts (Second Edition), by David Yates

Homelessness, by David C. Hoath

Human Rights and Europe (Second Edition), by Ralph Beddard

Immigration Law (Second Edition), by John Evans

Mortgages (Second Edition), by P. B. Fairest

Natural Justice (Second Edition), by Paul Jackson

Registered Land (Third Edition), by David J. Hayton

Remedies for Breach of Contract, by Hugh Beale

Small Businesses, by M. Chesterman

Strict and Vicarious Liability, by L. H. Leigh

The Protection of Privacy, by Raymond Wacks

Squatting, by A. Prichard

Taxation and Trusts, by G. W. Thomas

TABLE OF CASES

Amalgamated Investment and Property Co. (in liquidation) *v.*
    Texas Commerce International Bank (1981) 127
Appleton *v.* Appleton (1965) 35

Bailey, *Re* (1977) 198, 218
Balfour *v.* Balfour (1919)... 102, 106
—— *v.* Welland (1809) 178
Bannister *v.* Bannister (1948) 118, 183, 184, 186
Barclay *v.* Barclay (1970)... 95–6, 179
Barnett *v.* Hassett (1981)... 124, 179
Bedson *v.* Bedson (1965) 67
Bendall *v.* McWhirter (1952) 81, 200, 201, 208
Bernard *v.* Josephs (1982)..76, 79
Bernbaum *v.* Bernbaum (1949) 75
Beswick *v.* Beswick (1968) 150
Binions *v.* Evans (1972)....................... 118, 127, 182–5, 193, 202, 218
Bird *v.* Syme-Thompson (1979) 159
Boyle's Claim, *Re* 161
Bradley-Hole *v.* Cusen (1953) 218
Brown *v.* Brown (1981)... 79, 124
Buchanan-Wollaston's Conveyance, *Re* 63, 64, 67, 78
Bull *v.* Bull (1955)...................................... 71, 78, 93–5, 96, 178, 216
Burgess *v.* Rawnsley (1975) 138, 150
Burke *v.* Burke (1974) 65, 78
Burston Finance *v.* Godfrey (1976) 219

Carson *v.* Carson (1981) 124
Caunce *v.* Caunce (1969) 159–60, 165, 166, 167, 179
Cedar Holdings *v.* Green (1981) 173
Cetrax Trustees *v.* Ross (1979) 219
Chaffer and Randall's Contract, *Re* (1916) 178
Chandler *v.* Kerley (1978)................................104–5, 107, 127, 192
Christie, *Re* (1979) 151
Clore *v.* Theatrical Properties (1936)................................125, 181
Cobb *v.* Cobb (1955) 124
Combe *v.* Combe (1951) 127
Cook, *Re* (1948) 150
Cooke *v.* Head (1972)... 40, 43, 76
Cousins *v.* Dzosens (1981) 78, 79
Coventry, *Re* (1980) 151

Cowcher v. Cowcher (1972) 40, 41, 42, 58, 73
Crabb v. Arun District Council (1976) 127

D.H.N. Food Distributors v. Tower Hamlets London Borough
    Council (1976) 193
Daubney v. Daubney (1976) 73
Dennis v. McDonald (1981) 71–2
Densham (a bankrupt), Re (1975) 42, 43, 44, 58, 206, 218, 219
Dillwyn v. Llewehlyn (1862) 112, 115, 117, 127, 150, 219
Diwell v. Farnes (1959) 77
Dodsworth v. Dodsworth (1973) 76, 120, 122–3, 127, 128, 150
Dougall, Re (1981) 150
Dummer v. Pitcher (1832) 74
Dunford v. Dunford (1980) 124
Dyer v. Dyer (1788) 32

Ebrand v. Dancer (1680) 74
Edwardes v. Barrington (1901) 126
Elias v. Mitchell (1972) 179
Errington v. Errington and Woods (1952) 123, 150, 183, 188–9,
                                                 191, 192
Evers' Trust, Re (1980) 64, 65, 66, 78
Eves v. Eves (1975) 40, 43, 44–5, 46, 59, 67, 77, 106

Falconer v. Falconer (1970) 36
Ferris v. Weaven (1952) 123, 179
Finch v. Finch (1975) 36
First National Securities v. Hegarty (1982) 180

Gissing v. Gissing (1971) 35, 36–8, 41, 42, 43, 58, 75
Gonin, Re (1979) 127, 150
Gordon v. Douce (1983) 78
Gough, Re (1972) 218
Greasley v. Cooke (1980) 115–16, 127, 150
Grey v. Grey (1677) 74
Griffiths v. Williams (1977) 118–19, 127, 150

Halden v. Halden (1966) 124
Hall v. Hall (1971) 124
—— v. —— (1981) 59, 78
Hanlon v. Hanlon (1978) 124
Hardwick v. Johnson (1978) 102–3, 126, 182, 192, 193
Hardy's Trusts, Re (1970) 66
Harman and Uxbridge & Rickmansworth Railway Co, Re (1883) ... 178
Harnett v. Harnett (1974) 124
Harvey v. Harvey (1982) 79
Hazell v. Hazell (1972) 39
Henderson v. Eason (1847) (Chancery) 78
—— v. —— (1851) (Exch.Ch.) 125

Heseltine *v.* Heseltine (1971) 36
Hine *v.* Hine (1962)..35, 76
Hodgson *v.* Marks (1971)..160, 165
Holliday (a bankrupt), *Re* (1981)...........................66, 78, 198–9, 218
Holloway *v.* York (1877) 218
Horrocks *v.* Forray (1976)....................... 105–6, 107, 140, 150, 192
Hounslow London Borough Council *v.* Twickenham Garden
    Developments (1971) 101, 125, 128
Hunt *v.* Luck (1902) 154, 178
Hurst *v.* Picture Theatres (1915)..100–1
Hussey *v.* Palmer (1972) 40, 46, 120, 121

I.R.C. *v.* Rennell (1964) 219
Inns, *Re* (1947) 125
Inwards *v.* Baker (1965) 115, 118
Irani Finance *v.* Singh (1971) 208, 211, 219
Ives (ER) Investments *v.* High (1947)................................179, 193

Jackson *v.* Jackson (1971) 66
Jenning's Trustee *v.* King (1952) 218
Jones *v.* Challenger (1961) 63, 64, 67, 78, 125
—— *v.* Jones (1977) 67, 71, 139–40, 150
—— *v.* Padavatton (1969) 102

Kirk *v.* Webb (1698) 30

Landi, *Re*, (1939) 125
Leake *v.* Bruzzi (1974) 69, 70
Lee *v.* Lee (1952) 124
Levermore *v.* Levermore (1979) 219
Liverpool City Council *v.* Irwin (1977) 109
Lloyd *v.* Spillett (1740)..30, 32, 74
Lloyds Bank *v.* Bundy (1975) 169, 179
—— *v.* O's Trustees (1953) 150, 218
Lowne, *Re* (1981)...199, 218

McCarthy, *Re* (1975) 218
M'Mahan *v.* Burchell (1846) 78
Maddison *v.* Alderson (1883) 127
Marshall *v.* Crutwell (1875) 74
Marvin *v.* Marvin (1976)..76, 77
Mayo, *Re* (1943) 63, 64, 67
Mens *v.* Wilson (1973) 189
Mesher *v.* Mesher & Hall (Note) (1980) 124
Midland Bank *v.* Farmpride Hatcheries (1981) 219
Midland Bank Trust Co. *v.* Green (1981) 110, 171, 172, 173, 179
Miles *v.* Bull (1968) 179
Montgomery *v.* Montgomery (1965) 124

National Provincial Bank *v*. Ainsworth (1965)..........25, 81–2, 179, 181,
182, 183, 200–1, 218
National Westminster Bank *v*. Allen (1981) 219
Neilsen-Jones *v*. Fedden (1975)..138, 150
Nixon *v*. Nixon (1969) 39

Oughtred *v*. I.R.C. (1960) 77

Pascoe *v*. Turner (1979)............ 76, 117, 122–3, 126, 127, 145, 150, 187,
205, 219
Paul *v*. Constance (1977) 76
——— *v*. Paul (1882) 73
Peffer *v*. Rigg (1977) 179
Pettitt *v*. Pettitt (1970) 35, 36–8, 39, 40, 43, 54, 58, 73, 75, 77
Power's Will Trusts, *Re* (1947) 125
Practice Note (Family Division) (Matrimonial Home: Exclusion:
Injunction) (1978) 124
Pritchard *v*. Briggs (1980) 182

Rainbow *v*. Moorgate Properties (1975) 219
Ramsden *v*. Dyson (1866).............................. 112–14, 219
Rawlings *v*. Rawlings (1964) 78
Richards *v*. Dove (1974).......................................45, 76
——— *v*. Richards (1982) 124
Rider *v*. Kidder (1805) 74
Rimmer *v*. Rimmer (1953) 35, 41
——— *v*. Bailey (1942) 219
Roberts Petroleum Ltd. *v*. Bernard Kenny Ltd. (1983) 219
Robinson *v*. Bailey (1942) 219
Rogers' Question, *Re* (1948) 78
Ross *v*. Caunters (1980) 180

Savva *v*. Costa and Harymode Investments (1980) 120–1
Sharp *v*. Sharp (1981) 73
Sharpe (a bankrupt), *Re* (1980)......................121, 203, 218
Solomon, *Re* (1967) 218
Spiro *v*. Lintern (1973) 179
Steadman *v*. Steadman (1976)...........................127, 189
Stephens *v*. Hutchinson (1953) 219
Stewart *v*. Stewart (1948) 124
Strachan *v*. Strachan (1965) 124
Strand Securities *v*. Caswell (1965) 161, 179
Suttill *v*. Graham (1977) 69, 70, 78
Syer *v*. Gladstone (1885) 149

Tankard, *Re* (1942) 149
Tanner *v*. Tanner (1975).....................45, 104, 106, 107, 140, 150, 192
Taylor *v*. Taylor (1968) 168, 179

Taylor's Fashion *v.* Liverpool Victor Trustees Co. (1981) 127, 179
Tennant *v.* Trenchard (1869) 219
Terrunanse *v.* Terrunanse (1968) 150
Thomas *v.* Sorrell (1673) 97
—— *v.* Times Book Co. (1966) 77
Thompson *v.* Park (1944) 128
Turner, *Re* (1977) 218

Ulrich *v.* Ulrich and Felton (1968) 76, 77

Vandervell *v.* I.R.C. (1967) 75
Verrall *v.* Great Yarmouth Borough Council (1981) 193

Wachtel *v.* Wachtel (1973) 27
Waller *v.* Waller (1967) 125
Walsh *v.* Lonsdale (1882) 126
Warr *v.* London County Council (1904) 125
Webb *v.* Ledsam (1855) 178
—— *v.* Pollmount (1966) 193
Western Bank *v.* Schindler (1977)..................................... 214–15
Westminster Bank *v.* Lee (1956) 123
Wilkinson *v.* Hartley (1852) 178
——, *Re* (1977) 151
Williams *v.* Hensman (1861)... 137–8, 150
—— *v.* Staite (1979) 123
—— *v.* Williams (1976) 64–5, 66, 78
Williams and Glyn's Bank *v.* Boland; Same *v.* Brown (1981) 84, 158,
                                159, 160, 163, 164, 165, 166, 167, 169, 170, 174,
                                                         175, 178, 179, 214, 216
Windle, *Re* (1975) 219
Wood *v.* Leadbitter (1845).. 99, 100, 126
Woodcock (Jess B.) & Sons *v.* Hobbs (1955) 123
Wroth *v.* Tyler (1974) 124, 179

TABLE OF STATUTES

1535 Statute of Uses (26 Hen. 8, c. 10) ...29, 73

1677 Statute of Frauds (29 Cha. 2, c. 3) 30

1705 Administration of Justice Act (4 & 5 Ann., c. 3) 125

1832 Representation of the People Act (2 & 3 Will. 4, c. 45) 16

1856 Settled Estate Act (19 & 20 Vict., c. 120) 2

1857 Matrimonial Causes Act (20 & 21 Vict., c. 85)......20, 85
ss. 32, 45 25

1873 Custody of Infants Act (36 & 37 Vict., c. 12) 123

1877 Settled Estate Act (40 & 41 Vict., c. 18) 2

1878 Matrimonial Causes Act (41 & 42 Vict., c. 18) 22
s. 4 124

1881 Conveyancing Act (44 & 45 Vict., c. 41) 24, 152
s. 36 178

1882 Settled Land Act (45 & 46 Vict., c. 38) 16, 17
s. 3(i) 24
Married Women's Property Act (45 & 46 Vict., c. 75(—
s. 17 .... 27, 34–6, 66, 75, 82, 85

1886 Guardianship of Infants Act (49 & 50 Vict., c. 27) 123

1890 Intestates Estate Act (53 & 54 Vict., c. 29) 123

1893 Trustee Act (56 & 57 Vict., c. 53)...152, 178
s. 20 178

1894 Building Societies Act (57 & 58 Vict., c. 47) 5

1914 Bankruptcy Act (4 & 5 Geo. 5, c. 59) 194
s. 4 217
s. 18 196
    (1) 218
s. 26(4) 217
s. 33(1)(a),   (b); (3) 217
s. 38 218
s. 42 205–7
s. 54 218
s. 62(1) 196
s. 130 150
Sched. II 217

1925 Settled Land Act (15 & 16 Geo. 5, c. 18) 17, 92, 118, 119, 151, 155, 184, 185, 186, 187–8
s. 1 118–19
s. 13 187–8
s. 19(1) 126
s. 36 90
s. 38 24
    (1)............127, 193
ss. 65–67 24

1925 Trustee Act (15 & 16
         Geo. 5, c. 19) 172
      s. 14 ... 24, 153, 156, 157,
                    158, 170, 178

      Law of Property Act
         (15 & 16 Geo. 5,
         c. 20) 62, 151,
                    155, 172
      Pt. I 172
      s. 1 24
      s. 25 91
      s. 26(1) 178
         (3)............. 95, 156
      s. 27 ......170–1, 172, 175
      s. 30 .....61–3, 65, 66, 68,
            72, 91, 94, 119, 139,
            197–8, 204, 211, 212,
                    216
      s. 34 24
      s. 35 91
      s. 36(2) 137
      s. 40 190
         (1) 141
      s. 53(1)(*b*)..... 28, 41, 42,
                    43, 51
         (*c*) 51
         (2) 43
      s. 63(1)................ 173–4
      s. 101(1)(i) 212
      s. 103 .... 150, 212–13
      s. 149(6) 193
      s. 172 207
      s. 205(1)(xxi) 171, 172

      Land Registration Act
         (15 & 16 Geo. 5,
         c. 21) 156, 157, 174
      s. 3(xv) 174
         (*a*) 158
      s. 43 218
      s. 49 210
         (3) 158
      s. 70(1)(*g*)....... 159, 162,
            163, 174, 175, 181,
            182, 187, 188, 190
      s. 74 156–7
      s. 86(2)............ 174, 188

1925 Administration   of
         Estates Act (15 &
         16 Geo. 5, c.
         23) 18, 73, 92, 128
      s. 25 150
      s. 33(1) 149
      s. 34(1) 150
      s. 35 134
         (1),(2) 149
      s. 39(1)(i) 143
      s. 45 25
      s. 46 .... 132, 143
         (2),(3) 149
      s. 47A 149
      s. 55(1)(i), (ii), (x)   149
      Sched. 1, Pt. I .. 143, 149
            Pt.II 131,
                  134, 143
      Sched. 2, para. 1(4) 149

1933 Housing   (Financial
         Provisions)   Act
         (23 & 24 Geo. 5,
         c. 15)   5

1938 Inheritance   (Family
         Provision) Act (1
         & 2 Geo. 6, c. 45) 146

1948 Companies Act (11 &
         12 Geo. 6, c.
         38)—
      s. 187 217

1952 Intestates' Estates Act
         (15 & 16 Geo. 6 &
         1 Eliz. 2, c. 64) 132
      Sched. 2 133
            para. 1(1)   149
            para. 4(1),
            (3), (5) 149

1964 Law of Property (Joint
         Tenants) Act (c.
         63) 150

1965 Matrimonial   Causes
         Act (c. 72)—
      ss. 27–28A 146

1966 Family Provision Act
         (c. 35) 149

1967 Matrimonial Homes
      Act (c. 75) ...82, 83–4,
             85, 158, 159, 164,
             177, 179, 180
      s. 1 85
         (1) 124
         (5) 215
      s. 2 83
         (5) 83
      Leasehold Reform Act
         (c. 88) 2

1969 Family Law Reform
      Act (c. 46)—
      s. 14 149

1970 Administration of Jus-
      tice Act (c. 31)—
      s. 36 .... 149, 215
         (1).............213–14
      s. 39(1) 219
      Matrimonial Proceed-
      ings and Property
      Act (c. 45) 26, 83
      s. 37 ....75, 76

1971 Administration   of
      Estates Act (c.
      25)—
      s. 9 150

1972 Finance Act (c. 41)—
      s. 75 56
      Land Charges Act (c.
      61) 166, 171, 172
      s. 1(6) 164
      s. 4(6) 171
      s. 6 210
      s. 17(1) 164

1973 Administration of Jus-
      tice Act (c. 15)—
      s. 8(1) 214
      Matrimonial   Causes
      Act (c. 18) 21, 26,
             66, 103, 206
      s. 24 ....35, 65, 70, 73, 85
      s. 25 39
      s. 31 73
      s. 39 219

1974 Finance Act (c. 30)—
      Sched. 1, para. 4(1)
         (a), (4) 77
             para. 5(1)   77

1975 Finance Act (c. 7) 135
      s. 37(3) 149
      Sched. 6, para. 1(1)   149
      Inheritance (Provision
      for Family and
      Dependants) Act
      (c. 63) 132, 145–9
      s. 1(1)(a) 150
         (b), (c), (d)   151
         (2)(a), (b), (c),
         (e) 151
         (3) 147
      s. 2 148
      s. 3 147
      s. 9 148
      s. 10 148–9
         (2)(a) 151
      s. 15 151

1976 Finance Act (c. 40) 149
      Domestic   Violence
      and Matrimonial
      Proceedings Act
      (c. 50) 86

1978 Domestic Proceedings
      and Magistrates'
      Courts Act (c. 22)   86
      Employment Protec-
      tion (Consolida-
      tion) Act (c. 44)—
      ss. 121–127 217

1979 Charging Orders Act
      1979 (c. 53) 208–11
      s. 2....................208–9
         (1)(a)(ii) 208
         (b)(ii) 208–9
         (iii) 209
      s. 3(3) 208
         (4) 219

1980 Limitation Act (c.
      58) ...122, 128, 145, 150

1981 Matrimonial   Homes
          and Property Act
          (c. 24) 83, 215
      s. 4 .... 124, 158
      s. 7 66

      Finance Act (c. 35)—
          s. 24 77
          s. 92(1)(*a*) 149
          Sched. 13 149
1982 Finance Act (c. 39)—
          s. 91 149

TABLE OF STATUTORY INSTRUMENTS

1980   Supplementary Ben-
        efits (Requirem-
        ents) Regulations
        (S.I. 1980 No. 1229)
        regs. 14(1)(*b*), 16 ...   13
1981   Family Provision (In-
        testate   Succes-
        sion) Order
        (S.I. 1981 No. 82) ... 149

1981   Family Provision (In-
        testate   Succes-
        sion) Order
        (S.I. 1981 No. 255)   149

TABLE OF RULES OF THE SUPREME COURT

1937   Rules of the Supreme
        Court (No. 3)
        (S.R. & O. 1937 No.
        1150)
        O. 54, rr. 12A, 22A   75

1965   Rules of the Supreme
        Court (Revision)
        (S.I. 1965 No. 1776)
        O.88 219

"If a healthy race is to be reared, it can be reared only in healthy homes; if infant mortality is to be reduced and tuberculosis to be stamped out, the first essential is the improvement of housing conditions; if drink and crime are to be successfully combated, decent, sanitary houses must be provided. If "unrest" is to be converted into contentment, the provision of good houses may prove one of the most potent agents in that conversion."

George V, *The Times*, April 12, 1919.

Chapter 1

THE RISE OF OWNER-OCCUPATION

(1) *Introduction*

In the nineteenth century, only a small percentage of homes were occupied by their owners. Today over 50 per cent. of homes are owner-occupied, about half of which have oustanding mortgages and the vast majority of which having been acquired by means of an instalment mortgage, usually obtained from a building society. This transformation is of crucial importance for understanding how and why the law of the family home has developed as it has.

Industrialisation and population growth in the nineteenth century fuelled the demand for houses, especially in the rapidly growing urban area. But building in the nineteenth century was largely for private renting. In some parts of the country, this was co-ordinated by large, aristocratic landowners. In Edgbaston near Birmingham, for example, the Calthorpe family over a long period developed a large suburban estate. In Huddersfield, for most of the nineteenth century, development was in the control of the Ramsden family. Mayfair was owned by the Grosvenor family, and The Park in Nottingham was owned by the Newcastles. Such landowners tended to control quite carefully the layout and tenor of these estates. Not all significant development involved major landowners: a notable example of smallscale piecemeal development was the building of Hampstead.[1]

Although large landowners played an important role in the development of housing estates, this did not mean that housebuilding itself took place on a large scale. Speculative building on a relatively small scale seems to have been more common.[2]

The traditional pattern involved the landowner granting a building lease to speculative builders.[3] In some cases their ability to do so was hampered by settlements of their land, in which case either a Private Act was needed or a breaking of the settlement until the Settled Estate Acts implied such powers (though permitting exclusion by the settlor).[4] Where the building lease, usually for 99 years, was used, the builder would construct housing, paying a ground rent to the landowner, and once built, the builder could let the house or sell the lease. The landowner's right to regain the unencumbered freehold at the end of the lease lasted unimpaired until the Leasehold Reform Act 1967. Estate planning was possible by a landowner laying out an estate, even where a number of different builders were involved, by the insertion of covenants in the leases, to attempt to ensure uniformity or complementarity in layout and design.

For the duration of the building lease, there would thus be a form of split ownership, with the landowner entitled to his ground rent and the owner of the lease entitled to the higher occupancy rent for the duration of the term. The occupant would commonly rent from the owner of the lease, often on a short term. Status conscious Victorians considered it undesirable to have a lease for more than two or three years, so that as the circumstances of the family improved it would be possible to move to higher quality accommodation.[5]

Thus in the nineteenth century, although owner-occupation of the home was not unknown and indeed became more common in the course of the century, there was by no means as firm a link as today between ownership and occupation of the home.[6] But houses were in a significant way a source of revenue through rents for their owners either in the form of ground rents or occupancy rents; in other words, for many of the "propertied classes," houses or the land on which they were built, comprised part of the family property and might well be settled on trust to provide a secure income[7];

a very different picture from the contemporary one in which the home comprises the only significant capital asset of the family, and is not, for most of the owner's life cycle, an asset which normally yields an income.

This pattern was transformed in the twentieth century. Building for sale became more common, and few landowners in England sought to emulate their predecessors and develop housing estates in which they retained ground rents. So far as large aristocratic landowners were concerned, their planning and coordinating role was increasingly usurped by local councils and the growth of regulatory public health and planning controls.[8] Equally, as reversions fell in, property came to be transferred to the owner-occupied sector. These movements were part of the general decline of the private rented sector, which was spurred on by the introduction and retention of rent control and statutory security of tenure. Thus in the twentieth century, fewer and fewer new houses were built for private renting, while at the same time, existing properties were progressively transferred from private renting to owner-occupation. This has not been unequivocally beneficial, either for the housing stock or the occupants, as the impact of this change upon some inner city areas like Saltley vividly illustrates.[9]

This shift towards owner-occupation cannot adequately be explained solely with reference to the impact of the Rent Acts. While rent control did influence the objectives of speculative builders, other forces were at work in the first three decades of this century which led to much developed and undeveloped land coming on to the market for the first time. In particular, the great landowners withdrew on a large scale. The Ramsdens sold their whole estate to Huddersfield Corporation in 1920; the Westminsters sold off parts of their Mayfair estates and many other London landowners disposed of some or all of their estates. What led to these changes is disputable; the general climate for private landownership by individual families had become less favourable—the enactment of estate duty in 1894; the threat of a tax on land values, finally introduced in the People's Budget[10]; the rise of local government and the corresponding erosion of initiative and independence on the part of landowners. The pace and predictability of change was such that many landowners were less willing than in the nineteenth century to plan long-term (a strategy which was inherent in the notion of the building lease) and what took place represented a "conscious decision to restructure and rationalise their assets."[11] The less indebted of the landowners who sold invested their proceeds in colonial and overseas shares.[12] The withdrawal of many large landowners and the marked decline of the employment of the building lease, greatly increased the supply of land for owner-occupation development. But what made it possible, in a climate in which owners wished to sell, for owner-occupation to develop on the scale in which it did was the spectacular growth of the building society movement, accomplished with active government support from the end of the First World War.

(2) *The rise of the building society and home ownership*[13]

As the name indicates, a building society was originally an association of individuals who came together in order to build houses. The early societies were "terminating" societies. The members would subscribe regular contributions in order to build a house each time sufficient money had been contributed. Each accumulated fund would be allocated, usually by ballot, to one of the members, who would be advanced the money as a loan in order to build a house for his own occupation or for renting. Such societies had a limited lifespan, and a small number of members.

The origin of the modern building society is to be found in the shift to permanent societies, which dates from 1845. Such societies are permanent lending and saving institutions, competing with other institutions such as banks to attract savings, and lending some of their funds on the security of mortgages. These societies had a chequered start: between 1874–1894 for example, there were many failures, often due to defective securities and malpractice on the part of officers, the most spectacular of which being the fall of the Liberator in 1892. These failures led to spasmodic government regulation to curb abuses, most significantly in the Building Societies Act 1894. A further setback occurred in 1911 with the fall of the Birkbeck Society. This pattern of collapses and recoveries left its distinctive mark upon the main form of state regulation of the societies. Successive statutes have been designed primarily to protect investors. Thus they have regulated the kinds of securities upon which building societies can lend, the amount of liquidity they must maintain, and the kinds of borrowers to whom they can lend. Even today, regulation of access to home purchase finance is minimal.[14]

It was only after the First World War that the societies came into their own. Post-war governments promoting house building and subsidised private house-building as well as building by local authorities. The boom period was in the 1930's; funds flowed into the societies, which were attractive because of their security and interest rates relative to company shares or government securities. As real income rose for those in work, falling prices and building costs fuelled the supply of houses, while public sector expansion was curtailed by withdrawal of government subsidies under the 1933 Housing Act. Building societies embarked upon an extensive campaign to promote home ownership, and in this wave of expansion mortgages became cheaper and easier in order to widen the net of those who could afford to take them on— mortgage terms were extended in length, and mechanisms were devised to increase the percentage loan which a borrower might raise, in collaboration with insurance companies or speculative builders keen to sell the houses they built.[15] As a result of these changes, owner-occupation rose from 10 per cent. in 1914 to somewhere between 25 per cent. and 33 per cent. in 1938. During the same period, total building society assets rose from £76m in 1910 to £756m in 1940 (an increase of 400 per cent. in constant prices) while the number of societies fell from 1,723 to 952, a process of concentration and amalgamation which has continued to the present day.

Until this boom between the wars, building societies had largely been indifferent to whether building was for renting or owning. The link between building socieities and home ownership was forged in these boom years, and from that time on, building societies and their Association have become the main proponents and advocates of the ideology of home ownership. After the Second World War, a Labour Government was returned committed to expansion of the public sector. Though from 1945 to 1951 private building was stagnant, building societies thrived on the business generated by sales of existing houses by private landlords, spurred on by the continuation of rent control. Under the succeeding Conservative Governments, owner occupation and the building societies thrived. It should, however, be noted that there were significant regional disparities in these developments, which still apply today. While 53·6 per cent. of the total housing stock in 1977 was owner-occupied, the figure was only 34·1 per cent. in Scotland, 47·5 per cent. in Greater London, and over 60 per cent. in the south east (excluding London) and the South West.

The building societies dominate the provision of finance for loan purchase (from 64 per cent. of net amounts loaned in 1959 to 95 per cent. in 1978) and are one of the major institutions for investment from the personal sector (an average of 29 per cent. between 1966 and 1978, though fluctuating considerably—21 per cent. in 1974, 39 per cent. in 1977) and their assets were about 28 per cent. of the total assets of all institutions holding mainly personal savings in 1978, rivalled only by insurance companies.

Moreover, increasing concentration of assets has led to

a relatively small number of societies effectively forming policy. Out of a total of 339 societies in 1977, the five largest (The Halifax, Abbey National, Nationwide, Leeds Permanent and The Woolwich) held 53·6 per cent. of all building society assets, and the largest 20 societies held around 84 per cent. Lending policies, given the importance of these societies, not only affect who can enter the market, but have considerable impact upon the provision of housing generally. The 1977 Green Paper[16] envisaged an even more significant role for the societies in the future, contemplating that the owner-occupied sector will comprise 58·8 per cent. of the total housing stock by 1986.

As a result, building societies exercise a great influence over effective demand in the housing market, that is, over the demand for houses which can be realised in practice. The societies' main sources of funds from which new loans are provided are net receipts of investment, mortgage repayments of capital sums advanced and interest on outstanding mortgages. The last two are relatively stable over time, but net receipts (investments minus withdrawals) are increasingly unstable.

Integration into the general finance market has meant that building societies are increasingly vulnerable to fluctuations in interest rates, and subject to these fluctuations, face increased competition for investment from other institutions. Although, as we have seen, building societies are one of the primary destinations for personal sector savings, fluctuations in receipts (*e.g.* 39 per cent. of total personal sector savings of £1,916m in 1977, only 26 per cent. of £2.130m in 1978) render the supply of finance for home purchase irregular and unpredictable. It has been argued that the resulting instability of effective demand has its own impact upon the structure of the construction industry, which is characterised by labour intensity, low capital investment and a high level of subcontracting; and the instability also leads to a slow and cautious response by builders to changes in demand.[17]

In the short term, the movement of house prices is

strongly influenced by the availability of mortgages. Thus, when interest rates are low and the building society share rate is attractive to investors, the funds of societies tend to swell, and more money is available for lending on mortgages. When this happens, effective demand is increased, and house prices tend to rise. This pattern lay behind the 1972–73 boom in house prices, which rose by 31 per cent. in 1972 and by 35 per cent. in 1973, to be followed by a slump in lending as interest rates rose sharply in late 1973. Over a time, the ratio of house prices to annual earnings has remained fairly constant (from just over 3:1 in 1956 to over 7:2 in 1976), but in the boom of 1972–73, the ratio surged to nearer 9:2.

(3) *The structure of home purchase finance*

Common to most forms of mortgage available is the object of spreading acquisition costs through time. For the duration of the loan, interest will be payable to the lender on the outstanding capital. The overall effect is that, since normally the size of periodic payments are fixed at the outset, on the assumption that wages rise, the burden of repayment relative to income diminishes through time.

The most common repayment device is the capital repayment mortgage (66 per cent. of new loans in 1978 were made in this way). Payments are made to the society each month, the amount being fixed in advance. These repayments comprise both capital and interest outstanding on the unrepaid capital advanced. Therefore in early years, since interest will be high, most of the periodic repayment will be interest and only a small amount capital. As capital debt is reduced, so the interest component in the period payment will be less, permitting the borrower to make correspondingly greater progress in reducing the capital debt.

The second main type of mortgage, the endowment mortgage, combines an insurance element. The borrower only pays interest to the society on the capital advanced;

to pay off the capital, periodic payments are made to an insurance company for an endowment policy which runs for the length of the mortgage, yielding a capital sum at the end of the period from which the capital due is paid.

(4) *Tax subsidies*

Although building societies are not directly controlled by the state (though their powers are restricted by law), home ownership is subsidised by the state, especially by means of exemption from various kinds of taxation.

(a) Income tax

The interest payments on capital payment mortgages are deducted from gross income; that is, they are effectively paid out of untaxed rather than taxed income. This particularly benefits higher-tax payers, though since 1974 relief has been confined to interest on loans of £25,000 maximum and in respect of the principal residences of the taxpayer (or of a dependent relative of a divorced or separated wife). On endowment mortgages, further tax relief is available in respect of the insurance premium component.

(b) Capital gains tax

Increases in house prices mean that in the course of a few years, a home owner, even with an outstanding loan on the property, will stand to make a substantial capital gain on a sale. Since 1965, when capital gains were first taxed, the gain realised on a sale of the main or sole residence has been exempted from tax.

(c) Imputed rental income

One of the advantages of home ownership is that the owner does not have to pay rent to occupy his home.

Thus, use of the house involves a cash benefit in the form of the saved rent which the owner would otherwise have to pay. Until 1963, owner-occupiers paid tax under Schedule A on the imputed rent (which was based on out-dated valuations of the market rent). This was abolished in 1963, and since that time tax is payable only on actual rental income and not on imputed income. This exemption, combined with the tax relief in respect of mortgage interest, means that owner-occupiers are treated more favourably than tenants, whose rent is not tax deductible but must be paid out of taxed income.

(5) *Other government involvement*

Government involvement in the promotion of owner-occupation goes beyond subsidising home ownership through tax concessions. Although we have indicated that building societies are vulnerable to general fluctuations in the finance market, they are to some extent "sheltered" by comparison with other institutions. First, building societies enjoy various tax advantages over their competitors. Secondly, they have in the past been excluded from various credit controls which have been imposed upon banks and other financial institutions. In 1973 and 1974, when net receipts slumped, the government provided direct financial assistance to the societies.

Apart from these privileges and support of societies by the state, informal mechanisms have been developed with a view to controlling the supply of loan finance and achieving greater stability. In 1975, the Building Societies Association–Government Joint Advisory Committee (set up in 1973) agreed to make periodic estimates of the appropriate level of lending and to try to ensure that individual societies did not exceed these limits. Until 1978, actual lending did not reach the level of the periodic estimates, but in 1978, and the beginning of 1979, the Committee agreed a policy of self-restraint in artificially limiting the amount of loans made in response to the government's fear about a further price explosion.

(6) *The significance of owner-occupation*

The success of the promotion by successive governments and the building society movement of the goal of home-ownership is undeniable. But is the change to home-ownership merely one of form or also a change of substance? For the duration of the mortgage, the "home owner" is effectively paying rent to a financial institution. As Karl Renner wrote in a slightly different context "mortgage and lease . . . in most cases are nothing but two forms of the same thing."[18] From this point of view, the distinction between the private rented sector and owner-occupation is largely formal, and the primary significance of the change which has taken place relates rather to the character of the "effective owner." From this perspective, landowners and speculative builders are displaced by increasingly concentrated financial institutions as effective owners. The point is not without significance for the development of the law: if we take the view that "home ownership" is little more than a matter of form, it may be inappropriate to invoke the freedom or rights of private property in the course of resolving disputes concerning the family home.

Of course, for the duration of the mortgage, the owner occupier is paying a rent.[19] Equally, both lease and mortgage provide formal mechanisms whereby capital can control the conduct of the occupant and the use the occupant makes of the property. But over a longer time span, the growth of owner occupation may prove to have significant consequences. In the nineteenth century the family home was in no sense a capital asset for many occupying families. Inter-generational financial security was usually achieved through the preservation of a guaranteed income by means of family settlements, in which capital in the form of funds or houses was preserved and transmitted from one generation to another. In this respect owner occupation is different. Through the instalment mortgage the family is able in the course of a generation to acquire a capital asset in such a way that family income is transformed through time into family capital. If family inheritance takes place largely within the core members of the family unit, the family, after two generations of separately funded home acquisition, is likely to have accumulated significant capital for transmission to the third and fourth generations. So long as investment in homes continues to be one of the most secure and attractive forms of long-term capital appreciation, the increased supply of funds could fuel demand for homes and further increase house price inflation. Such a trend could increase the disparities in opportunity between those who have substantial deposits through inheritance and those who without such deposits have much greater difficulty in entering home ownership. Recent estimates suggest that the amounts in question are now quite considerable—in 1976 35 per cent. (£1,770m) of building society lending went to purchasers of existing housing which was not being sold by owner occupiers who were moving. The sales, in other words, were mainly sales of the homes of deceased owners. However, this pattern of capital accumulation may be offset where home owners choose to decapitalise towards the end of their lives, for example on retirement, by turning a capital asset into a supplementary income. The recent growth of a market in annuities is a part of this countervailing trend.

Notes to pages 1–12

[1] See generally David Cannadine, *Lords and Landlords: The Aristocracy and the Towns 1774–1967* (1980). See also C. Stephenson, *The Ramsdens and their Estate in Huddersfield* (1972); K.C. Edwards, "The Park Estate, Nottingham" in M.A. Simpson and T.H. Lloyd (eds.), *Middle Class Housing in Britain* (1977); F.M.L. Thompson, *Hampstead: Building a Borough 1650–1964* (1974).

The prevalence of aristocratic landownership may have been less than was assumed in the turn of the century political debates: see Cannadine, "Urban Development in England and America in the Nineteenth Century" Econ.Hist.Rev., 2nd ser. XXXIII (1980), 309 and Avner Offer, *Property and Politics 1870–1914* (1981). A good example of anti-landlord polemic is Frederick Pollock, *The Land Laws* (1896), pp. 156 *et seq.*

[2] Cannadine, *op. cit.* Chap. 26.

[3] The 90 year building lease was particularly common in London and was sometimes called the "London Lease." Whether the effects of the system were good or bad was much contested; compare the Majority of Minority views of the *Select Committee on Town Holdings* (P.P. 1888, XXII).

[4] Settled Estate Acts 1856 and 1877.

[5] John Burnett, *Social History of Housing 1815–1970* (1980).

[6] Thus as late as 1914, the Land Enquiry Committee observed: "A small minority only of the actual occupiers of property are also the owners of it," *The Land* Vol. II Rural (1914), p. 348.

[7] Technically, the house is owned by the owner of the land. But in the urban context, for practical purposes, a distinction can be drawn between "owning" the ground rent (*i.e.* the land) and the occupancy rent (*i.e.* the building for the duration of the lease). References to "freeholders" in the historical literature refer to people who had the rental income from both. For present purposes, it is the prevalence of rental income which is important, rather than the different forms such income assumed.

[8] Cannadine, *op. cit.* Chap. 27.

[9] Ann Stewart, *Housing Action in an Industrial Suburb* (1981); Benwell Community Project, *Private Housing and the Working Class* (1978).

[10] For the political resonances, see Douglas, *Land People and Politics* (1976), Chap. 8.

[11] Cannadine, *op. cit.* p. 424.

[12] *ibid.* See also F.M.L. Thompson, *English Landed Society in the Nineteenth Century* (1963), pp. 307–308.

[13] See especially Cleary, *The Building Society Movement* (1965) and Boddy, *The Building Societies* (1980), upon which the following account draws heavily.

[14] See Boddy, *op. cit.* Chap. 5.

[15] See, for example, Jackson, *Semi-Detached London* (1973).

[16] *Housing Policy: a consultative document*, Cmnd. 6851 (1977).

[17] See Boddy, *op. cit.* pp. 95–98.

[18] *The Institutions of Private Law and their Social Functions* (Kahn-Freund ed.) (1949), p. 158.

[19] At least as regards interest payments to the lender—as recognised in social security law: see reg. 14(1) (*b*) and reg. 16, Supplementary Benefits (Requirements) Regulations 1980 (S.I. 1980 (S.I. 1980 No. 1299).

Chapter 2

THE ORIGINS OF THE MODERN LEGAL FRAMEWORK

Two distinct streams of twentieth century legal development converge around the family home—the reform of the land laws and the formulation of a code of family law. The shape of these distinct but overlapping bodies of law was obviously affected by the conditions in which they emerged.

A. SETTLEMENTS AND LAND LAW REFORM

The corollary of the small scale of owner-occupation of houses in the nineteenth century was, as we have suggested, the extensive use of private renting. This pattern of nineteenth century property relations left its imprint upon the design of land law reform. Since most land, farms as well as houses, was occupied by tenants, the majority of owners of land enjoyed their property in the form of rent. We have briefly considered the different forms of rent—farm rents and urban ground rents (associated particularly with the landed aristocracy and gentry) or capitalist occupation rents enjoyed by speculative builders and purchasers of long leases or freeholds. We must now introduce a further, pervasive dimension of these traditional property relations—the prevalence of different forms of settlement of rental income.

   Two features of such settlements stand out. First, they provided a mechanism for the transmission of the family property on or before death from one generation to another.[1] Secondly, they provided a legal form in which the family property—especially its rental income—could be apportioned between the members of the family. Although the evidence suggests that a wide variety of

14

forms of settlement were employed, we can distinguish two broad types of settlement.

The basic distinction was between partible and impartible inheritance. Impartible inheritance—or strict settlement—aimed at ensuring that the family estates devolved through the senior male line. This involved considerable complexities in drafting such settlements, since the conveyancer had to think ahead and consider how the estates should devolve should this or that contingency arise. In the normal case, such settlements were made on the marriage or coming of age of the eldest son, and were intended to last at least a generation.[2] Provision for other family members was enshrined in the settlement in the form of various charges, which would be paid either directly out of the income of the tenant for life or by mortgages raised, in effect, by anticipating future income.[3]

Since one of the central objectives behind such settlements was to ensure that the settled lands remained in the family, it was necessary to limit the ability of the head of the family for the time being to dispose of the land. This was inherent in the use of a series of successive entails which established an order of priority as to who would succeed on the death of the head of the family, who would normally have under the settlement a legal life estate in possession which enabled him to take the rental income as it arose (subject to the family charges diverting income elsewhere). The legal title was thus fragmented into a series of successive legal estates. Unless the tenant for life was expressly given a power of sale, it would be difficult to alienate the land for the duration of the settlement unless a Private Act of Parliament was obtained.

By contrast, partible inheritance involved the apportionment of rental income, usually on an equal basis, among the next generation. It was commonly associated with settlements of personalty, but also with the use of a tenancy in common of the freehold or leasehold estate. Where this form of settlement was practised, the share in the rental income could itself become subject to a subsequent settlement, as well as being mortgaged or sold. This form of settlement thus involved a different kind of fragmentation of title, where, if a fee simple or entail was held in common, the title could come, through time, to be vested in an ever expanding group of individuals, and became increasingly difficult or hazardous to sell on the market.[4]

Settlement was rooted in a system of property relations where a central concern was the security and predictability of the return upon capital, and when the ownership of property meant the right to an income from the property. The reform of the land laws was aimed at simplifying the conveyancing difficulties which these settlements generated without altering the systems of family ownership as such. In dynastic settlements the price paid was the loss of inalienability.

In the nineteenth century, the idea of such reforms had been controversial and politicised. Both before and after the 1832 Reform Act, political power was, to a considerable extent, concentrated in the hands of the aristocracy and gentry and the basis of their power was seen to lie in their possession of landed estates which were, through the practice of primogeniture and entail, enabled to pass from generation to generation without being broken up. Not only were these features of settlement said to consolidate the power of the landed classes, but they were thought to impede agricultural and urban development because of the limited powers of the tenant for life, requiring an expensive Private Act in order to override the settlement. Nineteenth century reformers generally succeeded in getting legislation passed which overrode the fetters imposed by settlement, culminating in the Settled Land Act 1882, which gave the tenant for life a power to sell land held in strict settlement. More radical (if symbolic) attempts to 'abolish' primogeniture came to nothing.[5]

Whatever the political resonances of the reform of the strict settlement in the nineteenth century, the issue of reform had become by the twentieth largely a technical matter for conveyancers. This technical issue did acquire a certain political momentum of its own, focussed around the solicitors' monopoly over land transfer,[6] but the political dimension concerning the power and influence of the landed interest was absent. This was partly because the connection between landownership and political power had diminished[7] and partly because the attack on the landed interest came to centre around taxation policy rather than the elimination of primogeniture and entail.[8]

In part, the 1925 code conveyancing reforms simply effected further modifications of what was achieved in the reforms of the 1880s.[9] But a more concerted attempt was made to tackle the conveyancing difficulties resulting from the practices of settling real estate which we have already outlined. Thus, whereas, for political reasons, the strict settlement had been at the core of the debates on reform in the previous century, the uncontentious tenancy in common constituted a major concern of the architects of the 1925 code. One of these, Sir Arthur Underhill, was explicit on this point[10]:

> " . . . my experience is that settlements with all their complexities give less trouble in investigation of title than the tenancy in common, which, after all, is substantially a settlement on people concurrently instead of successively, but without a tenant for life with whom one can deal under the Settled Land Act."

The strategy of the technical reformers was based upon a number of key changes. First, the number of legal estates was reduced to two.[11] Thereafter, the successive interests contained in a strict settlement would operate in equity only. The legal title was to be vested in the tenant for life, who would have a largely unfettered ability to sell and give a good title.[12] Secondly, the maximum number of concurrent holders of a legal estate was limited to four,[13] which was linked with a third element, the abolition of the legal tenancy in common.[14] Thenceforth, tenancies in common would take effect by means of some kind of trust; purchasers would have to deal only with a limited number of trustees, who would be in a position to give a good title on transfer. In both cases, the new system was buttressed by the principle of overreaching.[15] This would ensure that purchasers took free of the claims of beneficiaries and were not required and indeed were unable to investigate the position of the beneficiaries behind the trust. The beneficiaries were safeguarded by requiring that the purchaser would only be protected if he had a receipt for the purchase money from two trustees.[16] As Holdsworth percipiently observed, this, along with other legislative changes, beginning in the 1880s, led to the increased importance of equity; thenceforth, possession of the legal estate merely denoted the ability to give title, and all questions of substantial ownership became the province of equity.[17]

In succeeding chapters, we will examine in detail the types of trust employed in the 1925 scheme. For the moment, it is sufficient to recall that the reforms, and therefore the structure of the 1925 code, were aimed at rationalising the conveyancing difficulties arising out of settlements of rental income. The use of the trust substituted a trustee-beneficiary relationship for a common law relationship, and made questions of rent entitlement largely equitable. The only significant change in 1925 in the substance rather than the form of property rights concerned the changes in the rules of intestate succession in the Administration of Estates Act 1925, whereby the old distinction between personalty and realty was abolished, and the rules relating to personalty made to apply to land as well. In this limited sense, primogeniture in respect of land was 'abolished.'[18] The 1925 code was thus neither premised upon the existence of mass owner-occupation, nor aimed at providing a legal framework to govern such a pattern of ownership.

This brief discussion of the 1925 code and its objectives

suggests that it was not concerned to provide a conveyancing regime tailored to the needs of the modern owner occupied sector. Rather, the code was constructed against the background of the late Victorian and Edwardian system of family property law.[19] This raises difficult questions about the proper approach to interpretation of the code in present-day conditions and in particular should encourage a certain caution in speaking of "the policy of 1925" in the context of disputes concerning the family home. Nor is there any reason to suggest a close correlation between the conveyancing reforms and the rise of owner occupation. The code reached the statute book at a time when the upswing in owner occupation and building society activity was already under way. The yet more dramatic upsurge in the 1930s was more influenced by economic factors and the promotion of home ownership than the elimination of problems of title. Equally, the shift in the form of tenure from short leasehold to freehold or long leasehold is more connected with the withdrawal of the landed interest than with changes in the law. Indeed the most important contribution which law reform has made to the transformation of land ownership in Britain was those reforms aimed at granting statutory powers to tenants for life under strict settlements. In this respect the withdrawal of the landed interest especially from urban land would have taken place in the 1880s if the land market had been sufficiently buoyant.[20] This is not to say that the reduction in the fragmentation of legal title achieved by the 1925 code did not reduce the potential hazards involved in land transfer. The simplification of conveyancing, especially with regard to the period of search and the execution of mortgages, must have facilitated the growth of owner occupation, but this can be exaggerated. In particular, it is to be noted that while "drudgery relief" reduced the workload involved in completing land transfer, it was accompanied by an improvement in the fees lawyers were able to charge for their services.[21]

B. THE FAMILY LAW CODE

It is probably fair to suggest that the main features of the modern law governing owner-occupation emerged most sharply in the operation of a quite different stream of legal development—the experience of matrimonial disputes, which has left its mark upon the shape of the modern law.

The area of family law which has most significantly impinged upon home ownership is the approach to financial provision and property adjustment on divorce. The statutory law in this field goes back to vesting the courts with a complete jurisdiction over questions of civil divorce, initiated in the Matrimonial Causes Act 1857. The statutory framework for financial provision on divorce, which remained, in formal terms, unchanged until 1970, was rooted in practices of settlement which became increasingly unworkable with the growth of mass owner-occupation on the one hand and large-scale divorce on the other.

In many ways, the mid-nineteenth century code mirrored the practices enshrined in marriage settlements by giving the courts power to order adjustments in the organisation of family income on the dissolution of the marriage.[22] While, in the nineteenth century and for much of this century, the question of divorce and the grounds on which it could be obtained or denied were the main source of controversy, the problems consequent upon divorce were essentially questions of income redistribution between the former spouses which were the converse of settlement. So far as this question was concerned, the position of the courts was not greatly different whether faced with a separation or a divorce. Thus, divorce was not simply *confined* in practice to the upper classes (because of the expense of litigation, etc.); it was designed for the upper classes and gave expression to their aspirations and concerns. In this sense, its emphasis upon maintenance—income security—for the divorced wife, while signalling the dependency of upper class women, was rooted in the particular social reality of settlement.

Now since, as we have already suggested, private renting was the dominant mode of tenure until the years between the wars, it is perhaps obvious that maintenance awards or alimony were quite compatible with the form of housing provision. On a divorce, when one household became two, the residential consequences of divorce were not especially intricate or complex. By the 1950s with the spread of owner-occupation, the focus upon maintenance came to seem anachronistic, and to run up against a serious practical difficulty—the disposition of the former matrimonial home.

The spread of divorce after the war, facilitated in part by the availability of legal aid from 1949,[23] meant that a régime aimed at the needs and practices of the wealthy of an earlier time had to be used to make adjustments consequent upon the break-up of a working class or lower middle class marriage. Here, the only family income would be earned income and the only capital asset would be the family home acquired or being acquired on an instalment mortgage, that is, by means of earned income. Moreover, the capital asset—the home—did not yield or produce the family income. The position was reversed; the family income—wages and salaries—produced, went to purchase the family asset. At the time of divorce, that process of acquisition would often still be in motion.

Thus, disputes about the ownership and occupation of the matrimonial home came increasingly to be intertwined with marital breakdown, until, under the new code (now contained in the Matrimonial Causes Act 1973) the courts were empowered to make a property adjustment order on divorce, the main subject-matter of which would normally be the former matrimonial home.

Children

The other dimension to the evolution of modern family law is the increased concern of the state with the preservation and welfare of children, commonly through the agency of the mother. Apart from the somewhat distinct concerns of the Poor Law, this orientation can be traced back to the establishment of the "alternative jurisdiction" for matrimonial disputes—the use of magistrates' or "police" courts, inaugurated in the Matrimonial Causes Act 1878. This empowered magistrates' courts to make orders that a wife was not obliged to cohabit with a husband convicted of criminal assault upon her. The scheme of this Act—separation order, maintenance order and custody of children vested in wife—became the model for a frequently expanded jurisdiction contained in the Summary Jurisdiction (Separation and Maintenance) Acts 1895 to 1949. These reforms aimed at ameliorating the conditions of working class families, with particular emphasis upon the conditions of life of wives and children. They also marked the beginnings of a complex network of surveillance of the family by different "expert" institutions. The orientation of these interventions could variously be expressed as enhancing social control or preserving children (sometimes with explicitly eugenicist overtones).[24] Modern family law developed within this orientation, infused with a combination of moralism and demographic engineering.[25] Intervention and reform spanned juvenile justice, social security law and family allowances, all of which formed part of a complex system designed to be instrumental in what Jacques Donzelot has aptly described as the "policing" of families.[26] The field of adjustment on divorce came increasingly to be subsumed within a concern with the destinies of children. In other words, as the *grounds* for divorce were liberalised, and the courts given greater powers, the fate of children became progressively the guiding principle as to the *consequences* of divorce.[27]

As the environmentalist idea that children did not just need a home but needed to remain in the same home after their parents separated gathered momentum, a firm connection between family law and property law was forged, albeit, as the succeeding chapters suggest, some-what ambiguously. This movement has been particularly evident in the way in which doctrine has been modified or reshaped in processing intra-familial disputes. This is examined in the next three chapters. These changes have had effects in the commercial field, where the owner-occupied home is a valuable commercial asset, and is the subject of purchases, mortgages, or the target of creditors. How this spillover has taken place is considered in the final three chapters.

Notes to pages 14–23

[1] The effect of marriage and inheritance upon the social distribution of land and the "rise of great estates" has been a particular concern of economic historians, especially with reference to the eighteenth century. The seminal article was Habakkuk, "English Landownership 1680–1740" Econ.Hist.Rev. X (1940) 2. See also his "Marriage Settlements in the Eighteenth Century" Trans. of the R.H.S. 4th ser. XXXII (1950) 15 and his revised position "The Rise and Fall of English Landed Families, 1600–1800" Trans. of the R.H.S. 5th ser. Vol. XXXI (1979) 195; *cf.* Clay, "Marriage, Inheritance and the Rise of Large Estates in England, 1660–1815" Econ.Hist.Rev. 2nd ser. XXI (1968) 503; Beckett, "English Landownership in the Later Seventeenth and Eighteenth Centuries: The Debate and the Problems" Econ.Hist.Rev. 2nd ser. XXX (1977) 567; Bonfield, "Marriage Settlements and the Rise of Great Estates: The Demographic Aspect" Econ.Hist.Rev. 2nd ser. XXXII (1979) 483. Some have suggested that the strict settlement of land may not have been as ubiquitous, at least in the nineteenth century, as was supposed at the time—see especially E. Spring, "Landowners, Lawyers and Land Law Reform in Nineteenth Century England" 21 *American Journal of Legal History* (1977) 40.

[2] See Bonfield, *loc.cit.*; E. Spring, "The Settlement of Land in Nineteenth Century England," 8 *American Journal of Legal History* (1964) 209; for an exchange about *when* such settlements were made, see English and Saville, "Family Settlements" and the "Rise of Great Estates" Econ.Hist.Rev. 2nd ser. XXXIII (1980) 556 and Bonfield's, "Rejoinder" *ibid.* 559. The *duration* of settlements of course was affected by demographic hazard—see Clay, *loc.cit.* and E. Spring, "Landowners . . .," *loc. cit.*

[3] The effect of such charges upon the estate is much discussed in the literature—see F.M.L. Thompson, "The End of a Great Estate" 1 Econ.Hist.Rev. 2nd ser. VIII (1955) 36; *cf.* D. Spring, "English Landownership in the Nineteenth Century: A Critical Note" Econ.Hist. Rev. 2nd ser. IX (1957) 472 and Cannadine, "Aristocratic Indebtedness in the Nineteenth Century: The Case Re-opened" Econ.Hist.Rev. 2nd ser. XXX (1977) 624; D. Spring's, "Comment" Econ.Hist.Rev. 2nd ser. XXXIII (1980) 564 and Cannadine's, "Restatement" *ibid.* 569. For the effects of charges upon estate administration, see D. Spring, *The English Landed Estate: Its Administration* (1963), pp. 34–40.

[4] There are obvious difficulties in assessing how common any of these forms of settlement were. The case studies of economic historians (conducted within a different "problematic"), have shed some light on the strict settlement. Beyond this, there is only the historical residue of lawyers' perceptions of what people did or should do in different circumstances, as mirrored in, for example, the many editions of Davidson's *Precedents in Conveyancing*, or of Lord St. Leonard's *Handy Book on Property Law*. How far they can provide a clue to what people did remains problematic.

[5] On the significance of primogeniture in political discourse, see F.M.L. Thompson, "Land and Politics in England in the Nineteenth Century," Trans of the R.H.S. 5th ser. XV 15 (1965) 23.

[6] Offer, "Origins of the Law of Property Acts 1910–1925" 40 M.L.R. 505 (1977).

[7] F.M.L. Thompson, *English Landed Society in the Nineteenth Century* (1963), pp.269–291, 325–326; Mingay, *The Gentry* (1976) pp.173–178; though *cf.* Newby *et al. Property, Paternalism and Power*, (1978) for the persistence of "paternalist" influence at the local level.

[8] Offer, *Property and Politics* (1981), Pts. III-V. Douglas, *Land People and Politics* (1976), Chaps. 7 and 8. Otherwise, the increasingly "punitive" nature of estate duty, more than anything, seems to have led to the decline of the strict settlement of land and, more generally, the rise of the discretionary trust: Sanford, *Taxing Personal Wealth* (1971), Chap. 2; see also Titmuss, *Income Distribution and Social Change* (1962), Chap. 5.

[9] Both in terms of building upon the technical changes in the later nineteenth century Conveyancing Acts, and in tightening up the machinery of the Settled Land Acts.

[10] (1920) 36 L.Q.R. 107, 108.

[11] s.1 L.P.A. 1925.

[12] ss.38, 65, 66, 67 S.L.A. 1925. *cf.* s.3(i) S.L.A. 1882.

[13] s.34 L.P.A. 1925.

[14] s.34 L.P.A. 1925.

[15] See *infra* p. 91

[16] s.14 Trustee Act 1925 and see *infra* pp.152–157.

[17] Holdsworth, "Equity" (1935) 51 L.Q.R. 142, reprinted in his *Essays in Law and History* (1946), p.165.

[18] s.45 A.E.A. 1925. "Limited," because by definition the change was only relevant in the absence of a will or settlement.

[19] As Lord Wilberforce has observed: See *National Provincial Bank* v. *Ainsworth* [1965] A.C. 1175, 1244.

[20] A point repeatedly emphasised in the literature—see F.M.L. Thompson, *English Landed Society in the Nineteenth Century,* 319–320; Mingay, *op. cit.* see *supra* at p.171; Cannadine "Lord and Landlords . . .," pp. 418–420.

[21] Offer, *loc. cit.*

[22] s.32 Matrimonial Causes Act 1857, *cf.* s. 45.

[23] Gibson and Beer, "The Effect of Legal Aid on Divorce in England and Wales, Part II: Since 1950" (1971) 1 Fam.Law 122; Chester, "Divorce and Legal Aid: A False Hypothesis" (1972) 6 *Sociology* 205.

[24] See especially J. Lewis, *The Politics of Motherhood* (1980).

[25] See E.S.P. Haynes, *Divorce Problems of Today* (1910).

[26] Donzelot, *The Policing of Families* (1979).

[27] See Murch, *Justice and Welfare in Divorce* (1980), pp. 185–208.

Chapter 3

A SHARE OF THE EQUITY

A. INTRODUCTION

English law has traditionally recognised no special law of
property to be applicable in domestic relations, although
prior to 1882, this was subject to one significant exception—the law of married women's property, in which, in
various ways, the ownership or control of a married
woman's property vested in her husband for the duration
of the marriage.[1] English law firmly set its face against the
introduction of any kind of "community property" between spouses, or mandatory partible inheritance in the
transmission of property from parents to children.[2] In
theory this position still applies today, although the Law
Commission has now recommended a regime of statutory
co-ownership of matrimonial property (subject to the
ability to opt out).[3] Since 1970, however, the general law
of property has most clearly been overridden in the field
of divorce.

Since the enactment of the Matrimonial Property and
Proceedings Act 1970 (now codified in the Matrimonial
Causes Act 1973) the courts have been given a jurisdiction
to make a property adjustment order on divorce.[4] In this
matter, the courts have a complete discretion as to the
type of order made, although, once made, it cannot be
altered by a subsequent order.[5] This is to be contrasted
with the position on maintenance, where unless a consent
order has been made, a maintenance order can normally
be reviewed in the future.

Three main forms of order are used where something
other than giving the former matrimonial home outright
to one of the spouses is deemed appropriate: first, a

co-ownership order, with or without an immediate sale; secondly, a deferred charge, either of a lump sum or of a proportion of the equity value; thirdly, (perhaps rarely) a more elaborate settlement of the matrimonial property.[6]

It is difficult to offer any general summary of how the courts proceed in making these orders—the evidence suggests that the practice of judges and registrars, and even the guidelines formulated in the Family Division and the Court of Appeal, vary considerably.[7] While in most of this chapter we are concerned solely with the question of how a successful claim to a share of the equity in a house can be established, in the divorce field, this question is usually linked to the question of whether or not, or how much, maintenance should be ordered in favour of the wife (or occasionally the husband) after the dissolution of the marriage.[8]

In the early days of administering the new jurisdiction it seemed as if the courts would first seek to ascertain the respective property rights of spouses under the general law (normally under the summary procedure contained in section 17 of the Married Women's Property Act) and then determine an appropriate re-allocation.[9] In *Wachtel* v. *Wachtel*[10] this practice was disapproved, and the courts were encouraged to take a broader approach in assessing the relationship between financial contributions to the marriage and the form the property adjustment order should take.[11]

The consequences of the way in which this jurisdiction has been set in motion by the courts is that in many disputes between husband and wife as to the future ownership of the family home, the property law questions which form the core of this chapter are side-stepped. The reach of property law has in this sense been narrowed, and is largely applicable only to disputes between other family members, or quasi-marital or other cohabitees. The property law questions are still germane, so far as spouses are concerned, however, where the question of a share of the equity arises in the context of a dispute involving a stranger—creditors, purchasers or mortgagees or on the bankruptcy of one of the spouses. Although the fundamental issues of law and policy here concern the question of priorities between occupants and strangers, it may in some cases be necessary to turn to the general law of property, which governs the existence of a share in the first place.

B. Express Trusts

If two or more people are buying a house together, the simplest way in which each can acquire a share of the equity is for the house to be bought in their joint names on trust for themselves as joint tenants or tenants in common.[12] In unregistered conveyancing, these trusts will normally be declared in the conveyance of title, or alternatively (which would be preferable if anything complicated is envisaged) in a separate trust instrument. In registered conveyancing, something similar will usually be contained in the deed of transfer executed on completion, but the Registrar will exclude references to the trusts from the Register. The best practice is to enter a restriction[13] on the title, specifying that at least two trustees are required for any future disposition of the property.

An express trust can also operate if the house is transferred to one person who declares himself a trustee for the other or for them both concurrently. To be enforceable, this declaration must be evidenced in writing (section 53(1)(*b*) of the Law of Property Act 1925). This is a perfectly effective way of constituting a trust, but suffers from the disadvantage that the beneficiary is not on the title, and therefore the trustee may deal with a stranger on the basis that he is the sole beneficial owner.[14]

However an express trust comes into existence, once constituted, it remains fixed and the courts cannot subsequently alter the shares or vary the trusts in any way (except under the divorce jurisdiction discussed above).[15] This is today particularly important for unmarried cohabitees. The only way in which a declaration of trust can be combined with allowing for a change of circumstances in the future is either to include a joint power of revocation or to provide that the trusts are determinable on the occurrence of a specified event or events, in which case the property is to be held upon different trusts. Thus it could be provided that the trusts are determinable upon separation of the couple, or the termination of cohabitation. These devices are probably rarely employed in the ordinary situation of home ownership.[16]

Sometimes the house may be put in the joint names but no trusts expressly declared. Here, the trusts will have to be ascertained by implication from the circumstances. Primarily, this is done by looking at the intention of the parties and the size of their respective contributions to the costs of acquisition. In this respect, the legal issues are similar to those which arise where a claim is made for a share of the equity based on an implied trust when the home is vested in the sole name of one of the parties to the dispute. There are certain differences, however, discussion of which is postponed until the question of implied trusts has been examined.

C. IMPLIED TRUSTS

1. *The Resulting Trust*

(1) *The origins of the resulting trust*

The resulting trust has a more complicated lineage than most of the concepts with which we are centrally concerned in this book. Just as the trust was fashioned by analogy with the medieval "use," so the circumstances giving rise to a resulting trust were originally similar to those leading to a resulting use prior to the Statute of Uses of 1535.[17] There were, however, certain important differences. If a grant was made for good consideration,[18] no resulting use would arise in favour of the grantor. Such consideration came commonly to be expressed in the deed evidencing or making the grant. In certain circumstances, however, a resulting *trust* would be imposed on the grantee even though the grant was expressed to be made for consideration. These circumstances were stated categorically by Lord Hardwicke in *Lloyd* v. *Spillett*.[19] First, where an estate was purchased in the name of one person, but money or consideration was given by another, a trust resulted in favour of the person providing the money or consideration. Secondly, where a trust was declared only as to part of an estate, and nothing was said with regard to the rest, what remained undisposed of resulted to the heir-at-law.[20]

The Statute of Frauds, however, was taken by the courts of the eighteenth century to limit the freedom with which they could seek evidence to raise a resulting trust. In particular, the courts were reluctant to deprive a grantee of his grant contrary to the terms of the deed under which he took. First, it was laid down in *Kirk* v. *Webb*[21] that if the pecuniary consideration was expressed in the deed to have been paid by the person in whose name the conveyance was taken, and nothing appeared in the conveyance to raise a presumption that the money was paid by someone else, then parol evidence was inadmissible after the death of the nominal purchaser to prove a resulting trust in favour of the person who advanced the purchase money. Conversely, if it appeared on the face of the conveyance (by recital or otherwise) that the purchase was made with money of a third person, a resulting trust woul be imposed in favour of that person. But if, during his lifetime, the nominal purchaser declared himself a trustee, or confessed that he took as trustee, the Statute no longer applied. Subject to these evidentiary problems, the clear rule was established that *a trust resulted to the person who paid the purchase money.*

(2) *Advancement and the resulting trust*

The courts developed a particular way of dealing with disputes about the ownership of family property, which links up with the question of pre- and post mortem inheritance which has already been introduced. If, for example, someone bought stocks or bonds in the name of his children, who owned the property on the death of the purchaser? The fundamental approach was to give effect to the purchaser's intention, but since, in many cases, firm evidence of actual intention might not be available, the courts proceeded by way of presumptions. In the family context, they asked whether a trust arose in favour of the purchaser, or whether the transaction was to be taken to be an *advancement* in favour of the children. Where the property in question was copyhold, it could be particularly difficult to answer these questions. There were special complexities involved in the purchase and settlement of copyholds because of the form of tenure involved. Copyholds could not be transferred by a simple grant. First, in order to sell a copyhold, it was necessary to surrender it to the lord of the manor who would then "admit" the purchaser (which would often involve paying a "fine," to the lord of the manor). Secondly, the custom of the manor determined the rights of the copyholder, and a common custom was that grants of copyholds had to be made for three successive lives. Thus, if someone wished to purchase a copyhold where such a custom prevailed, the vendor would have to surrender to the lord, who would then admit, upon payment of the fine, the purchaser, and make a grant to him of the copyhold for the three lives successive. This would mean that the purchaser needed in effect to find two nominees in order to take the grant. If he, having paid the fine, chose two strangers, it would be quite clear that they were not entitled to take anything beneficially; it was less clear if the nominees were his wife or children.

Consistently with the rule laid down by Lord Hardwicke, (in *Lloyd* v. *Spillett* (*supra*)) a resulting trust could always be raised in these cases in favour of the person who provided the purchase money. The difficulty was in determining what would rebut the presumption of that trust. Here we can observe a clear difference of approach between the resulting use and the resulting trust. This was stated in the judgment of Eyre C.B. in *Dyer* v. *Dyer* which has come to be regarded as the leading case.[22]

It would have been simplest to follow the approach of the use, which was to say that if good consideration could be shown, the trust would be rebutted. (No resulting use would in any event have been presumed in an analogous situation because the necessary consideration to rebut the presumption would have been supplied by the blood relationship.) There was one obstacle to following the resulting use so closely. The approach to consideration in that context had come to depend upon the consideration for which the conveyance was *expressed* to be given. In the case of the grant of copyhold for successive lives, or the purchase of bonds in joint names of purchaser and other relatives, the consideration for adding the names of non-purchasers was rarely expressed. In refusing to adopt a simple rule that as between the real and nominal purchasers, the presence of a blood relationship was sufficient to exclude a resulting trust, the courts were thus in part responding to the fact that the absence of expressed consideration meant that no direct analogy with the old rules for uses was adequate.

Instead, where there was a blood relationship, the courts asked whether this was to be treated as an advance, (*i.e.* a gift) from the real purchaser to the nominal purchaser. As Eyre C.B. acknowledged, this approach to the question led to "some very nice distinctions" finding their way into the case law.[23]

The exclusion of the resulting trust thus became primarily a question of evidence which turned mainly upon whether the circumstances permitted the court to treat the transaction as an advance of the property to the nominal purchaser or not. This question was itself predicated upon a notion (implicit in the terminology of advancement) that certain members of the family had "something coming to them" from the family estates, and conversely, that some had no such legitimate expectations, or had already received what was their due. Thus while the courts insisted that their priority was to ascertain the intention of the real purchaser, and all the circumstances were simply means of effecting that ascertainment, they inevitably approached the question on the basis of certain "paradigm" or "normal" notions of how property should be distributed within the family.

The main scope for advancement was in the relationship between parents and children—advancement was often linked with "emancipation." For example, the courts asked whether a son was already fully advanced (*i.e.* had all that he was due) and emancipated, or advanced only in part, or not at all. If either of the latter, then the general approach was to treat the transaction as effecting a further, partial or complete, advance in favour of the son. If the son was already fully advanced, then a trust was raised for the father, "as much as if it had been in the name of a stranger, because in that case all presumptions or obligations of advancement cease."[24] This would all yield before clear evidence that the son was a mere nominee.

This test combined two inter-related but distinct assumptions: (i) an obligation to support—a relationship of dependency (which was the aspect of advancement which permitted its later extension to wives) and (ii) a legitimate expectation to receive some of the family estates—a notion of inheritance which would rarely have applied to wives.[25] Thus where a grandfather took bonds in the names of his grandchildren, the case was made to turn on whether the children's father was alive at the time or not. If dead, then the transaction was to be regarded as a provision for the children, but if he was still alive, a resulting trust would arise.[26]

Children would commonly meet both of these criteria and were perhaps, in the eyes of the law, the most "favoured" advancees. The position of wives was perhaps more ambiguous: certainly the nineteenth-century case-law shows decisions going either way, apparently turning on whether a provision was intended by the husband for the wife, which required investigation of the surrounding circumstances.[27] By contrast, if a man bought an annuity for his mistress in her name, she held it as a trustee for him and his estate.[28]

(3) *The emergence of the modern resulting trust*

Until the 1970s, the majority of the modern cases in which arguments concerning the scope of the resulting trust arose between husband and wife upon the break-up of marriage and came to the courts by means of the summary procedure in section 17 of the Married Women's Property Act 1882. These disputes centred around the extent to which financial or non-financial contributions by a spouse towards the acquisition or maintenance of the family home would lead to that spouse being credited with a share of the equity in the family home arising by implication.

Section 17 had, in the context of the "legal emancipation" of married women in the nineteenth century, enacted a summary procedure for adjudicating property disputes between spouses. Before the Second World War, section 17 applications appear to have been of a fairly routine "administrative" nature, involving the compilation of household inventories, etc.[29] The surge in the divorce rate during and after the war, coupled with the growth of owner-occupation from the nineteen thirties, led increasingly to section 17 applications being used with a view to determining the ownership of the family home.

The scheme of trust or advancement has proved to be somewhat awkward in this context. This is often said to be because advancement is not consistent with modern ideas of equality between the sexes. Whether or not this is so, the real difficulties are rather different. They centre around two things. First, the family home is normally purchased by instalments, not outright. Secondly, the inheritance dimension of advancement is effectively absent in modern disputes. In the old cases, it was largely a question of identifying the real purchaser and applying then prevalent notions of intergenerational transmission of property. Today, the second is irrelevant and the first contentious.

Perhaps for these reasons, considerable differences in the proper approach to section 17 applications surfaced in the courts, and no consistent test can be found in the cases in the years leading up to the House of Lords decisions in *Pettitt* v. *Pettitt*[30] and *Gissing* v. *Gissing*.[31] It also suggests that some judges considered that doctrinal purity would produce unfair or unsatisfactory results. The confusion which ensued was partly a result of the absence of any statutory jurisdiction to re-allocate property on divorce, which now exists under section 24 of the Matrimonial Causes Act 1973.

Several approaches under section 17 were taken:

(1) The broadest approach under section 17 was that the judge should do what was fair and reasonable between the parties, and this was sometimes coupled with an explicit assumption of a re-allocative jurisdiction on the basis of the discretion as to orders contained in section 17 (an interpretation which was unanimously repudiated in *Pettitt* by the House of Lords). See for instance *Hine* v. *Hine*[32] and *Appleton* v. *Appleton*.[33]

(2) The principle of equality, which verged upon, in some judgments, a presumption of equality. In *Rimmer* v. *Rimmer*,[34] for example, Evershed M.R. used the maxim "equality is equity" to award equal shares where the ratio of contributions between the spouses was unclear. Denning L.J., by contrast,

used as a starting point the presumption of equality. This latter emphasis came to be linked to the
notion of the home as a family asset and its
acquisition as a joint venture or a family partnership. See for example *Heseltine* v. *Heseltine*,[35]
Finch v. *Finch*[36] and *Falconer* v. *Falconer*.[37]

(3) A third, to some extent overlapping test, was to use
an "imputed common intention," where the shares
were to be determined with reference to what
reasonable spouses in the position of the parties
would have intended. See for example Lord Reid
and Lord Diplock in *Pettitt* v. *Pettitt*.

(4) A final test was to look for the "actual common
intention" of the parties, which was favoured by
the majority in *Pettitt* and *Gissing*.

(4) *Pettitt and Gissing: The modern rules*

Where the property is conveyed to a spouse as sole
beneficial owner, then prima facie that person is absolutely entitled to the equitable estate. Equally, if no mention
is made in the conveyance as to the equitable ownership it
would normally be assumed that the legal owner was so
entitled, provided that the intention of the transferor was
that the equitable ownership should pass.[38]

In *Pettitt* v. *Pettitt* a house was transferred into the name
of a wife alone. The husband contested that he had a share
in the equity value, by virtue of his contributions to
improvements which took the form of doing the garden-
ing, plus handy work round the home. The House held
that this was not sufficient to give him an equitable
interest in the house. The majority emphasised the need
for an agreement or a common intention between the
parties before a resulting trust will be implied, to be
ascertained at the time of the initial purchase. In their
view, the courts could not ascribe to the parties intentions
which they demonstrably never had. J. Gareth Miller
summarises this approach as follows[39]:

"When no express agreement can be established the spouses may, nevertheless, have formed a common intention that the beneficial interests in the land should be vested in them jointly without having used express words to communicate this intention to one another or their recollections of the words used may be imperfect or conflicting by the time the dispute arises. In such cases it may be possible to infer their common intention from their conduct and from the surrounding circumstances. However, where it is clear that the spouses never had a common intention, no such intention can be inferred."

The minority view in *Pettitt* (Lords Reid and Diplock) was that the court should impute to the parties a common intention, which in fact they never formed, by forming its own opinion as to what would have been the intention of reasonable men and women.[40] On the facts of *Pettitt* itself, despite the differences, no real difficulty arose because the court felt the husband's contributions to the improvement of the property were insufficient to suggest any entitlement to an equitable interest in the property.[41]

In *Gissing* v. *Gissing* the House of Lords refused to award an equitable interest in a property to a spouse (this time a wife) who claimed to have made contributions towards the acquisition of the matrimonial home. The parties had married in 1935. The wife had worked throughout the marriage and had been instrumental in getting her husband a job with the same firm as herself. The house in dispute was purchased in 1951. The wife had made no direct contributions to the acquisition costs but had paid for some fittings for the house and had paid for a lawn to be laid. She also paid for her own clothes and those of their son. The majority, reaffirming *Pettitt*, rejected her claim, but there are fundamental ambiguities in the reasons. The rejection of a resulting trust may have been based on the fact that no direct contributions were ever made by the wife and therefore no inference of a common intention could be made.[42] Alternatively, the wife's contributions may have been too insignificant to permit an inference giving her an interest in the matrimonial home.[43] Yet again, her money contributions to the household budget, although relieving her husband of expenditure, may have been insufficiently connected with the purchase of the property to raise the inference of some sort of common intention between the parties.[44] The Law Lords disagreed on this last point. Lords Reid and Pearson felt that, if a husband was relieved of all household expenditure on the basis that he pays the mortgage instalments, this should be sufficient to raise an inference that the property was being acquired by their joint efforts.[45] Lord Diplock was close to this view in his judgment, although he suggested that an actual adjustment to the household expenses which is referable to the acquisition costs must have been made in order to raise this inference.[46] It seems therefore from *Gissing* that there must be a causal connection between the making of any payments and the acquisition of the property under an implied trust. The difficulty with these decisions is ascertaining precisely what the right test is for implying a resulting trust.

(5) *Remaining difficulties*

The crucial difficulties are twofold. First, what kind of contributions to acquisition are envisaged; secondly, can the trust be based on intention alone irrespective of contributions?

(a) Direct/indirect contributions

A different way of formulating the problem would be to ask what kind of family arrangement would come within the scope of the *Pettitt* resulting trust? Compare the three following models:

In *Family One*, both husband and wife work full-time,

pool their resources and pay for all outgoings, including the mortgage repayments, from a joint account. Clearly this is within *Pettitt*, and the only questions for further scrutiny would concern quantum of interest.

In *Family Two*, the wife works part-time and her earnings are used to pay for holidays, utility bills and children's clothes. Most of these payments are payments which the husband would have to meet if the wife did not, although some (*e.g.* holidays) could be regarded as optional. Equally, all of these payments could either be payments which the husband could not meet without the wife's assistance, or they could be payments which the husband could make as well as the mortgage instalments. Is the crucial question then whether the wife *has* to work in order for the family to achieve their desired standard of living? Many of these questions remain unresolved but it should be noted that in involving themselves in such questions the courts have moved away from a pure property approach (*i.e.* from the norms of the nineteenth century family settlement) towards an evaluation of the sexual division of labour in a marriage, and of family aspirations.[48]

In *Family Three*, the wife stays at home and makes no financial contribution to the family's outgoings. Perhaps in many cases it would be difficult to argue that the husband could not pay off the mortgage without the wife's assistance in the provision of domestic services. However even those services could be viewed as having a "cash value"—see, for example, Lord Denning in *Hazell* v. *Hazell*[49] and also *Nixon* v. *Nixon*[50] (and note its inclusion in section 25 of the Matrimonial Causes Act 1973). Whether the legal recognition of the "paid housewife" is desirable is much debated.[51]

So far, we have considered the question of how the boundary is to be drawn between what can be treated as a contribution towards acquisition and what cannot. When both parties make substantial contributions over a long period of time, some rough and ready answer can usually be found as to the existence of shares, even if quantification can be difficult. Finally, we should take note of two particular problems. First, does it follow that any contribution to mortgage repayment will result in some kind of interest? The answer seems to depend on the intention of the parties and the surrounding circumstances.

First, there are some suggestions that both parties must be jointly liable to the mortgagee, notably by Bagnall J. in *Cowcher* v. *Cowcher*.[52] This seems to be too stringent a requirement.[53] But if payments are normally made by one party (as in *Cowcher*) and the other makes one or a few payments, it may, depending on the circumstances, be appropriate to treat these payments as loans of definite sums of money rather than as giving rise to an interest. This may be linked to a right to remain in the home until repayment, but not the acquisition of a share of the equity (see Chap. 4).

Secondly, there is the question of repairs and improvements. In *Pettitt* v. *Pettitt*, Lord Upjohn stated that contributions to these were quite different in quality from contributions to acquisition, and at most operated by way of estoppel, not trust.[54] Insofar as this meant that, as a matter of law, such contributions could *never* give rise to a trust, it has been reversed by statute so far as spouses are concerned. It is difficult to tell whether the same approach would prevail today, although most recent cases concerned with improvements have been couched in terms of estoppel.[55]

In *Cooke* v. *Head*,[56] what appears to be a resulting trust arose partly on the basis of helping to build the home, but this could be viewed as part and parcel of the process of acquisition (though strictly speaking, from a legal point of view, building a house *de novo* on land is no different from improving an existing one).[57] The strongest cases are perhaps *Eves* v. *Eves*,[58] where a woman's physical labour on repairs and decorations were one factor in awarding her a share, and *Hussey* v. *Palmer*,[59] where money spent on building an extension was held to give rise to a trust.

We consider these further under the heading "constructive trust."

Despite Lord Upjohn's categorical statement, the question must surely be viewed as dependent on the circumstances of the case. If X acquires a run-down property and, as part of a joint venture, Y expends considerable time, effort and perhaps money in refurbishing it, it may surely be appropriate to infer an intention of shared beneficial ownership. The answer should depend on what the court's best estimate of what the intention is.

(b) Actual common intention

(i) The narrow view: *Cowcher* v. *Cowcher*[60]

In *Cowcher* Bagnall J. undertook a close examination of the judgments in *Gissing* and canvassed two alternative interpretations: that the common intention or agreement of the parties (between which he drew no distinction, substituting the term "consensus") was either (a) a consensus as to the proper shares in which the parties were to be taken as having provided the purchase money (which he termed "money consensus") or (b) a consensus as to what the beneficial interests of the purchase money were to be ("interest consensus"). Bagnall J. considered that 'money consensus' was the test contemplated. "Interest consensus" amounted to an express declaration of trust and thus written evidence of the declaration was required complying with section 53(1)(*b*) of the Law of Property Act 1925 (though the declaration itself could be informal and arise by conduct).[61] For Bagnall J. the classic instance for the inference of a "money consensus" was "a system of all purchases out of a common fund." Otherwise, it would be difficult to invoke such a consensus. Bagnall J. also felt that the maxim *equality is equity* (as used in *Rimmer* v. *Rimmer*),[62] survived only "if consensus that both spouses are to be treated as making substantial contributions is established, but the proportions cannot be precisely quantified."[63]

(ii) The wide view: *Re Densham*[64]

In *Re Densham*, Goff J. disagreed with *Cowcher*, because "in the vast majority of cases, parties do not direct their minds to treating the money payments as notionally other than they are."[65] For him, if the evidence pointed to an agreement, the inference would, in practical terms, be an interest consensus. If such an agreement was found, it would be unconscionable for a party to set up the statute (s.53(1)(*b*)) and repudiate the agreement, and so, if interest consensus was established in evidential terms, the legal owner would become a constructive trustee.

Though the judgment is fairly brief on these points, its effect appears to be, first, that the court must look for evidence of actual agreement (and it may, cynically, be suggested that the parties will readily admit such agreement when the dispute as in *Densham* involves a stranger); secondly, that the agreement is to relate to their respective interests; thirdly, that insofar as such an agreement amounts to a declaration of trust, a constructive trust will be used so as to circumvent any difficulty concerning formal requirements. Goff J. was able to find ample dicta in *Gissing* to support most of this analysis.

(iii) A better view?

Which is to be preferred (leaving on one side for the present the bankruptcy context of *Densham*)—money consensus or interest consensus? The problem with the latter is that it does, as Bagnall J. suggested, seem to amount to an express declaration of trust, and therefore, if purely oral, fall foul of section 53(1)(*b*) of the Law of Property Act 1925. Moreover, there is no explanation of how we move from agreement to unconscionability. Other constructive trust cases (notably *Cooke* v. *Head*, *Eves* v. *Eves*) contain elements of detriment, reliance or change of position; the facts of *Densham* may have been amenable to such an analysis, but Goff J. did not make this an integral part of his reasoning. If we treat such trusts as a species of estoppel, their use may perhaps escape the reach of *Pettitt* and *Gissing* and of section 53(1)(*b*): but to equate agreement, without more, with unconscionability leaves no apparent room at all for declaration of trust. In *Densham*, it is unclear whether a resulting trust based on actual common intention (interest consensus) is envisaged which can take effect without written evidence (s.53(2) L.P.A. 1925) or whether an express trust fails for want of evidence (s.53(1)(*b*) L.P.A. 1925) and a constructive trust arises in its place. If the latter, some reason should be offered as to why circumvention of the statutory formalities is justifiable.

The *Densham* interpretation thus envisages a resulting or constructive trust arising solely by virtue of an agreement, apparently irrespective of direct or indirect contributions and without any need to show unconscionability. One justification offered by Goff J. for interest consensus is that to search for any other form of evidence is unrealistic. While such a view is probably correct, it is difficult to see how this constitutes a sufficient justification for ignoring the distinction between resulting and express trusts.

What of Bagnall J.'s money consensus? It possesses at first sight the merit of preserving a distinction between express and resulting trusts. But the kind of consensus he envisages is quite artificial and tenuous. If the parties have a joint bank account (*i.e.* "common fund") from which all household outgoings are paid, then it would seem that money consensus would apply (at least, nothing in his judgment indicates why it would not) irrespective of their proportional inputs into that account, Significant consequences, in other words, could turn upon contingencies.

(iv) Implied trusts where the home is in the joint names

The modern resulting trust was developed in the context of disputes when the home was vested in the name of only one of the parties. Should the position be different when the house is in the joint names and no trusts are expressly declared? Here it is easier, without doing violence to the distinction between express and implied trusts, to find joint beneficial ownership. The choice is between a trust based on the respective contributions of the parties (when the evidence suggests that this is what was intended) and finding that, whatever the respective contributions, joint beneficial ownership was intended, in which case the larger contributor will be taken to have made a gift *pro tanto* to the other party.

The basic presumption of equity, if contributions are unequal, would be to find unequal beneficial shares proportionate to the respective contributions. If one party has paid all the acquisition costs, it would thus be appropriate to invoke a resulting trust of the traditional kind. But often, this will give way before contrary evidence—that, for example, the house was put in joint names so that the survivor would take it absolutely on the death of the other.[66] It is not necessary here to invoke the terminology of 'advancement'—simply that it is common practice, especially for married couples, to put the home in the joint names so that, irrespective of contributions, it belongs to both jointly.[66a] By contrast, when the house is in the name of one party only, the other must rely upon contributions (however defined) in order to invoke a trust, unless the broader approach of *Densham* is followed.

2. *The Constructive Trust*

This appears to be a second type of implied trust by means of which a share of the equity can be claimed. It is similar to estoppel, *i.e.* based in some way on unconscionability.

A classic example is *Eves* v. *Eves*[67] where a house was

bought by a man and a woman who originally intended to marry when they were both free to do so. The conveyance was taken in the man's sole name because the woman was under 21 (in 1968) and therefore unable to appear on the legal title to the property. There were two elements in the Court of Appeal's decision that the woman was entitled to a one-quarter share of the property. The first element was the fact of the assurance given to her by the man that the property would be put into joint names when it was legally possible to do so. The second element was the element of contribution to the purchase of the property by the woman. The plaintiff in *Eves* made no direct contribution in money, but she helped with the extensive renovation which the property required, as well as having two of the defendant's children.

The Court of Appeal held that these events warranted the imposition of a trust upon the legal owner. Brightman J. emphasised the evidence of agreement between the parties and the element of a joint venture; Lord Denning M.R. emphasised joint efforts but also the reliance of Janet Eves, evidenced by her "hard work" and encouraged by the man's representations. The decision is thus an amalgam of common intention and unconscionability.[68]

The problem with a move beyond common intention, for all its difficulties, towards unconscionability lies in assessing precisely what the boundaries are between conduct or reliance resulting in an award of an equitable share and conduct which results in protected occupation or nothing. For example, in *Richards* v. *Dove*[69] Walton J. found that the property was not acquired by the joint effort of the parties. All the female partner did in that case was pay for the food and cook it and make a small cash loan towards the deposit. In *Tanner* v. *Tanner*,[70] another case involving an unmarried couple, the Court of Appeal rejected a trust analysis, distinguishing *Eves* v. *Eves* on the basis that in *Eves* "the man and his mistress obtained the house in contemplation of marriage."[71]

This distinction between cases where an unmarried

couple intend to marry "when they are free" and where no such intention is evident is somewhat problematic. If the intention to marry is harnessed to a common intention test as to shares, it becomes part of the evidence going to the existence of that requisite common intention as to ownership. In this sense, it indicates a perception on the part of the courts as to what people in particular situations can be expected to intend. If however, "marriage" in the above sense is coupled with reliance or unconscionability, its role is surely more unsatisfactory. At most it might be suggested that the expectation of marriage is evidence of the expectation of a permanent union and thus reinforces the evidence that there was significant reliance.

The cases are too few and the judgments too diffuse (based as we have seen on an amalgam of different elements) to predict future developments with any confidence or to extract firm principles. It may be that some of the judges are feeling their way towards a distinction in viewing unmarried couples between the quasi-marital and the non-marital. Certainly, in *Eves* v. *Eves*, Lord Denning M.R. compared the position of a couple like the Eves whose relationship had broken down and the approach of a court in the event of marital breakdown. It is also to be noted that the concept of the quasi-marital has acquired considerable vitality in other common law jurisdictions.[72]

At its most extreme the constructive trust may be used as a kind of remedy, and as such, has been heavily criticised. In *Hussey* v. *Palmer*, for instance, Lord Denning M.R. awarded a beneficial interest by way of constructive trust to a mother-in-law, who had paid for the construction of a bedroom for herself in her son-in-law's house. The mother-in-law seems to have viewed the transaction as a loan but Lord Denning found a trust on the basis that it would be "entirely against conscience that (the son-in-law) should retain the whole house and not allow (the plaintiff) any interest in it."[73] More usually, however, it would seem that mere reliance or unconscionability give rise to occupation rights rather than a successful claim for a marketable share of the equity in the home.

Statutory co-ownership

The Law Commission has proposed automatic co-ownership of the matrimonial home (or homes, if the spouses have more than one).[74] This would normally operate behind a trust.[75] Thus, if the legal title to the home is vested in one spouse, these proposals would make that spouse automatically a trustee holding on trust for himself and his wife as equitable joint tenants. An express declaration of trust would in effect be deemed to have taken place.[76] This would operate either when the home is acquired after marriage, or upon marriage where, prior thereto, one of the parties owns a home which subsequently becomes the matrimonial home.[77]

Various ways of excluding statutory co-ownership are, however, also proposed. Either spouse can exclude statutory co-ownership if he or she owns the property prior to marriage and makes a written declaration excluding the scheme from applying to that property.[78] Secondly, a donor can exclude the scheme, whether the gift takes effect prior to or after the marriage.[79] The proposals also envisage exclusion by mutual agreement between the spouses.[80] It is not contemplated that statutory co-ownership should affect the freedom of the courts to make a property adjustment on divorce.[81]

D. VALUATION

1. *Introduction*

Prior to the modern period, there was no difficulty in ascertaining the quantum of the interest behind an express trust, and resulting trusts would simply involve asking what size of contribution to the purchase price was made by the person claiming a share. Whether the property in question was land or personalty, the question was relatively straightforward. When we turn to the modern position, more fundamental problems arise out of the relationship between the formal legal analysis of home ownership and the practical realities of modern home purchase. It is necessary to consider this carefully before returning to how the courts have approached questions of valuation in particular cases.

2. *General Issues*

For the majority of people, home purchase is by instalments. In practical terms, on completion of the purchase, the purchaser acquires the ability to occupy the house. In this sense, from the time of transfer of occupancy, the home "belongs" to the purchaser; but if he has bought by means of a mortgage, then should he default on his repayments, the property will probably have to be sold, and should he sell voluntarily, he will not retain all the proceeds but only the net proceeds after, in particular, the discharge of the mortgage. The mortgage instalments really represent the "buying-back" from the building society of a *pro rata* share of the equity value. In formal legal terms, however, the building society is not a co-owner of the property; the charge is simply security for the money advanced and owed; title (and full ownership) passes on completion or thereabouts (there are differences here between the two systems of conveyancing, which are not significant for present purposes)[82]; the mortgage is secured on this title.

The "practical realities" of home purchase can be expanded. First, in most cases, the purchaser will have provided a deposit. Secondly, in recent years the effect of a rapid increase in house prices has meant that through time the ratio of the amount lent to the market value of the house diminishes irrespective of loan repayments. In other words, mere retention of the capital asset leads to capital appreciation. The practical position can be represented as follows, using the example of a capital repayment mortgage.

Figure 1—Repayment Mortgage

(1)	(2)	(3)	(4)
Deposit	Windfall (due to increase in house prices)	Reduced Capital Debt (the equity, 'bought back' from the building society)	Outstanding Mortgage Debt

Total Equity Value,
i.e. total value of property

This indicates how the proceeds of sale will be divided between home-owner and building society. (2) will increase with inflation in house prices; (3) will increase slowly in the early years of a mortgage, when the bulk of the repayment is interest, but in the later years will increase substantially as the capital:interest ratio in the repayments alters significantly in the direction of capital. The value of (4) as a proportion of the total equity value will diminish through time as (2) expands due to inflation.[83]

3. *Valuation and Express Trusts*

The issues which arise here highlight the disparity between the practical realities of home purchase and the formal legal analysis of home ownership. On transfer of title, H becomes absolute owner in law and equity and this is the position for at least a moment in time before the mortgagee's charge takes effect. This may have important consequences so far as priorities between claimants and strangers are concerned; for the moment we concentrate upon its impact upon the subject-matter of the trust.

We have already suggested that where the home is bought on instalment, in reality H owns only the equity of redemption, and the mortgage instalments represent the buying back from the building society of the equity in the home. But analytically, because H becomes absolute owner at the time of transfer, he is free to don the mantle of trustee of the property. Three situations must be distinguished:

(1) *Where the house is put in the joint names*

Here H and W become joint owners in law and equity, but the building society will normally insist that W is joined in the mortgage deed and therefore takes subject to the charge. Thus she is in exactly the same position as H, and practically, therefore, the value of her interest at any point in time is confined to half share of the equity of redemption. This will be so whether the trust is express or implied.

(2) *Declaration of trust prior to transfer of title where the house is transferred to H or W in his or her name*

There may be a properly evidenced declaration of trust in favour of the other party. This situation (more than any other) points to the curious consequences of the dislocation between the theoretical and practical positions as regards home purchase. From the time of exchange of contracts, H (the intending purchaser) has something of value capable of forming the subject-matter of a trust (and, equally, capable of assignment): a valuable right to specific performance of a contract for the sale of land at a determinate price. From that time on, it follows that H can declare himself trustee (in whole or in part) of his equitable interest which arises at that point. (Whether such a declaration need only be evidenced in writing (s.53(1)(*b*) L.P.A. 1925) or needs to be made in writing (s.53(1)(*c*) L.P.A. 1925) can be ignored for present purposes—the answer is not altogether clear on present authority).[84] In this event, it is presumably the case that on transfer of title to H, the declaration will bite on the title, and H will hold as trustee *pro tanto*, and thus W acquires a share of the whole equity value of the house and not just the equity of redemption.

Alternatively, and more simply, H can declare himself trustee for W at any point in time prior to the transfer of title, such that on acquiring title on completion, the trust will instantaneously bite on the title in favour of W. Provided the intention continues up until the time H acquires the title, the property will be impressed by the trusts.[85]

(3) *Declaration of trust after transfer of title*

H could declare himself trustee at any time after he has acquired the title. The difference between this situation and the two preceding ones is that such a declaration means that W can never take priority over the building society's charge, which already affects the title.[86]

In the first two examples, irrespective of H's actual financial outlay on intitial acquisition, he can in theory "settle" by means of express declaration (say half of) the equity value which he does not in any practical sense himself have (see Fig. 1 above). While such a declaration will be voidable if it comes within the scope of bankruptcy and related jurisdictions[87] such jurisdictions are limited in scope and in certain circumstances the analysis presented above may have important consequences. If, by contrast, the subject-matter of the trust was regarded as the equity of redemption, W's share could never exceed in value the quantum of the equity which H, in a practical sense, has at any point in time vis-à-vis the building society. This leaves outstanding the problem of second mortgages, which are necessarily secured upon what the lender supposes to be the value of the equity of redemption rather than, as in the case of a first mortgage, the value of the property itself. So far as the security of such mortgages are concerned, it must turn *exclusively* upon the rules concerning priorities between beneficiaries and strangers.[88]

4. *Valuation and Implied Trusts*

As pointed out earlier in this chapter there are several types of implied trust and these will be examined separately in this section. They are (i) the implied trust based on direct/indirect contributions; (ii) the implied trust based on an actual common intention of the parties and (iii) the constructive trust. In every instance it is assumed that the mortgage is a capital repayment mortgage, *i.e.* each instalment consists of an element of capital and interest. In the early years of the mortgage the interest element will form nearly the whole of the instalment whereas towards the end of the life of the mortgage, the capital element comprises the major part of the instalment.

(1) *Contribution based*

Title to the home is vested in H as sole beneficial owner. He has bought the home by means of an 80 per cent. mortgage from the building society. W has acquired an interest behind a trust by means of one of the methods considered above. There are various different possibilities.

(a) Deposit

W pays the whole of the 20 per cent. deposit in cash on a house costing £20,000 (*i.e.* £4,000), and there is no evidence to suggest that a gift to H is intended. This will, by means of a resulting trust, give W 20 per cent. of the equity value or total value of the property. Thus the value of her share will increase through time (*i.e.* her interest will include an entitlement to the windfall element (2) above). If H and W pay one-half each of the 20 per cent. deposit, then each will have a 10 per cent. share in the equity value of the property.

(b) Contributions to mortgage repayments

H and W make equal contributions to the monthly repayments. These can be considered separately from deposit contributions. How big a share does W thus acquire? The simplest answer is to credit her with a half share of (2) and (3), *i.e.* the windfall element and the equity bought back from the building society: a half-share of (3) because her repayments have led to half the reduction in the capital debt, a half-share of (2) since it is the mortgage repayment which has permitted the windfall to be gained. This can be represented as follows:

Figure 2—Effect of contributions to mortgage repayments

	1975	1981
Total equity value (1, 2, 3 and 4)	£20,000	£30,000
20% deposit (1)	4,000	6,000
Repaid capital, equity brought back (3)	—	2,000
Outstanding debt (4)	16,000	14,000
Total windfall (2)	—	10,000
Windfall apportionable to mortgage repayments	—	8,000
Windfall apportionable to deposit	—	2,000

Some comments must be made about this method of valuing the shares. First, it draws no distinction between the interest component and the capital component in the monthly repayments. This could become important as the following example illustrates. Suppose that from 1970–76, H and W made equal contributions to repayment, but from 1976–81, H alone repaid. Suppose further that the evidence suggested that the parties intended that a strict inquiry into actual repayments should be made for valuation purposes (which might plausibly be the case between unmarried couples or co-owners in a non-marital relationship). The interest component in the 1970–76 payments would normally be higher than in the 1976–81 payments. It would, however, be unsatisfactory to credit H with a larger share of (3) because of his greater contribution to actual debt reduction. Payment of interest is part of the totality of payments practically necessary in order to purchase the home. In other words, a strict valuation should give W one-quarter and H three-quarters of (3) and, if the argument above is followed, of (2) as well.

(c) A broader approach to valuation?

No doubt this kind of discussion seems artificial (hence, one of the reasons for the "joint venture" approach)[89] but the law should be capable of providing a satisfactory formula for conducting a strict valuation. The foregoing discussion was designed to clarify how such a strict valuation might be made. The evidence suggests, however, that even though the broad discretionary approach of the 1960s has been rejected (and reformulated for spouses on a statutory basis *via* the divorce jurisdiction) the courts will not treat the question of valuation in so narrow a way as suggested here. Thus in *Pettitt*, Lord Upjohn envisaged that when one spouse provided the deposit and the other kept up the morgage repayments, joint beneficial ownership might be inferred.[90] Lord

Denning has suggested that a strict approach is equally inappropriate today for unmarried couples.[91] We have already seen, however, that, where unmarried couples are involved, Lord Denning has confined the basis upon which the *existence* of a trust can be inferred, and we shall see below[92] that he has formulated a further distinction between married and unmarried couples so far as the relevant *time* for effecting the valuation of shares is concerned.

(d) Difficulties with a strict valuation

Three further issues should be noted which further complicate the possibility of conducting a strict valuation: first, the impact of fluctuations in interest rates; secondly, the question of tax relief; thirdly, additional complications which may arise where an endowment mortgage has been obtained.

(i) Interest rate fluctuations

It was once common practice for the interest rate to be set at the outset of the mortgage. As frequent variations in interest rates have become a more familiar aspect of modern economic life, building societies have adopted a flexible interest rate which rises and falls in accordance with the broader economic patterns. What consequences does this have for the question of valuation? There are two possibilities, resulting from a combination of the individual society's policy and the preference of the individual mortgagees. First, if monthly payments are held constant, variations in the maximum duration of the mortgage will occur (*i.e.* periodic adjustment in the capital interest ratio in the monthly payment). Secondly, the monthly payment may vary in quantum. The choice in a repayment mortgage usually lies with the mortgagor, who can either increase his payments or extend the term of the mortgage. If the payments are left static then this will require an adjustment to the calculation of shares as between H and W. If W's contribution to the instalments remains the same whilst H's increases to cover the extra interest, does this thereby entitle H to a larger share? These questions remain and it is difficult to give a definite answer to them. It may, of course, be simpler, given the rapidity with which interest rates have fluctuated in recent years, to ignore them.

(ii) Tax relief on the interest component

A further issue deserves mention. To what extent should the tax relief available on mortgage repayments be taken into the reckoning when valuing shares arising under implied trusts.

Interest is eligible for relief from income tax under section 75 of the Finance Act 1972, if it is paid by a person owning an estate or interest in land in the United Kingdom on a loan used to purchase land, or for improving or developing the land or the buildings thereon.

Certain restrictions should be noted. First, the land to which the loan relates must be the only or main residence of the borrower or of a dependant relative or former or separated spouse.[93] Secondly, relief is only available on loans up to £25,000.[94] There are special rules for joint borrowers, each of whom has to fulfil the conditions (as to main residence, etc.) and the £25,000 being apportioned between them. Where a person has two qualifying houses the £25,000 applies to the aggregate of such loans, which may limit the relief available where a husband proposes to buy a house for his (separated) wife to live in.

For the purposes of valuation the question is whether, if one of the co-owners has had all the tax relief, credit should be given to the other party in assessing the value of their respective shares.

(iii) The endowment mortgage

This is the other main type of mortgage used by home buyers. Whereas, in a repayment mortgage, the instalments consist of elements of both capital and interest, in an endowment mortgage the instalments cover merely interest. The mortgagor is obliged, by the terms of the mortgage, to keep up an "endowment" insurance policy which at the end of the term of the mortgage will produce a sum equal to the outstanding capital debt owing to the building society. Difficulties arise in valuing shares in this type of mortgage. Contributions to the instalments to the building society and to the premiums payable to the insurance company should surely produce a share which can be valued as a proportion of the total payments being made by H and W. Presumably, if a dispute arises before the end of the mortgage term, some calculation can be made as to an entitlement to the equity of redemption; but what about an entitlement to a share of the insurance policy?

There are other difficulties too. What about the profits, over and above what is required to repay the building society, which may arise on the maturing of the insurance policy (which depends upon the type of endowment policy used)? Again, should not the tax relief available in respect of the insurance premiums as well as the interest payments also be taken into account? Finally, what is the position of the parties if one of them contributes solely towards the insurance premiums whilst the other makes the payments to the building society?

The preceding discussion means that the value of W's share, at any point in time, is confined to (1), (2) and (3), *i.e.* to the (increasing) value of the equity of redemption. It does not mean that W acquires a half-share of the *total value* until the mortgage is discharged. In other words, whatever the position as to *priorities* between W and the building society, W cannot "overtake" "the first mortgagee" in terms of quantum, and the value of the security of the first mortgage will be preserved, unless house prices actually fall significantly.[95]

(e) The actual common intention trust

This "version" of the implied trust may modify the question of valuation in one of two ways. First, it may be used to obviate the need to carry out a strict valuation based on respective contributions to deposit and loan repayments. This much seems inherent in the majority judgments in *Pettitt* and *Gissing*.[96] Secondly, if the conflicting "glosses" upon *Pettitt* and *Gissing* in *Cowcher* and *Densham* are to be taken at face value, it might seem that, depending upon which approach was followed,[97] a significant divergence could emerge at the point of valuation. If we follow *Cowcher*, the position will be similar to that just discussed concerning implied trusts of the contribution-type. The actual intention of the parties and any agreement they may have made operates to give them a share of the equity of redemption. If we follow *Densham*, the position is apparently quite different and the actual common intention test will operate exactly like an express declaration of trust. In other words, it would seem that the trust could apply to the whole of the property, and not simply to the equity of redemption. (It should be noted that insofar as this type of trust is not based on actual contributions to the purchase price of the property it may be susceptible, as in *Densham*, to attack if one of the parties subsequently goes bankrupt).[98]

(f) The constructive trust

As we have previously pointed out, it is difficult to analyse the exact basis on which this type of trust operates. If, as seems likely, it is a reliance based trust, then presumably it can only operate on the equity of redemption. This presumption arises because it is difficult to see what W could be said to be depending on acquiring if not a share of the equity of redemption. In *Eves* v. *Eves*, the court assumed that the equity of redemption formed the subject-matter of the trust.[99]

(g) The relevant time for valuation

In times of considerable variations in house price inflation, it can be important to ascertain what is the relevant time for valuing a share. In the case of express trusts, the time for effecting the valuation will be when the trust is wound up, for example on a sale, although the courts may require an account between the parties.[1] Where the share is acquired under an implied trust, the position may be more difficult. The Court of Appeal has suggested that a distinction must be drawn between married and unmarried co-owners. In the former case, the trust determines on divorce; in the latter case, upon separation. The distinction appears to be based upon the intention of the parties—in the former case, the parties expect that the relationship will be permanent and therefore the trust terminates only when the relationship is permanently severed. Thus in *Hall* v. *Hall*,[2] where an unmarried couple lived together for seven years with no intention of marriage and then separated, the woman successfully claimed a half share of the equity on a resulting trust, but the share fell to be valued on the date of separation, when the house was worth £15,000, and not the date of trial, when the value had increased to £24,900. By contrast, in a later case, where the man moved out leaving his former mistress in the home, it was held that her share fell to be valued on the date of sale, since the intention of the parties or the purpose of the trust extended to providing a home for the woman until she could move to suitable alternative accommodation.[3]

Once again, the desirability of Lord Denning's emphasis upon marriage is open to dispute. These decisions point to serious difficulties about the appropriate way for the courts to proceed. We would argue that, at least when the implied trust arises because of quantifiable financial contributions to the deposit or mortgage repayments, it is unfair to "freeze" the value of the share at the moment of separation. Obviously, after the separation, the person who remains will often have assumed responsibility for all outgoings, and this too should be allowed for in resolving the dispute. The fairest solution would be to treat contributions to deposit and repayments separately. The portion of the value represented by the deposit should continue to appreciate in value until the final termination of co-ownership.

With regard to loan repayments, if, directly or indirectly, contributions were joint prior to separation and subsequently assumed by the person who remains, it would surely be fairer to take that part of the value at the time of trial attributable to repayments and apportion it in a way which corresponds to the ratio of repayments as between the parties over the whole period prior to trial. Thus, if the value attributable to repayments is £6,000 and the windfall apportionable to repayments is £8,000,[4] giving a total of £14,000, and X and Y were jointly responsible for five years and X solely responsible for one year, this part of the total equity value could be divided up as follows:

(1) $\dfrac{14,000}{6}$ = annual value acquired by repayments

(2)   Y therefore gets $\dfrac{14,000 \div 2 \times 5}{6}$

(3)   X therefore gets $\dfrac{14,000 \div 2 \times 5}{6} + \dfrac{14,000}{6}$

More elaborate formulae could take account of fluctuations in interest rates (and consequent variations in the capital interest ratio in the repayments) and of variations in house price inflation (with consequences for how the windfall could be apportioned from year to year), though it is not obvious that these factors should be accommodated in a valuation.

E. REALISABILITY

When someone has a share in the equity value of a house existing behind a trust, however it arises and however it is quantified, we must next ask whether, and if so, when, it can be realised. To what extent, in other words, is a share in the equity of the home something which can be turned into hard cash? The home will often constitute the main or only asset of the parties. The parties may agree a consensual termination of the equitable co-ownership, in that one party might buy the other party out. But if there is a mortgage outstanding on the property, it may well be that the party wishing to stay on the premises lacks the resources both to keep up the mortgage repayments and simultaneously to buy out the other party. In such circumstances, the only solution, if each is to realise his or her share, will be for the property to be sold. The corollary of sale as a method of realising shares is the protection of one party's ability to enjoy, at least in the short term, his or her capital asset. Sale and the protection of occupation of the home constitute the primary alternatives open to a court. It should be noted that an identical choice arises under the more flexible divorce jurisdiction, where no satisfactory solution has been found.[5] We concentrate on sale in this chapter and deal with the protection of occupation in the next.

1. *The Statutory Code: Section 30 of the Law of Property Act 1925*

When the equitable fee simple is held jointly or in common, the courts have held that, in the absence of an express trust for sale, the land is held on a statutory trust for sale.[6] Although there are no indications in the 1925 code that this was envisaged, this was probably an inevitable gloss on the statute unless further, substantial, modification of the 1925 conveyancing scheme was to be undertaken.[7] Bringing most co-ownership situations within the trust for sale framework of the Law of Property Act has profound implications upon the rights of beneficiaries to occupy the trust property and upon the conveyancing machinery, and we consider these in subsequent chapters.

For present purposes, it suffices to say that this means that disputes as to the realisability of a share of the equity can be processed through the broad discretionary jurisdiction conferred upon the courts by section 30 of the Law of Property Act 1925.

Section 30 provides:

> "If the trustees for sale refuse to sell or to exercise any of the powers conferred by either of the last two sections [powers of management of trustees for sale], or any requisite consent cannot be obtained, any person interested may apply to the court for a vesting or other order for giving effect to the proposed transaction or for any order directing the trustees for sale to give effect thereto, and the court may make such order as it thinks fit."

The statute gave no guidance as to how this discretion was to be exercised. It does seem however that the section was intended to permit a sale to be ordered by the court where, under the general law of trusts,[8] such a sale would not be possible. The most extreme example of this would be where the trustees agreed to exercise a power to postpone a sale. In these circumstances, it would be almost impossible for a beneficiary under the general law to persuade a court to challenge this exercise of discretion. Section 30, however, explicitly authorises the court to consider the question on its merits, thus justifying the court in taking a more active approach than usual to interfering with the exercise by trustees of discretion. According to Simonds J. in *Re Mayo*,[9] the discretion conferred by section 30 was to be exercised in the same way as a discretion which was exercisable by the court in the case of an instrument containing an express duty to sell coupled with a power of postponement. On this analysis, a formal approach to questions of sale should be adopted and where there is a conflict between power to postpone and duty to sell, the duty prevails.

There is perhaps general agreement that such an analysis is inappropriate when applied to the family home. Perhaps for this reason the courts have used section 30 to substitute their own view regarding the exercise of discretion for that of the trustee or trustees for sale.

2. *The Development of the Section 30 Discretion*

In time the appellate courts came to formulate their own guidelines to govern the exercise of the discretion, where there was a domestic dispute concerning the family home. In many respects, the turning point in judicial attitudes came in the case of *Jones* v. *Challenger*.[10] In this case a husband and wife had contributed equally to the purchase of the matrimonial home which was conveyed to them as joint tenants. The wife deserted the husband, who remained in occupation. The wife applied successfully for an order for sale under section 30. The importance of the case lies in the reasoning which was adopted to justify an order for the sale of the property. The following dicta of Devlin L.J. have been influential[11]:

"In the case we have to consider, the house was acquired as the matrimonial home. That was the purpose of the joint tenancy and, for so long as that purpose was still alive, I think that the right test to be applied would be that in *Re Buchanan-Wollaston's Conveyance*. But with the end of the marriage, that purpose was dissolved and the primacy of the duty to

sell was restored. . . . In these circumstances there is
no way in which the discretion can properly be
exercised except by an order to sell, because, since
they cannot now both enjoy occupation of the
property, that is the only way whereby the beneficiaries can derive equal benefit from their investment, *which is the primary object of the trust*." (italics
supplied).

Jones v. *Challenger* thus purported to follow the earlier
decision in *Buchanan-Wollaston*.[12] In the latter case there
had been a covenant between the parties to the trust
which governed the future disposition of the land subject
to the trust, and therefore, in refusing a sale, the court was
simply giving effect to a pre-existing legal relationship
between the parties. In "following" this case, Devlin L.J.,
in *Jones* v. *Challenger*, was in fact developing a more
flexible test for resolving disputes about sale. *Jones* v.
Challenger also involved a departure from *Re Mayo*. This
was justified on the ground that *Mayo* concerned "a
simple trust for sale" where no beneficiaries intended or
wished to occupy the property. Where, however, there
was a "secondary or collateral" object besides sale then
the simple principle could not prevail.

This notion of a secondary or collateral object lies at the
heart of the modern practice. In *Jones* v. *Challenger* the
secondary object was said to be the provision of a
matrimonial home and since that purpose had come to an
end then a sale should be ordered. This approach has been
broadened by two Court of Appeal decisions, *Williams* v.
Williams[13] and *Re Evers' Trust*,[14] in which the identifica-
tion of "purpose" has been broadened from "matrimonial" to "family" home. As Lord Denning M.R. expressed it in *Williams*[15]:

"When judges are dealing with the matrimonial
home, they nowadays have great regard to the fact
that the house is bought as a home in which the family
is to be brought up. It is not treated as property to be

sold nor as an investment to be realised for cash. . . .
The court in executing the trust should regard the
primary object as being to provide a home and not a
sale. Steps should be taken to preserve it as a home
for the remaining partner and children, but giving the
outgoing partner such compensation, by way of
charge or being bought out, as is reasonable in the
circumstances."

A similar approach was adopted by Ormrod L.J. in *Re
Evers' Trust.*

These reformulations of the "purpose" for which the
home is acquired, such that the purpose can continue after
marital breakdown, bear a close resemblance to the
Mesher order commonly made on divorce under section
24 of the Matrimonial Causes Act 1973.[16] This "assimila-
tion" of the two jurisdictions was further encouraged by
Lord Denning in *Williams*, when he urged that future
section 30 applications concerning the matrimonial home
should be initiated in the Family Division rather than the
Chancery Division. At present, it is unclear to what extent
the courts will apply this broader principle to unmarried
couples—but it should be noted that the Court of
Appeal's procedural recommendations can have only
limited applicability to unmarried couples, since the
jurisdiction of the Family Division in this area primarily
extends only to marital breakdown.

This formulation does involve a departure from traditional property principles insofar as it takes account of the
needs of the children, who will normally not be beneficiaries of the trust. Some appellate judges with a
Chancery background have objected that it elevates the
children in effect to the status of beneficiaries. Thus in
Burke v. *Burke*,[17] Buckley L.J. held that relatives or
children should strictly be taken into account only insofar
as they affected the equities as between the beneficial
owners. Refusal of an immediate sale might be justified if
there would be great difficulties in making proper arrange-

ments for rehousing (which suggests that only a short-term postponement should be permitted). Goff L.J. returned to this theme in *Re Holliday*[18]: "When the marriage is at an end . . . some very special circumstances need to be shown to induce the court not to order a sale."

However, there does seem to be agreement that, where possible, disputes between spouses should be heard in the Family Division rather than the Chancery Division. Goff L.J. suggested that if one spouse applied for a section 30 order in the Chancery Division, the other spouse should apply for a transfer to the Family Division.

Prior to the enactment of section 7 of the Matrimonial Homes and Property Act 1981 there was some doubt about whether the Court has jurisdiction to order a sale under the Matrimonial Causes Act 1973, and therefore it had been common for spouses seeking sale to apply either under section 30 or under section 17 of the Married Women's Property Act 1882 (before the decree absolute). *Williams* and *Evers* may partly have been influenced by this. The logic of Goff L.J.'s position is that, in matrimonial cases, a deferred sale should take effect under the 1973 Act and not under section 30.

3. *Departures from the "Purpose" Test*

Subject to these general guidelines, the following modifications or further considerations should be noted.

1. Irrespective of any collateral object, the court may exercise its discretion in accordance with the needs or conduct of the parties. See for example the case of *Jackson* v. *Jackson*[19] where after a marital breakdown a sale was ordered because the house was in excess of the wife's needs, and also *Re Hardy's Trusts*,[20] where Stamp J. refused an order for sale asked for by the husband until he had found alternative accommodation for his wife.

2. Even where a collateral object has ceased, a sale may be refused or postponed for a significant period, if a sale would be inappropriate, as, for example, where a sale

would cause more inconvenience or hardship to one party than postponement would to the other. This was the view adopted in *Eves* v. *Eves*, where a postponement was ordered on the basis that although the purpose of the trust had come to an end, (in that the parties had split up and both had subsequently remarried), Janet Eves was being supported by her new husband in a new home, whereas Stuart Eves had his new family to support in the old family home. On weighing these factors a postponement was considered appropriate, on the basis that Janet Eves would suffer less if a sale were postponed than Stuart Eves would if a sale were ordered, though this does not mean that an allowance will not be made to the non-occupying spouse for the period of non-occupation, when the property *is* finally sold.[21]

3. A sale will usually be ordered where there is a bankruptcy involved.[22]

4. A sale will probably be ordered if one party sells his/her share and that share thereby falls into the hands of a stranger. See *Jones* v. *Challenger*[23]; and *Bedson* v. *Bedson*,[24] where the court, assuming this to be the general rule, went so far as to issue an injunction to prevent the wife from severing her equitable joint tenancy. If the court are now more willing to look at all the circumstances before requiring sale, then sale might not be ordered as of course if a share of the property was acquired by a stranger. This is, however, a fairly unexplored area.

5. A sale may be refused if there is some overriding legal relationship external to the trust which is present, as in *Re Buchanan-Wollaston's Conveyance*[25] and *Jones* v. *Jones*,[26] where a sale was refused on the basis that an estoppel arose which prevented the trustee from asking for occupation of the premises.

4. *Conclusion*

The courts have moved a considerable way from the simple if formal approach of *Re Mayo*. Generally, the section 30 discretion is exercised so as to give effect to what the courts discern to be the intention of the parties or the purpose for which the house was acquired. The outstanding question is to what extent the courts in the future will be prepared to give effect to express agreements (made at the time of purchase) between the parties, especially if such agreements expressly provide for a sale on the termination of cohabitation. In the divorce jurisdiction, the needs of children have become increasingly paramount.[27] It is still unclear, under section 30, whether an agreement for sale would later be upheld if it would cause hardship, especially to the children.

F. Equitable Accounting and Occupation Rents

One complication which arises because of the instalment method of home purchase occurs where, prior to a sale or consensual termination, one party leaves and the other keeps on the mortgage payments where previously both had contributed. If the trust is implied, the question can be dealt with as one of valuation, at least where the trust is based upon contributions. Where the trust is express (for example, joint beneficial ownership) the court is constrained by the prior act of the parties and cannot simply adjust the shares as it deems appropriate. The position appears to depend upon the basis upon which the parties envisaged the financing of the purchase.

1. *Where Joint Contributions Contemplated*

Where a house is being acquired on this basis, and one party moves out leaving the other to see to the mortgage repayments, the court will give credit to the person who keeps up the loan repayments, in effect treating the payments as to half as those which he or she would have made anyway and as to the other half as having been made on behalf of the person who has left. Against this, it can be said that the person who remains has the exclusive use and benefit of the home and should in some sense account to the one who has left for this. The solution adopted by the courts is to distinguish between the capital and interest components in a normal repayment mortgage.

Thus in *Leake* v. *Bruzzi*,[28] the home was held by the husband on an express trust for himself and his wife as joint tenants. Both contributed to the mortgage repayments, but the express trust concluded the issue as to the existence and valuation of the spouses' equitable shares. The wife left the matrimonial home and the husband remarried and carried on paying the mortgage repayments. The question which arose was whether the wife's half-share in the proceeds of sale should be reduced by at least part of the mortgage repayments which the husband had made since she left. The Court of Appeal held that the wife should give the husband credit for half of that part of the mortgage repayments made in respect of capital, presumably on the basis that, had she remained, the wife would have contributed (half?) towards the monthly repayments which the husband had made on his own after her departure. No allowance should be made in respect of interest payments made however, in view of the fact that the husband had the whole house to himself and would, in any event, have had to pay rent elsewhere.

The husband's payments of interest thus constituted *pro tanto* an "occupation rent" to the wife. This approach has been confirmed by a differently constituted Court of Appeal in *Suttill* v. *Graham*.[29] The effect of these decisions is that when the property is sold, half of the capital element in the mortgage repayments made since the wife left would be deducted from the net proceeds of sale, and the remainder then divided equally between husband and wife.

These calculations, it must be said, are somewhat rough and ready. In practical terms, much will depend on how long the mortgage has been running, and therefore what is the balance of capital and interest in the monthly repayments. In the early years of the mortgage, most of the monthly repayment will be interest, and in the later years, the balance will shift towards capital. There seems to be no good practical reason for giving the person who remains and makes all the payments a significant amount of credit in the latter case and a negligible amount in the former. As we have argued above, it is somewhat artificial to distinguish the capital component and the interest component in the repayments—both form part of the total acquisition cost. Moreover, as we have seen, the capital interest ratios in the monthly payments will vary, according to the type of mortgage. In the capital repayment mortgage, it will alter through time as the interest component diminishes, whereas the ratio will remain constant in the endowment mortgage. Equally, the impact of fluctuations in interest rates will have arbitrary consequences.[30]

In *Leake* v. *Bruzzi* and *Suttill* v. *Graham*, both of which concerned former spouses, it was only necessary to resort to the general principles of equitable accounting because in each case one or both of the former spouses had remarried. As Ormrod L.J. observed in *Suttill*, had a prayer for a property adjustment order been included in the petition for divorce, all these questions would have been dealt with flexibly within the section 24 jurisdiction. But equitable accounting will be necessary where the parties seeking an account have never been married.

2. *Where no Joint Contributions Contemplated*

Where only one of the parties is responsible for the mortgage, the question of accounting will presumably depend upon the circumstances. Where that person remains in occupation after separation, it is difficult to see that there should be any form of account, since he or she still has the benefit of occupation, and the trust in such a case takes the form of a gift of a share to the other. By contrast, if the person responsible for the mortgage leaves, the other remaining in occupation, some form of adjustment would seem appropriate, whichever party keeps up the payments. One possibility, which in some ways is simpler and less arbitrary than the accounting procedures discussed above, is to require the person who remains to pay an occupation rent to the other.

3. *Occupation Rents*

In some cases, the fairly limited exercise of accounting may not go far enough. If, after the termination of cohabitation, the property is to remain unsold for a considerable time, it may be appropriate to order an occupation rent to be paid by the occupier to the person who has left. This issue can arise whether the trusts are express or implied.

In the old cases, a clear rule was stated that one joint tenant or tenant in common in occupation of the land is not liable to pay an occupation rent to his or her fellow tenants in common.[31] In *Bull* v. *Bull*,[32] Denning L.J. stated that the old common law rules concerning legal tenancies in common applied analogously to equitable tenants in common behind a modern trust. This was applied in *Jones* v. *Jones*[33] with the result that an equitable tenant in common in occupation was held not to be liable to pay rent to the other tenant in common who was not in occupation. It is to be noted that the facts of *Jones* v. *Jones* were somewhat unusual, since the equitable tenancies in common did not originate in a joint venture, or in cohabitation.[34]

More recently, there are signs that the courts may be ready to order actual payments to be made while the property remains unsold. This was the position in *Dennis* v. *McDonald*.[35] The case concerned an unmarried couple who had bought a house in 1970 with the intention that it should be their family home. The house was conveyed to them both as joint tenants on trust for themselves as tenants in common in equity. During the twelve years which followed, the plaintiff left the defendant on several occasions because of his violence towards her. Eventually she left for good taking all five children with her. The three older children returned to the house to live with their father whilst the mother kept the two youngest children. The defendant had kept up the mortgage repayments since 1974 (when the plaintiff left) and the mortgage had been discharged by 1980.

The plaintiff, having failed to obtain an order for sale under section 30, claimed that the defendant was obliged to pay to her an "occupation rent." Purchas J. held that credit should be given to the defendant for his mortgage payments between 1977–1980, and that thereafter the defendant should pay half the "fair rent" as agreed between the parties or assessed by a rent officer to the plaintiff. In making his refusal of a section 30 order, the judge said that this refusal was conditional upon the defendant giving and performing such an undertaking. Purchas J.'s judgment was affirmed in the Court of Appeal (although certain adjustments were made to detail).[36]

The basis for quantifying the rent is apparently related to the relative proportions of the shares of the parties. Thus a later court, applying *Dennis* v. *McDonald* in a dispute where the person who remained had a one-third share, ordered an occupation rent to be paid assessed at two-thirds of the fair rent for the property.[37]

Notes to pages 26–72

[1] For the law prior to 1882, see C.S. Kenny, *Effects of Marriage on Property* (1879); for the legislation see V. Ullrich, "The Reform of Matrimonial Property Law in England during the Nineteenth Century," 9 *Victoria University of Wellington Law Review* (1977) 13 and L. Holcombe, "Victorian Wives and Property" in Vicinus (ed.) *A Widening Sphere* (1977).

[2] Though the latter was a centrepiece of many political conflicts: see for example F.M.L. Thompson, "Land and Politics in England in the Nineteenth Century" *loc. cit.*

[3] Law Com. No. 86 (1978).

[4] s.24 Matrimonial Causes Act 1973.

[5] s.31 Matrimonial Causes Act 1973.

[6] See Hayes and Battersby, "Property Adjustment Orders and the Matrimonial Home" (1981) Conv. 404.

[7] See Cretney, *Principles of Family Law* (3rd ed., 1979), pp. 284–335; and see especially Ormrod L.J.'s observations in *Sharp* v. *Sharp* (1981) 11 Fam.Law 121.

[8] The increasing interest in achieving a "clean break" on divorce may alter this to some extent. See, for example, the Law Commission's recent recommendations (Law Com. No. 112 (1981)); G. Douglas, "The Clean Break on Divorce" (1981) Fam.Law 42. So long as maintenance for children continues to be thought desirable, however, a complete "clean break" will remain difficult to achieve: see, for example, Delphy, "Continuities and Discontinuities in Marriage and Divorce," in Barker and Allen (ed.) *Sexual Divisions and Society: Process and Change* (1976).

[9] *e.g. Cowcher* v. *Cowcher* [1972] 1 W.L.R. 425; [1972] 1 All E.R. 943.

[10] [1973] Fam. 72; [1973] 2 W.L.R. 366. See also *Daubney* v. *Daubney* [1976] Fam. 267, 274 *per* Cairns L.J.

[11] *cf.* Cretney, *op. cit.* pp. 300–303.

[12] The choice between these two forms of co-ownership ultimately depends on what the parties wish to happen in the event of the death of one of them. This is considered in Chap. 5.

[13] See Ruoff and Roper, *Registered Conveyancing* (4th ed., 1979), pp. 697, 763 *et seq.* and Chap. 6, *infra*.

[14] See further Chap. 6, *infra*.

[15] *Paul* v. *Paul* (1882) 20 Ch.D. 742; 51 L.J.Ch. 839 and see *Pettitt* v. *Pettitt* [1970] A.C. 777, 813 *per* Lord Upjohn.

[16] Paradoxically, while such determinable trusts should be valued as between unmarried couples, the new trusts may be void for illegality if the parties are married. In any case, when the parties are married, the judicial discretion on divorce or separation permits the court to override such settlements.

[17] Under the medieval common law, estates in land could be transferred, for example by livery of seisin, without the transferee needing to show consideration for the grant. With the development of the use, express uses could be declared on such a transfer, and the Chancellor would compel the grantee to hold the land to the uses declared. From this, the equity courts developed the notion of the resulting use. Where a feoffment occurred, and the feoffee did not provide consideration, and no uses were expressly declared, equity held that a use resulted to the feoffee. The corollary was that where consideration was provided, a use was raised in favour of those who provided consideration. The Statute of Uses 1535 executed many of these uses, including the resulting use, with the consequence that the

cestui que use now came to acquire, by virtue of the statute, the legal estate. This means that a legal estate would not pass unless consideration moved from the grantee, or unless a use was expressly declared on the grant. See Sugden's Introduction to Gilbert's *Uses and Trusts* (3rd ed., 1811). See also Simpson, *Introduction to the History of the Land Law* (1961) Chap. VIII.

[18] At this time, consideration had a different meaning from that commonly in use today. It meant in essence that there had to be some *good reason for the conveyance.* If there was not, and no express uses were declared, there would be a resulting use. Good reasons were taken to be pecuniary consideration (which by the eighteenth century could be nominal) or natural love and affection or marriage. All of these were good consideration, and where a conveyance involved such consideration, no resulting use arose. See Simpson, *op. cit.* p. 167.

[19] *Lloyd* v. *Spillett* (1740) 2 Atk. 148.

[20] The rules concerning succession to realty by the heir at law were abolished by the Administration of Estates Act 1925.

[21] (1698) Prec. Ch. 85.

[22] (1788) 2 Cox. Eq. Cas. 92; White and Tudor's *Leading Cases in Equity* (9th ed.) vol. II, pp. 749 *et seq.*

[23] (1788) 2 Cox Eq. Cas. 94.

[24] *Grey* v. *Grey* (1677) 1 Eq. Abr. 81.

[25] Lawyers appeared to regard the normal expectations of married women of the propertied classes as involving entitlement to a provision by way of a jointure in the marriage settlement. The interesting historical question is not how much of her husband's property a wife acquired, but how much of her own (or of that derived from her family) she was able to keep. The well-known equitable devices employed in this context in the nineteenth century—the settlement to her separate use, commonly coupled with a restraint against anticipation during marriage—were concerned with demarcating and protecting the wife's own property. Similarly, the later debate about the covenant to settle after acquired property concerned delimiting the circumstances in which spouses could be compelled to comply with the covenants in the marriage settlement, when the central purpose—the preservation of the family assets for the next generation—had failed through lack of children. The only significant discretionary remedial concept in use in the nineteenth century— the wife's equity to a settlement—was also a discretion exercised in respect of unsettled property which the wife had brought into the marriage. The general picture which emerges, then, is that wives did not have, in the minds of lawyers, legitimate claims upon their husband's property; which is not to say that the social reality corresponded.

[26] *Ebrand* v. *Dancer* (1680) 2 Ch. Cas. 26.

[27] See for example, *Dummer* v. *Pitcher* (1833) 2 My. & K. 262; *cf. Marshall* v. *Crutwell* (1875) 20 L.R. Eq. Cas. 328.

[28] *Mortimer* v. *Davies* cited in *Rider* v. *Kidder* (1805) 10 Ves. 360, 366.

[29] The history of this section is regrettably obscure. There are barely any *reported* decisions in the inter-war years, so that it is impossible to suggest (a) what kinds of property disputes came before the courts during the period (about realty or personalty; on separation/divorce or during the effective continuation of the marriage) or (b) whether the "broad-brush" approach of some of the post-war judges was new or merely the development of a pre-existing practice. Most relevant court records have been destroyed or, if available, are uninformative. We do know that in 1937 the Rules of the Supreme Court were changed (RSC Ord.54 r.12A (1937)) so as to permit Masters to deal with section 17 applications with all the powers of a High Court judge. Previously, it would seem, they were dealt with almost entirely by a judge in chambers. From this procedural change, one *may* infer that, in the High Court at least, there were a considerable number of section 17 applications (at least relative to the other business of the Court, or certainly enough to make devolving the work on to Masters worthwhile) and secondly, that the applications were of a fairly routine, "administrative", nature, involving the compiling of inventories, etc. This impression is confirmed by some later remarks of Denning L.J., when the validity of r.12A came to be challenged as *ultra vires*. In 1937, by RSC Ord.54 r.22A, a right of appeal was provided from the decision of a Master to the Divisional Court or a judge in chambers. Appeal to the Divisional Court was subsequently excluded in 1940. According to Denning L.J., this was because experience showed that it was most inconvenient that appeals from a decision of the Master under section 17 should be dealt with by the Divisional Court, owing to the amount of detailed investigation involved: *Bernbaum* [1949] P. 325, 329. But such inferences are little more than speculation; alternative explanations are possible, for example, that the change was due to an increase in *other* kinds of court work. The history of section 17 applications in the County Courts is even more shrouded in mystery.

[30] *Pettitt* v. *Pettitt* [1970] A.C. 777; [1969] 2 W.L.R. 966.

[31] *Gissing* v. *Gissing* [1971] A.C. 886; [1970] 3 W.L.R. 255.

[32] [1962] 1 W.L.R. 1124; [1962] 3 All E.R. 345.

[33] [1965] 1 W.L.R. 25; [1965] 1 All E.R. 44.

[34] [1953] 1 Q.B. 63; [1952] 2 All E.R. 863.

[35] [1971] 1 W.L.R. 342; [1971] 1 All E.R. 952.

[36] (1975) 119 S.J. 793.

[37] [1970] 1 W.L.R. 1333; [1970] 3 All E.R. 449.

[38] See *Vandervell* v. *IRC* [1967] 2 A.C. 291; [1967] 2 W.L.R. 87.

[39] J.G. Miller, *Family Property and Financial Provision* (1978), p. 22.

[40] [1970] A.C. 777, 823 *per* Lord Diplock.

[41] Subsequently reversed by s.37 Matrimonial Property and Proceedings Act 1970 see *supra*, pp. 40–41, 44–47.

[42] [1971] A.C. 886, 909 *per* Lord Diplock.

[43] *Ibid.* at p.900 *per* Viscount Dilhorne.

[44] *Ibid.* at p.901; *cf. Richards* v. *Dove* [1974] 1 All E.R. 888.
[45] [1971] A.C. 886, 896, 903.
[46] *Ibid.* at p. 900. See also his judgment in *Ulrich* v. *Ulrich and Felton* [1968] 1 All E.R. 67.
[47] In particular, income security and inter-generational transmission.
[48] For a recent sociological study of these matters, see particularly Edgell, *Middle Class Couples* (1980).
[49] [1972] 1 W.L.R. 301; [1972] 1 All E.R. 932 (C.A.).
[50] [1969] 1 W.L.R. 1676; [1969] 3 All E.R. 1133 (C.A.).
[51] For an overview, see O'Donovan, "Legal Recognition of the Value of Housework" (1978) Fam.Law 215. For the broader debate, see Molyneux, "Beyond the Domestic Labour Debate" 14 New Left Rev. 3 (1979) and Fox (ed.), *Hidden in the Household* (1980). For the broader undercurrents, *cf.* Sargent (ed.), *The Unhappy Marriage of Marxism and Feminism* (1981).
[52] [1972] 1 W.L.R. 425; [1972] 1 All E.R. 943.
[53] See Diplock L.J. in *Ulrich* v. *Ulrich and Fetton*[1968] 1 All E.R. 67, 73.
[54] [1970] A.C. 777, 818.
[55] s.37 Matrimonial Property and Proceedings Act 1970. Of the recent cases, see especially *Dodsworth* v. *Dodsworth* (1973) 228 E.G. 1115 (C.A.) and *Pascoe* v. *Turner* [1979] 1 W.L.R. 431; [1979] 2 All E.R. 945 (C.A.). See further Chap. 4. pp. 110–118.
[56] [1972] 1 W.L.R. 518; [1972] 2 All E.R. 38 (C.A.).
[57] Since anything fixed to the land belongs to its owner.
[58] [1975] 1 W.L.R. 1338; [1975] 3 All E.R. 768 (C.A.).
[59] [1972] 1 W.L.R. 1286; [1972] 3 All E.R. 744 (C.A.).
[60] [1972] 1 W.L.R. 425; [1972] 1 All E.R. 943.
[61] See now *Paul* v. *Constance* [1977] 1 All E.R. 195 (C.A.).
[62] [1972] 1 All E.R. 943, 955.
[63] *Ibid.*
[64] [1975] 1 W.L.R. 1519; [1975] 3 All E.R. 726.
[65] *Ibid.* at p.1525.
[66] *Cf. Hine* v. *Hine* [1962] 1 W.L.R. 1124; [1962] 3 All E.R. 345.
[66a] *Cf.* for married couples *Bernard* v. *Josephs* [1982] 2 W.L.R. 1052 (C.A.).
[67] [1965] 1 W.L.R. 1338; [1975] 3 All E.R. 768.
[68] Some elements of which can also be seen in *Cooke* v. *Head* [1972] W.L.R. 518; [1972] 2 All E.R. 38.
[69] [1974] 1 All E.R. 888.
[70] [1975] 1 W.L.R. 1346; [1975] 3 All E.R. 776 (C.A.).
[71] *Ibid.* at p. 1359 *per* Lord Denning M.R.
[72] *Marvin* v. *Marvin* 557 P. Rep. 2d. series 106 (Cal.Sup.Ct. 1976); Carol S. Bruch, "Property Rights of De Facto Spouses including Thoughts on the Value of Homemakers' Services" *Family Law Quarterly* X, 101 (1976); Susan Westerberg Prager, "Sharing Principles and the

Future of Marital Property Law" UCLA Law Rev.1 (1977); Herma Hill
Kay and Carol Amyx, "Marvin v. Marvin: Preserving the Options" 65
Ca. Law Rev. 937 (1977).

[73] See A.J. Oakley, *Constructive Trusts* (1978).

[74] The Law Commission *Third Report on Family Property* (Law Com.
No. 86) Part 1A.

[75] Although provision is made for a spouse who is not on the title to
apply to the court to be appointed a trustee: Law Com. No. 86, para.
1.293; cls. 19 and 20(5) of the draft Bill.

[76] Paras. 1.55 and 1.61; cl.6(1)(*c*). If the owning spouse has only an
equitable interest, statutory co-ownership operates as a partial assignment of the interest.

[77] Para.1.71; cl.5(2), 3(*a*), (4) and (5).

[78] Paras. 1.106—1.115; cl. 9.

[79] Paras. 1.116—1.126; cl. 10.

[80] Paras. 1.127—1.149; cl.11. The recommendations are quite complex: see Law Com. No. 86, pp. 114–116 for a useful summary.

[81] Para. 1.179.

[82] See the discussion of the "relevant time" in the two systems of
conveyancing, *infra*, pp. 161–163; 165–166.

[83] Obviously, this picture will be modified if, over the longer term, the
inflationary trend is modified or reversed.

[84] On the problem of "sub-trusts," see Pettit, *Equity and the Law of
Trusts* (4th ed., 1979), pp. 57 *et seq.* The point is in any case complicated
by Stamp Duty questions—see *Oughtred* v. *IRC* [1960] A.C. 206; [1959]
3 W.L.R. 898 (H.L.).

[85] This is to import into the law of trusts a basic principle of the
(common) law of gifts—see especially *Thomas* v. *Times Book Co.* [1966]
1 W.L.R. 911. The best trust analogies are in the area of fully secret
trusts and covenants to settle after-acquired property.

[86] The rules concerning priorities between beneficiaries and strangers
are discussed in Chap. 6.

[87] See *infra.*, Chap. 8.

[88] See *infra.*, Chap. 6.

[89] See, for example, Diplock L.J. in *Ulrich* v. *Ulrich and Felton* [1968]
1 All E.R. 67, 72, 73.

[90] *Pettitt* v. *Pettit* [1970] A.C. 777, 816, following Diplock L.J. in
Ulrich (see *supra*, n.89).

[91] *Eves* v. *Eves* [1975] 1 W.L.R. 1338; [1975] 3 All E.R. 768 where the
strict approach of *Diwell* v. *Farnes* [1959] 1 W.L.R. 624; [1959] 2 All
E.R. 379 (C.A.) is rejected.

[92] See *supra*, pp. 59–61.

[93] Finance Act 1974, Sched. 1, para.4(1)(*a*) and (4).

[94] Finance Act 1974, Sched. 1, para. 5(1), and Finance Act 1981, s.24.

[95] See further *infra.*, Chap. 6.

[96] See *supra*, pp. 36–38.

[97] See *supra*, pp. 41–43.

[98] See *infra*, Chap. 8.

[99] [1975] 1 W.L.R. 1338; [1975] 3 All E.R. 768.

[1] See *supra*, pp. 68–71.

[2] *Hall* v. *Hall, The Times*, April 4, 1981 (C.A.).

[3] *Cousins* v. *Dzosens, The Times*, December 12, 1981 (Ch.D.). *Cf. Gordon* v. *Douce, The Times,* January 18, 1983 (C.A.), where it was held that there is no rigid rule for the valuation date.

[4] See Figure 1, *supra*, p. 49.

[5] See *infra*, pp. 85–86.

[6] The reasons for this are examined *infra*, pp. 91–94; 152–157.

[7] The starting point is *Bull* v. *Bull* [1955] 1 Q.B. 234; [1955] 2 W.L.R. 78. *Cf. Re Roger's Questions* [1948] 1 All E.R. 328, which, in some respects, anticipated *Bull.*

[8] See especially, Hawkins (1967) 31 Conv. 117.

[9] [1943] Ch. 302; [1943] 2 All E.R. 440.

[10] *Jones* v. *Challenger* [1961] 1 Q.B. 176; [1960] 2 W.L.R. 695.

[11] *Ibid*. p. 183.

[12] *Re Buchanan-Wollaston's Conveyance* [1939] Ch. 738; [1939] 2 All E.R. 302.

[13] *Williams* v. *Williams* [1976] Ch. 278; [1976] 3 W.L.R. 494.

[14] *Re Evers' Trust, Papps* v. *Evers* [1980] 1 W.L.R. 1327; [1980] 3 All E.R. 399.

[15] [1976] Ch. 278, 285. *Cf.* the earlier decision of *Rawlings* v. *Rawlings* [1964] P. 398, 419 *per* Salmon L.J.

[16] See Cretney, *Principles of Family Law* (3rd ed., 1979), pp.192–193. See further *infra*, pp. 85–86.

[17] *Burke* v. *Burke* [1974] 1 W.L.R. 1063; [1974] 2 All E.R. 944.

[18] *Re Holliday* (a bankrupt) [1980] 3 All E.R. 385. Law. Com. No. 86, suggests codifying the wider view—see cl. 22(3) of the draft Bill.

[19] [1971] 1 W.L.R. 1539; [1971] 3 All E.R. 774.

[20] (1970) 114 S.J. 864.

[21] See *supra*, pp. 68–72.

[22] For example, See *Re Holliday, supra* and see *infra*, pp. 198–199.

[23] [1961] 1 Q.B. 176.

[24] [1965] 2 Q.B. 666; [1965] 3 W.L.R. 891.

[25] [1939] Ch. 738.

[26] [1977] 1 W.L.R. 438.

[27] See *supra* pp. 21–23 and not the Law Commission's recommendations conerning financial provision on divorce (Law Com. No. 112, 1981).

[28] [1974] 1 W.L.R. 1528; [1974] 2 All E.R. 1196.

[29] *Suttill* v. *Graham* [1977] 3 All E.R. 1117.

[30] See Denyer (1978) 128 New L.J. 828.

[31] See *Henderson* v. *Eason* (1847) 2 Ph. 308; *M'Mahon* v. *Burchell* (1846) 2 Ph. 127 and see *infra*, Chap. 4, pp. 88–90.

[32] [1955] 1 Q.B. 234, 237.

[33] [1977] 1 W.L.R. 438; (1976) 33 P. & C.R. 147.

[34] See further *infra*, Chap. 5, p. 129.

[35] [1981] 1 W.L.R. 810; (1981) 125 S.J. 308; *cf. Bernard* v. *Josephs* [1982] 2 W.L.R. 1052 (C.A.).

[36] A similar approach may be developing within the divorce jurisdiction, see *Brown* v. *Brown, The Times*, December 11, 1981 (C.A.); [1982] 3 F.L.R. 161; *Harvey* v. *Harvey* [1982] 2 W.L.R. 283 (C.A).

[37] *Cousins* v. *Dzosens, The Times*, December 12, 1981.

Chapter 4

PROTECTING OCCUPATION

A. INTRODUCTION

If entries in the Law Reports provide any kind of index, protecting occupation of the home has become a particular concern of the modern law, and indeed certain legal concepts—notably licences and estoppel—have been remodelled in recent years to as to provide a fairly flexible framework through which occupation disputes can be processed. This contemporary concern with residential security was largely absent in the rules and doctrines of family property law both before and immediately after the passing of the 1925 code. The main focus of the traditional law was upon pre or post-mortem inheritance (upon *inter vivos* settlements or the devolution of property on death). Residential security was a relatively unimportant concern of the old framework.[1]

The modern law has developed against the background of the changing tenurial context—the growth of owner-occupation and the decline of a free market private rented sector. The emphasis upon residential security can be traced back to the ways in which matrimonial law came to be modified as occupation of the matrimonial home became a central issue on marital breakdown.

B. MATRIMONIAL LAW

(1) *The common law and occupation*

At common law, a husband was under a legal duty to provide a home for his wife and children. In its original form, this duty was part of a broader framework in which the wife was subordinate to and dependent upon her

husband, which included the husband's right of chastise-
ment, the wife's duty to provide sexual services, the
husband's right of guardianship over children, and indeed,
in the absence of a suitable settlement, full ownership or
at least control by the husband of the wife's property for
the duration of the marriage.[2] In the latter part of the
nineteenth century different elements of this common law
framework were modified by successive statutes.[3] The
duty to provide a home survived unaltered into the
modern law and became particularly entwined with the
legal regulation of marital breakdown, especially desertion and separation.

(2) *Equity*

After the "fusion" of law and equity effected by the
Judicature Acts 1873–75, equitable remedies could be
sought to protect the infringement of common law rights.
Thus the common law duty to provide a home could be
protected by an injunction restraining the husband from
disposing of the home without providing alternative
accommodation. In the 1950s conflicting views emerged of
the scope of this equitable jurisdiction. Either it meant (as
in the law of nuisance) that equitable remedies were being
used to supplement the sometimes less satisfactory remedies previously offered by the common law; alternatively, it meant that a wife had an "equity," if she was
deserted by her husband, such that her occupation was
secure against mortgagees or purchasers of the home from
the deserting husband.

This latter view, the "deserted wife's equity," first
promoted by Lord Denning in *Bendall* v. *McWhirter*,[4]
flourished in some courts[5] in the 1950s, to be unanimously
repudiated in favour of the former view, that equity was
merely supplementing the common law remedy, by the
House of Lords in *National Provincial Bank* v. *Ainsworth*.[6]
The divergence of view, however, was only germane if the
husband subsequently sold or mortgaged the home after

deserting his wife; it did not affect the position in a dispute between husband and wife in which the duty to provide a home was clearly established. Put differently, the important question for many purposes, both before and after *Ainsworth*, was not the position of the wife vis-à-vis strangers, but whether, in one way or another, she could resort to the law to prevent her husband from dealing with the home. In this respect, two questions should be distinguished. First, can the wife seek an order restraining the husband from dealing with the home, thereby protecting her occupation? Secondly, will the law protect her occupation if the husband tries to sell or mortgage the home?

(3) *Protection during marriage*

(a) Section 17 Married Women's Property Act 1882

Under this section, the courts had a summary jurisdiction to determine, in a dispute between husband and wife, any question " . . . as to the title to or possession of property. . . . " A deserted wife could make an application seeking an undertaking from the husband to permit her continued residence in the house, unless he provided suitable alternative accommodation.[7] Equally, given the common law duty to provide a home, the husband would need to apply to the court under section 17 if he sought possession of the home.[8]

In practical terms, this jurisdiction remained important, even though, while the deserted wife's equity flourished, strangers might have been wary of dealing with the matrimonial home, and the courts might have protected the wife if a purchaser had sought possession. Following the collapse of the deserted wife's equity, the Matrimonial Homes Act 1967 was introduced as a simpler and more straightforward means of protecting occupation against dealing with the property.

(b) The Matrimonial Homes Act 1967 (as amended)

As between the spouses, the Act puts the old common law duty on a statutory basis, with the difference that it confers a right to occupy a *particular* home. In section 1 of the 1967 Act "statutory rights of occupation" in the matrimonial home are given to spouses in certain specified circumstances. Protection is only of occupation, not of shares in proceeds of sale.[9] The Act makes no distinction between wives and husbands; both enjoy a statutory right of occupation. A qualifying spouse who is in occupation of the matrimonial home has the right "not to be evicted or excluded from the dwelling-house or any part thereof by the other spouse except with the leave of the court." A spouse who is not in occupation, has the right "to enter into and occupy" the dwelling-house, but must first obtain leave of the court.[10]

Since 1967, the definition of "qualifying spouse" has been extended. Originally the 1967 Act only covered those spouses who had no legal or equitable interest in the house. By the Matrimonial (Proceedings and Property) Act 1970 this protection was extended to spouses who owned an equitable but not a legal interest in the house. Finally, by the Matrimonial Homes and Property Act 1981, protection is now given where neither spouse has a *legal* interest in the property, *e.g.* where the house is held by separate trustees on trust for the husband and wife. The Act does not apply where both spouses are on the title—in such cases, one spouse can at most deal with his or her equitable interest without the concurrence of the other.[11]

Under section 2 of the 1967 Act the statutory right of occupation may be registered as a class F land charge, if title is unregistered, or by a notice if the title is registered (registration of a caution is no longer possible after the 1981 Act)).[12] Once the right of occupation has been registered, it binds most third parties, except for a trustee in bankruptcy (section 2(5)). So far as the occupier is concerned this exception may be important. If for example a husband is unable to sell a property because of the class F charge registered on it by his wife, and he has to support another household too, he may well find the financial strain impossible and may be forced into bankruptcy, in which case the property would almost certainly be sold.

(c) Control over dealings during marriage

It is generally assumed that the main function of the Act is to enable a qualifying spouse to enter a charge or (after 1981) notice in the course of a matrimonial dispute, with a view to preventing the other spouse from disposing of the matrimonial home. In other words, registration is generally a "hostile" act; once undertaken, it will be virtually impossible for the owner to dispose of the property.[13] But in many cases, no doubt, a spouse will not register a statutory right of occupation unless there are marital difficulties.[14] In the words of Lord Denning M.R. in *Williams and Glyn's* v. *Boland*:

> "[T]he Act [of 1967] was of precious little use to [the wife], at any rate when she was living at home in peace with her husband. She would never have heard of a class F land charge: and she would not have understood it if she had."[15]

The Law Commission has proposed the introduction of a new registrable charge, which would have the effect of putting on a more formal basis a spouse's ability to consent to dealings by the other spouse with the matrimonial home. Where the statutory co-ownership scheme applies, failure to observe the requirement by the spouse in whom the home is vested would constitute, as between the parties, a breach of trust.[16] So far as purchasers and mortgagees are concerned, the Law Commission's proposals envisage that a stranger will only be affected if the consent requirement is registered. We postpone consideration of this aspect of the proposals to our discussion of the position of purchasers vis-à-vis beneficiaries behind trusts.[17]

The effect of non-registration is exactly the same as in the general scheme provided for by the 1925 legislation. Third parties will not be bound by the statutory right of occupation provided for in section 1 of the 1967 Act if that right has not been registered.

(4) *Protection on divorce*

The Matrimonial Homes Act ceases to apply after divorce. Before the changes in divorce law in 1969–1970, the courts had no power to order that the wife be permitted to remain in the former matrimonial home after a marital dissolution. If, however, she could establish that she had an interest in the home, she might be able to remain in occupation (this possibility is discussed in the next section). For this reason, it became common, in divorce proceedings to make an application under section 17. Provided that the application was lodged before the decree absolute, the court could hear the application, though section 17 ceased to apply after marital dissolution.[18] Alternatively, a wife seeking maintenance on separation or desertion from the magistrates' court or maintenance under the Matrimonial Causes Act 1857 might accept a reduced maintenance so long as she was allowed to remain in the home.[19]

Under the modern divorce code, the court has a much freer hand to make property adjustments on divorce (see s. 24 Matrimonial Causes Act 1973). One apparently common practice has been the development of *Mesher*[20] orders. A *Mesher* order means that, whatever share the wife receives under the property adjustment jurisdiction, her occupation will be protected until the children of the dissolved marriage are grown. Of course, this approach postpones the problem, and, recently, the question of

what should happen at the time a *Mesher* order expires
has been aired in the courts.[21] One answer canvassed
recently is that the wife should pay an occupation rent to
the husband, the house only to be sold in the event of her
non-compliance.[22]

(5) *Domestic violence and the protection of occupation*

One aspect of protecting occupation, though it can only
be considered briefly here, concerns the extent to which
the courts are able to exclude a cohabitee or a spouse from
the family home. The divorce courts could grant an
interim injunction, but only after divorce proceedings had
been commenced. These injunctions could be (and indeed
can be) used to exclude the husband from the matrimonial
home, but were (and are) used fairly infrequently because
of their supposed "drastic" nature.[23] The magistrates'
courts, in operating the alternative jurisdiction, were not
empowered to exclude a husband from the family home;
their powers were restricted to ordering maintenance for
the wife and suspending her duty to cohabit.[24]

The Domestic Violence and Matrimonial Proceedings
Act 1976 provided relief for the victims of violence in the
home, whether the parties were married or not, and
included protection for children.[24a] The mechanism used
to obtain this protection is again the injunction, to which a
power of arrest may be attached in extreme cases. Under
the 1976 Act, such injunctions can only be obtained from
the county courts or higher courts. This last defect has to
some extent been remedied by the Domestic Proceedings
and Magistrates' Courts Act 1978 which extends a similar
jurisdiction to the magistrates' courts, although this
jurisdiction is only available to married couples. These
two measures may then provide some protection of
occupation for the cohabitee or spouse, in that they may
exclude the other partner from the property, at least on a
temporary basis.[25]

C. BENEFICIAL OWNERSHIP AND OCCUPATION RIGHTS

Until the growth of mass owner-occupation, there was no particular connection between the ownership and occupation of houses. Houses were frequently the subject matter of a family trust, and held by trustees as a capital asset yielding an income to be distributed in accordance with the trust on which they held. Thus, if trustees under a duty to invest were not additionally empowered by the trust instrument to permit the beneficiaries to occupy a house comprised in the trust property, the court would not imply such a power or permit such an application of the trust property.[26]

There were, however, certain conventional ways by a settlor or testator could grant the right to occupy a particular property.

(1) *Traditional modes of securing occupation*

(a) Licences or life estates

Prior to the first major statutory reforms of the 1880s, it was a relatively simple matter to secure occupation, especially for widows on the death of a husband. In adopting a particular legal form, the primary question was whether the testator merely wished to give an option to reside, or whether, in addition, he wished that she should receive the net rents and profits for her lifetime, if she chose not to reside and a tenant was put in the property. Three main methods were available: (i) a devise of land on trust, empowering the trustees to permit the widow to occupy for her life. If she did not so wish, then empowering the trustees to pay the rents to other persons; (ii) the creation of a life estate in favour of the widow, determinable upon her ceasing to reside or, more probably, a similar life interest behind a trust; and (iii) a life estate or life interest behind a trust, the trustees being empowered to permit residence in a specified house. Prior to 1882, the practical effect of the first two possibilities was the same: the widow's rights would end on the termination of her occupation; by contrast, in the third case, she would be automatically entitled to the net rents and profits if she chose not to reside. The effect of the Settled Land Acts 1882–1925 was to assimilate the second method to the third rather than, as previously, to the first. This was because the scheme of the Acts was to override settlements which sought to place limits upon the power of tenants for life (*i.e.* the widow).

The main target of the Settled Land Acts was the reform of the nineteenth century strict settlement. Since the courts were reluctant to impede the effectiveness of these statutes, so far as the power of sale was concerned,[27] these relatively simple devices for protecting occupancy during widowhood tended to be brought within the Settled Land Act scheme, with the consequence that the widow would have all the powers of the tenant for life, and the right to call the legal estate to be vested in her.[28] The 1925 scheme did, however, permit a similar result to be achieved while avoiding the complications of the Settled Land Act: the land could be devised on trust for sale, the trustees being empowered to permit the widow to occupy, and making her consent requisite to any sale. Such a method may have been well-established before 1925.[29]

(b) Tenancy in common (or joint tenancy)

Under the pre-1926 law, the creation of legal co-ownership provided a convenient device for creating a joint right to occupy a property. Whichever form was chosen, each of the co-owners would be entitled to occupy the property concurrently with the others. However, although today we tend to associate the tenancy in common with concurrent occupation of property, it is important to remember that in the nineteenth century, the tenancy in common was often used as a means of settling and apportioning rents or revenue from real estate between members of the family. Where land was settled in this way, each tenant was entitled to occupation of the property or to his due share of the rents and profits therefrom. The choice between the two forms depended upon precisely what the settlor envisaged. If the concurrent interests were for life, then if granted by way of joint tenancy, the whole rental income would go to the life tenants until the death of the last lived; if granted by way of tenancy in common, each life tenant would have a fixed share of the income, and on the death of one, that share would pass to the reversioners (subject to accumulation powers, etc.). If the concurrent interests were absolute, then the choice between the two forms depended quite simply on whether the settlor wished the right of survivorship to apply between the grantees.[30]

Occupation or receipt by one was treated by the common law as occupation or receipt by all, and no tenant out of possession could maintain an action against one in possession. The relations of concurrent owners *inter se* were largely left to private arrangement. Agreements as to occupation rents would be enforced, but occupation by one in the absence of such agreement would not enable the other tenants to sue the occupant for rent. If, however, one tenant was excluded by another, an action for ejectment was available.

The other situation in which the law intervened in the mutual dealings of tenants in common or joint tenants related to the receipt of rents by one. Statutory provision was made in 1705[31] whereby if one tenant received more than his just share of the rents or profits of the land, the others could seek an account to redress the balance. For procedural convenience, such accounts were normally sought in Chancery, but disputes as to entitlement were matters for the courts of common law.[32] Thus, although, traditionally, the tenancy in common was a means for permitting joint occupation, it was, from a legal point of view, primarily a means of settling rents.

A further use of the tenancy in common was in the context of strict or dynastic settlement. A common provision in such a settlement, especially if made upon the marriage of the expectant heir, was that, in the event of there being no sons of the marriage, the estate would pass to the daughters as tenants in common in tail male, with cross-remainders over. This form of limitation might mean that the family property would eventually come to be concentrated in the hands of one male, but, in the meantime, the tenancy in common provided a useful means for apportioning the rents, which would be necessary since, if the daughters married, they might all live away from the family estates.[33]

Reform of the legal tenancy in common centred around eliminating the fragmentation of legal title which it involved. This was achieved by separating the right to beneficial enjoyment from the possession of legal title, by imposing a trust. To simplify, the aim seems to have been to effect a significant change from the technical point of view of conveyancing, while leaving unaltered the practical ability to enjoy the property. Under the old framework, the right to enjoy the property (occupation or receipt of rents) derived from possession of a legal estate, and the right to ensure apportionment of rents was a creature of statute. The 1925 legislation substituted a new framework. First, the legal estate was to be vested in trustees, who were obliged to apportion the rents among all the tenants in common on the basis of a fiduciary duty. The 1705 Act was abolished and replaced by an action to account rooted in a trustee-beneficiary relationship. The same pattern was adopted in the case of a former strict settlement, when the tenancies in common in favour of the daughters took effect in possession upon the failure of male issue. Under the Settled Land Act, s.36 the legal estate vested in trustees, and not, as in other cases under the Settled Land Act, in the tenant(s) for life. In each case, the trust imposed by statute was a trust for sale.

(2) *The statutory trust for sale*

In the quest to eliminate the fragmentation of title associated with the tenancy in common, the trust for sale was a convenient mechanism for the conveyancers responsible for the 1925 reforms. Under the statutory trust, the trustees were " . . . to stand possessed of the net proceeds of sale . . . and of the net rents and profits until sale after payment of rates . . . and other outgoings. . . ." (s.35 L.P.A. 1925). The apportionment of rent could be achieved just as easily by the statutory trust for sale, since the trustees were empowered by section 25 of the Law of Property Act 1925 to postpone sale and exempted from all liability for choosing to postpone. But the technical change of form made a significant difference from the point of view of alienability. The entire estate, under the old law, could not be sold to a purchaser unless every tenant in common participated; under the new statutory trust for sale, the interests of the beneficiaries would be "overreached" (converted into purchase money) in a sale by the trustees.[34] If there was a dispute as to sale, the court was empowered to order or refuse a sale "as it thinks fit" (s.30 L.P.A. 1925).

So far as alienability was concerned, the trust for sale had a further advantage. Trustees who sold did so in performance of their duty and it was the obvious device to employ, in the light of nineteenth century conveyancing practice, for keeping trusts off the title.[35]

Conversion and reconversion[36]

The introduction of the trust for sale brought with it a particular feature which has bedevilled much of the modern law. The trust for sale was introduced to facilitate the transfer of a good title on sale. Whether express or statutory, the trustees were under a fiduciary obligation to pay the rents and proceeds to the beneficiaries, but, strictly, the beneficiaries did not have equitable interests in the land held by the trustees pending sale. Before 1926, when, in the event of intestacy, realty descended to the heir-at-law and personalty to the next of kin, an interest of a person behind a trust for sale descended to the next of kin, since the trustees were under a duty to convert into personalty. This was an example of the doctrine of conversion, which operated, in devolution on death, to direct the property to go to those entitled after the conversion was completed. The rule was previously of some importance on intestacy, but since the Administration of Estates Act 1925, the rules for descent on intestacy of realty have been assimilated to those of personalty. Consequently, as Lightwood remarked in 1927[37]: "The disappearance of the distinction in cases of intestacy between the devolution of real and personal estate makes this branch of equity, and the decisions on which it was founded, obsolete." The doctrine of conversion is still relevant when, in a will, devises or bequests are couched in general terms. Strictly speaking that is all that the doctrine ever achieved; it regulated the devolution of land subject to a duty to convert, and served to identify the relevant class of beneficiaries. It did not serve, pending conversion, to affect the rights of the beneficiaries behind the trust for sale, whose rights, as we have stated, were to the net rents prior to and the proceeds of sale.

It was long established that the beneficiaries, if all *sui juris* and interested in possession, could elect to take the land as land, and thereby frustrate a sale. This rule may have survived into the post-1925 law, enabling, for example, the beneficiaries behind an express trust for sale to demand a conveyance of title from the trustees, to hold on the statutory trusts, or creating a settlement operating under the Settled Land Act.

(3) *The right to occupy property held subject to a trust for sale*

We have already seen that under the old law the right to

possession went with the legal estate. After 1925, this right passed to the statutory trustees, who had no express power by statute to permit the beneficiaries to occupy the trust property pending sale, although, if all the beneficiaries were *sui juris*, it would seem that none could have complained of a breach of trust if one or more were permitted to occupy before sale, if all acquiesced in such a course of action. This scheme may have made sense in the light of the objectives of the reformers in 1925, but it is less attractive as a legal framework for modern owner-occupation of the family home. If today people buy a house together, they usually do so with the intention of occupying. In such circumstances, who has the right to possession? If the house is in the joint names of the parties, then under the old rule, they are jointly entitled to possession. The more difficult question is where both parties have share of the equity, but the house is in the name of one of the parties only.

The problem first surfaced in *Bull* v. *Bull*.[38] In *Bull*, a mother and son both contributed towards the cost of acquisition of a house with a view to them both living in the property. The conveyance, however, was taken in the son's name alone. The court described them as each having in equity "an undivided share in the house."[39] The son then married and his wife and mother-in-law fell out. The son then sought a possession order against his mother. In denying the order, the Court of Appeal looked at authority on the mutual rights of tenants in common before 1925 and concluded, "each of them is entitled to the possession of the land and to the use and enjoyment of it in a proper manner . . . Until a sale takes place these equitable tenants in common have the same rights to enjoy the land as legal tenants in common used to have."[40]

It followed from this that the son was refused an order because the mother was equally entitled with the son to possession of the house. The only way in which the son could proceed to sell the house with vacant possession would be to obtain the mother's consent to such a sale. If such consent were unforthcoming, then, assuming the land to be held on trust for sale as a result of the implied trust, the son would have to apply to the court for an order for sale under the section 30 jurisdiction. It would then be up to the court to decide whether to set aside the mother's refusal to consent.

There are two strands to this decision. The first concerns the rights of equitable tenants in common and the second concerns the rights of beneficiaries under a trust for sale vis-à-vis the trustee. These are examined in turn.

(4) *The rights of equitable tenants in common*

In *Bull*, Denning L.J. suggested that the abolition of the legal tenancy in common was largely a change of form, not substance. This is inconsistent with the old rule that possession follows the legal estate, and has been criticised on that basis.[41] Against this must be set the simple argument that in many situations the parties intend a joint right of occupation.

It may be possible to take a narrower view of this strand of the decision in *Bull*. In *Bull*, the son did not come to court in order to exercise one of his statutory powers. He did not come to court in his capacity as trustee. Rather, he came to court *qua* beneficiary in order to obtain exclusive use of the trust property. In such circumstances, it is legitimate to look at the old learning on the legal tenancy in common and to hold that the son has no right to exclusive possession, but rather, as equitable tenant in common had equal rights to possession with his mother, given the absence of any independent legal relationship. This need not involve any erosion of the principle that the statutory scheme takes priority. Thus, if the son had come to court *qua* trustee, the issue should have been determined with reference to the statutory scheme and not with regard to the relationship between mother and son *qua* equitable tenants in common. It is this distinction that the reasoning in *Bull* obscures.

(5) *The statutory position*

The next question is whether a trustee who seeks possession from a beneficiary is entitled to the order he seeks. *Bull* was not clear on this point. By section 26(3) of the Law of Property Act 1925, the trustee is under a duty to consult the beneficiaries in possession. The court may grant an injunction to ensure performance of this duty prior to any disposition by the trustee.[42] Denning L.J. suggested that the trustee could not sell without the consent of the beneficiary; this seems to put the position too strongly, since under a statutory trust for sale, the beneficiary does not have a veto over sale, just a right to be consulted, and section 26(3) provides that the wishes of the beneficiaries with the largest share should prevail.

It is also clear that the trustee cannot sell with vacant possession unless the court will give a possession order evicting the beneficiary from the home. *Bull* may be authority for the view that the court will not give possession to a sole trustee, and that a second trustee should be appointed before the Court should consider making such an order. The courts have, at the instance of a beneficiary, granted an injunction forbidding sale by a sole trustee so that the beneficiary can have the protection of a second trustee.[43]

The ambiguities of *Bull* can be highlighted by comparing it with the later case of *Barclay* v. *Barclay*.[44] In *Barclay*, an express trust for sale of a bungalow was created by will, in favour of a number of descendants of the testator. One of these descendants was actually living in the bungalow and the personal representative of the deceased (also a tenant in common under the will) sought a possession order from the court. In order to resist this application the defendant sought to rely on *Bull* v. *Bull i.e.* the right of every tenant in common to possession of the property. The Court of Appeal distinguished *Bull* on the basis that in *Bull* the tenancy in common was of the house, whereas in *Barclay* it was of the proceeds of sale. Therefore it was right in *Barclay* to order the tenant in common in occupation to vacate so that the property could be sold and the proceeds realised for distribution.

Although, in common-sense terms, the two cases are different, we must now consider what the legal basis might be for permitting the beneficiary to remain in occupation as in *Bull* and evicting him as in *Barclay*.

The most satisfactory explanation seems to be that the purpose for which the trust came into being was different in the two cases.[45] In *Bull*, the property was acquired for the purpose of cohabitation by mother and son. In *Barclay*, the trust for sale arose in a will under which the property was to be sold and the proceeds divided among the beneficiaries. Put another way, in *Bull*, the trust for sale was purely a conveyancing device imposed by statute, whereas the testator in *Barclay* specifically intended a sale. It is to be noted that this is not the same as a distinction between a statutory and an express trust for sale. In the case of a joint purchase of the family home, it is common for the title to be taken by the puchasers expressly on trust for sale. Where, however, occupation by the purchasers is envisaged, it is still appropriate to describe the trust for sale as a conveyancing device. The true distinction thus seems to be whether, when the trust came into being, occupation or sale was primarily envisaged.

D. CONTRACTUAL LICENCES

(1) *The "licence" and property law*

The licence, like the resulting trust, has been modified as the courts have been faced with disputes concerning the family home. The licence has been displaced from its previously peripheral role in English property law, and become a substantial right analogous to a tenancy but with remedial undertones. In traditional English jurisprudence, a "licence" was only defined in a negative way. A licence negatived the doing of an unlawful act; the licensor, having licenced a person to enter upon his land, could not, for the duration of the licence, treat the licensee as a trespasser. The classic statement of this position is often said to be found in Vaughan C.J.'s judgment in *Thomas* v. *Sorrell*[46]: "A dispensation or licence properly passeth no interest, nor alters or transfers property in any thing, but only makes an action lawful, which without it had been unlawful."

Thomas v. *Sorrell* was concerned with the relationship between the royal prerogative and statute, and the question was whether James I could validly licence the Company of Vintners in the City of London, incorporated under letters patent from him, to sell retail wine, or whether the licence was void as conflicting with the earlier statute of 7 Ed. 6 c. 5. Vaughan C.J. sought to determine the boundaries of the King's dispensing power by drawing an analogy between the proper sphere or patrimony of the King and the individual subject; the King could dispense, just like any *paterfamilias*, with what was his own: "The King cannot dispense in any case, but with his own right, and not with the right of any other."[47] The attempt to equate the dispensing power of the Crown with the ability of a private subject to license the commission of acts in respect of which only that subject might maintain an action obliquely reveals the nature of the licence: "As a licence to go beyond the seas, to hunt in a man's park, to come into his house, are only actions, which without licence, had been unlawful."[48] The important distinction was between a mere licence and something which amounted to a grant:

> "But a licence to hunt in a man's park, and carry away the deer kill'd to his own use; to cut down a tree in a man's grounds, and to carry it away the next day

after to his own use, are licences as to the acts of
hunting and cutting down the tree; but as to the
carrying away of the deer kill'd, and tree cut down,
they are grants."[49]

It is this distinction between a licence and a grant which
provides us with the second important sense in which the
licence, traditionally, had a largely negative character. A
licence was a transaction which did not involve the
transmission of a proprietary right. A licence did not
involve the creation of an easement or a profit, or a lease.
It was, in other words, defined by what it was not.

A pure licensee then was simply someone whose entry
was not trespass, but whose entry was equally not
attributable to a grant of some proprietary right to enter.
A licence might, however, be ancillary to a grant as with a
licence to enter ancillary to a grant of the right to take
timber. A licence coupled with a grant involved the
creation of a definite proprietary relationship, within the
purview of property law, while a mere licence preserved
intact the proprietary rights of the licensor, although, if he
revoked the licence, the licensee had to be permitted a
reasonable time to leave the land.

The position becomes more complex if the licence is
coupled with a contractual relationship, or if some equity
arises in the course of dealings between licensor and
licensee. The latter is considered below; for the moment
we concentrate upon the "contractual licence."

(2) *Contractual licences*

There is no particular difficulty in speaking of contracts
or licences—but the amalgam contractual licence has
given rise to some confusion, especially so far as revocability is concerned. A contractual licence involves a
binding contract, whose content involves the entry of one
party upon the land of the other, but in circumstances
where property law denies that any proprietary rela-

tionship has been established. This can be observed in cases where the issue for the court is whether a particular transaction creates a lease or a licence. The question arose in a number of cases concerned with the legal effect of "front-of-house" rights in theatres. The courts consistently held that these arrangements constituted licences and therefore did not involve the grant of any proprietary interest in favour of the licensee.[50]

One conclusion can be drawn at this stage from the preceding discussion. Whatever the content of the contract, a licence was denied the status of a proprietary relationship by property law. At the same time, however, the contractual licence involves positive rights arising out of the contract. The first question, then, is how extensive are these rights, as between the original parties? Does one emphasise the contractual relationship—and thus directly enforce the promises of the parties; or the licence aspect, and emphasise, from the point of view of property law, the vulnerability of the licensee to have his permission to enter withdrawn? This question was squarely addressed when the courts had to decide whether licences were always revocable.

(a) Revocability

The traditional view was that a licence as such was always revocable, unless it was connected with the grant of some proprietary right. In the latter case, revocation of a licence which was incidental to a grant would not be permitted since it would constitute a derogation from the grant. In this respect, there were two prerequisites before a licence was irrevocable. First, that it was ancillary to a grant, secondly, that the grant was of something which did lie in grant, like a recognised easement or profit (such as a right to take timber). If the right in question did not lie in grant, then the licence was revocable. Could a licence which was not attached to a grant be revoked? The old view can be seen in *Wood* v. *Leadbitter*,[51] which concerned a licence to enter an enclosure at the Doncaster races. The question was whether, after a purported revocation of the licence, the licensee could lawfully be expelled. The Court of Exchequer held that he could, since upon revocation he became a trespasser. The decision was narrow but clear: a mere licence is always revocable; a licence coupled with a grant duly made is not.

In *Hurst* v. *Picture Theatres*,[52] the majority considered that the Judicature Acts altered this position, so that if the licence was contractual, an injunction was available to restrain revocation. The reasoning is somewhat confused. Alderson B. had stated in *Wood* v. *Leadbitter* that a right to watch the races, if claimed as an indefeasible right, was at least a right of way, and thus, to take effect as a grant, should be made by deed. In *Hurst*, the majority seemed to suggest that after the Judicature Acts, a grant would no longer fail for want of a deed. Therefore, it followed that *Wood* v. *Leadbitter* was no longer good law. "It cannot be said as against the plaintiff that he is a licensee with no grant merely because there is not an instrument under seal which gives him a right at law," *per* Buckley L.J.[53]

The majority's approach blurs some important distinctions. Subject to the discretionary nature of specific performance, a contract for a grant is, after the Judicature Acts, more or less as good as a grant in any court of law as well as equity, because equity prevails over law. In this sense, the want of a deed is immaterial (though in practical terms, there are a number of respects in which someone with a deed is better off than someone relying on a contract).[54] The important distinction in modern law is whether there is a contract to make a grant of a proprietary right (be it an easement or whatever) or a contract to license entry upon land for a definite or indefinite duration. The former is a contract to grant, and here it may be that, after the Judicature Acts, if the contract is specifically enforceable, a licence coupled with a contract to make a grant is in broad terms as irrevocable as a pre-Judicature Acts licence coupled with a grant. But the Judicature Acts can have had no effect upon the latter contract, because a mere licence, according to Alderson B., did not depend for its revocability upon questions of formality but upon the fact that it was not a grant[55]: " . . . a licence under seal (provided it is a mere licence) is as revocable as a licence by parol."

Until recently, there was still hesitation over the question of revocability, linked to a certain confusion about whether the recognition of irrevocability would transform the licence into a proprietary interest. But the matter has been put beyond doubt by Megarry J. in *Hounslow* v. *Twickenham G.D. Ltd.*[56] From this case it follows *only* that the licensor will be prevented from obtaining possession of the property for the period specified in the contract. As we shall see, when the contract is informal, this will involve in effect the exercise of discretion by the court. For this reason, some uses of the licence can be regarded as remedial.

(b) Exclusive possession

The second relatively novel feature about the modern contractual licence arises from the fact that it apparently can (and often will) involve, as one of its terms, the licensee having exclusive possession of the property. Hargreaves has argued that, in the old law, "exclusive possession" was the yardstick to determine whether a person on the property of another was a tenant or a licensee.[57] Thus exclusive possession was used as the test in the old "front-of-house" cases. This test has largely been eroded. Exclusive possession is now only a necessary, not a sufficient, condition for a tenancy. Overriding it is a resort to the intention of the parties, to be discerned (especially for present purposes) from the circumstances of the relationship. Against the background of statutory control of residential tenancies, the courts have come to view family arrangements as licences not tenancies and as therefore falling outside the Rent Acts.[58]

(c) Intention to create legal relations

The deployment of the family/commercial distinction in the law of landlord and tenant as a basis for discerning the intention of the parties cut across, somewhat paradoxically, an older doctrine designed to limit the intervention of the law of contract into domestic relations, as expressed, for example, in *Balfour* v. *Balfour*,[59] and some judges have shown reluctance to find or infer contracts in family disputes (see Lord Denning in *Hardwick* v. *Johnson*,[60] Danckwerts L.J. in *Jones* v. *Padavatton*[61]).

However, the refusal to analyse a relationship in contractual terms no longer means that the court will not interfere in some other way (for example, inferring an "equitable" licence[62]). Such hesitation as persists about the *Balfour* guideline leads only to render the analysis of disputes more erratic.[63]

(d) The modern case law

Subject to the foregoing considerations, it is quite straightforward for parties to enter into an express and relatively formal written contract providing for joint or exclusive occupation by one party of the home. But in many of the reported disputes, the relationship between the parties has been informal and the courts have proceeded by way of inference from the facts—from evidence of intentions and circumstantial evidence. For this reason, as we try to indicate in the discussion which follows, it is sometimes difficult to tell whether the modern law is concerned with finding express or implied agreements or with using "contract" as a convenient starting point from which to award the remedy which seems appropriate in the circumstances. Viewed in the latter way, the line between contract and estoppel becomes very fine indeed.[64]

A good illustration is to be found in *Hardwick* v.

Johnson.[65] The husband's mother agreed to purchase a house for her son and daughter-in-law on the understanding they paid her £28 per month. The conveyance was taken in the mother's name. The husband left the wife and the wife offered to continue paying the monthly sums. The mother-in-law sought possession and the question for the court was whether the daughter-in-law had any right whereby she could resist this claim for possession. No clear agreement had ever been concluded as to the nature of the legal relationship between the parties. Lord Denning M.R. eventually described the relationship as an "equitable licence" whereas Roskill and Browne L.JJ. called it a contractual licence. The majority view meant that there was a contractual licence made between the mother-in-law and the husband and wife in consideration of the payment of £28 per month. Since the licence was apparently not conditional on the marriage continuing, the wife was entitled to stay if she was prepared to make the same payments.

It should further be noted that the court expressly refused to put a limit on the duration of the licence, thereby leaving its termination or revocability in the air. Whether or not this is fair so far as the mother is concerned is debatable, but we can observe that this is an example of a desire on the part of the courts to avoid a definitive determination of many of these disputes (especially where children are involved) and to favour rather the preservation of some jurisdiction to "look again" and make a new determination if and when the circumstances alter. There is a certain similarity here with the exercise of the matrimonial jurisdiction under the Matrimonial Causes Act 1973, which leans against the sale of the matrimonial home until the children are grown up.[66]

More generally, it should be noted that the court assumes a narrow brief and answers only the immediate question before it—will an order for possession be given or not? The court does not spell out the totality of the rights and obligations of the parties—for example, obligations as to repairs and maintenance of the family home. Indeed, it would be difficult to articulate the relationship of the parties in great detail, given that the court proceeds almost entirely by inference. To do other than this would overtly amount to writing an express agreement for the parties.

This remedial approach is also illustrated by *Tanner* v. *Tanner*.[67] The plaintiff bought a house for the defendant (his mistress) and their two daughters to live in. Again the house was registered in his sole name. The defendant gave up a rent-controlled tenancy to live there. The Court of Appeal held that the inference to be drawn from the circumstances was that the defendant had a contractual licence to occupy the house for so long as the children were of school age. Because she had already given up possession of the house, having been evicted by the County Court, the Court ordered £2,000 compensation to be paid to her for the loss of her contractual licence. Lord Denning's judgment was couched in terms of some species of equitable principle of implying contracts based on the actions of the parties. Indeed, although the analysis turns on agreement, the discussion was suggestive of estoppel, insofar as it emphasised the money which the defendant had spent on the property and the fact that she had given up good accommodation to live there. Brightman J. viewed the giving up of the accommodation as consideration on the part of the defendant and therefore implied a contract.

A definite time limit was put upon the duration of occupation in *Chandler* v. *Kerley*.[68] The defendant and her husband bought a house together. Two years later the husband left, and soon after the defendant became the mistress of the plaintiff. The husband and wife agreed to sell the house to the plaintiff after unsuccessfully putting the house on the open market. He paid less than the husband and wife had paid for the house three years earlier, but this was not regarded as relevant by the court when the new relationship broke up, and, in the dispute which followed, the plaintiff sought possession from the defendant and her two children.

Lord Scarman in the Court of Appeal rejected all the claims of the defendant which were couched in proprietary terms, though the only explanation offered for this was that "if the defendant can establish a licence for life, there is neither room nor need for an equitable interest . . . ".[69] The case was made to turn on the scope of the licence to be inferred from the surrounding circumstances. First, the plaintiff had invested capital and "in the absence of express stipulation," could not have intended to have "frozen" his capital indefinitely. Although the plaintiff was aware that the defendant and her children wished to continue in occupation at the time he bought the house, "it would be wrong to infer in the absence of an express promise that the plaintiff was assuming the burden of housing another man's wife and children indefinitely, and long after his relationship with them had ended."[70] On the basis of these factors, Lord Scarman held that a contractual licence did exist (presumably because her occupation was contemplated) but that it envisaged occupation terminable on reasonable notice, which he put at twelve months. It is perhaps interesting to note that Megaw L.J. explicitly stated that the Court specified the maximum duration only at the invitation of counsel, and suggested that otherwise there would have been a question as to whether the court "could or should" have taken that decision upon themselves.

Where is the boundary drawn between protected occupation and a bare licence? In *Horrocks* v. *Forray*[71] a man bought a house for his mistress and their daughter to live in. The man had told his solicitor that the house was for them, but it was registered in the man's sole name for tax purposes. The man was killed in an accident and had by will left all his property to his wife. The wife sought a possession order for the house, claiming that the mistress's licence to occupy had been brought to an end by her husband's death. The mistress contended she had a right to remain so long as her daughter was of school age. In the Court of Appeal none of the judges felt able to infer a contractual licence in the circumstances. Megaw L.J. stated[72]:

> "In order to establish a contract, whether express or implied, there has to be shown a meeting of the minds of the parties with a definition of the contractual terms reasonably clearly made out and with an intention to affect the legal relationship . . . there must be consideration moving in order to establish a contract."

Scarman L.J.'s approach was similar although his reason for not implying a contract lies in the lack of intention to create legal relations because of the nature of the domestic or family arrangements between the two parties (*cf. Balfour* v. *Balfour, supra*). The net result was that the mistress and her daughter were not entitled to remain.

Most of these decisions can only be explained in terms of the inferences as to intention which judges will make in a commonsense or intuitive way. In this respect, of course, they inevitably reflect the judges' own perceptions of "normal" conduct and social relations between the sexes. Thus, in *Tanner* v. *Tanner* Lord Denning dismissed any proprietary claim (by analogy with *Eves* v. *Eves*[73]) by emphasising the lack of marriage plans in the former relationship. Equally, in *Horrocks* v. *Forray*, Scarman L.J. rejected a contract partly by pointing to the element of bounty in the relationship, and the "luxurious" style in which the woman was being maintained. This intuitive approach, apparently focussed upon the perceived merits, makes it difficult to detect many coherent principles of law. Although a common thread running through all these "family arrangements" (from the Rent Act cases, *Balfour*, through to the imposition of a contractual licence) is an emphasis upon giving effect to the intention of the parties, this will be difficult to ascertain in some cases, particularly where the relationship has changed through time. Thus, in *Chandler* v. *Kerley*, the focus is upon the intention of the owner of the house, in *Tanner* upon the woman's reliance, in *Horrocks* v. *Forray* upon the man's generosity.

One final point to be mentioned concerns another distinction drawn by Scarman L.J. in *Horrocks* v. *Forray* between that case and *Tanner*. *Tanner*, he said, was a case of arms-length dealing, where "the relationship of man and mistress was either broken or on the point of collapse. The parties to the relationship . . . had to consider what best should be done for the innocent product of their relationship, the illegitimate children . . . [they] were making arrangements for the future at arm's length."[74] By contrast, it was difficult to infer a contract in *Horrocks* v. *Forray* because "the relationship was continuing until the unhappy and unexpected death of the man."[75] The difficulty with this view of *Tanner* is that, although, since these analyses are based on inference, subsequent conduct after occupation has commenced is relevant to the legal interpretation of that occupation, it is generally assumed in the cases that the analysis explains the nature of that occupation from the outset (excepting, of course, cases explicitly based on a subsequent change of position).[76] Commencing the analysis at the moment of break-up introduces new difficulties: for example, if the primary consideration to support the contract in *Tanner* was the giving up of the rent-controlled flat, it would be past consideration on the dissolution of the relationship and could not support a contract at that stage. Consideration could perhaps be found elsewhere—for example, in the woman undertaking to bring up the children in return for guaranteed occupation. If this is to be the analytical approach, it further reinforces the idea that one of the central objectives in this area is protecting children. Whatever the conceptual problems involved, Scarman L.J.'s dicta perhaps draw attention to the real basis of the approach of the courts in these cases—that they examine the position on the merits as they see them at the time it comes to court.

(e) Licences and control over dealings

So far, we have considered the extent to which the courts have been prepared to protect the occupation of a licensee against the legal owner of the family home. A subsidiary question which arises is to what extent occupation will be indirectly protected by preventing dealings with the property by the legal owner which might imperil the continuation of the occupation. We consider in Chapter 7 the position as between licensee and purchaser/ mortgagee of the home; here the question concerns whether a proposed sale or mortgage by the legal owner is subject to the jurisdiction of the court in order to prevent potential disruption of the occupation.

At this stage, we must distinguish *de facto* and *de jure* control over dealings. Let us take the case of a sale. If the priority rules are such that some occupants take precedence over purchasers (see Chapter 6 below), then the practical effect of placing the risk upon the purchaser is that pre-sale inquiries will usually be made of all occupants. Since claims that an occupant might have upon the vendor will often depend on transactions or dealings between occupant and vendor which are beyond the possible knowledge of the purchaser, any occupant *may* be able to exercise a veto against dealings, if a cautious purchaser insists upon the occupant's consent to the transaction. This is simply a consequence of risk allocation between occupant and purchaser; in other words *de facto* control over dealings.

But what is the position if the owner proposes to sell to a purchaser who is willing to take a risk, or who is ignorant of the existence of the licensee? Obviously, one practical problem is how the occupant will discover what is in the wind. The position if the transaction goes through is discussed in Chapter 7. But what steps, if any, can the occupant take if he or she discovers that a sale is about to take place? Can the occupant seek an injunction against (a) the licensor or (b) the intending purchaser to restrain the transaction?

(i) A remedy against the licensor

The starting point here must be to ask what are the terms of the contract, if one exists, between the parties? What is the duration of the occupation envisaged? Let us assume that the answer is, for life, or so long as the occupant wishes. A sale might imperil this occupancy, but it is not obvious that the contract is such as to prevent a sale by the licensor. It might be considered a term of the contract that so long as occupation continued, the licensor would not voluntarily dispose of the home: given the way that the courts infer the terms of the contract from the surrounding circumstances, it is not clear what kind of factors would need to be present in order to infer such a term. It might be suggested that lifetime occupation necessarily implies such a further term. In *Liverpool City Council* v. *Irwin*,[77] a term was implied in a contract that a landlord should keep the common parts of a block of flats in good repair. This obligation appeared to arise because of the nature of the relationship of the parties rather than as any strict principle of law. Without it, the choice for the court is between granting an injunction and awarding damages against the licensor for breach of contract if subsequently the purchaser succeeded in evicting the occupant. If the licensor has already exchanged contracts, that might be a basis for denying the injunction (which is of course discretionary).

From the occupant's point of view, the choice of whether to go to court for an injunction is rather like a throw of the dice, given the present state of the law. If he or she does so and fails, then it is likely that occupation will have to be given up, even if the occupant is compensated financially; if he or she waits, then the question will be whether the courts will give priority to the occupant or purchaser when the latter seeks a possession order.

(ii) A remedy against the purchaser

It is most unlikely in the normal case that any remedy would be available like against the purchaser, with whom, after all, the occupant is not in privity of contract. In rare circumstances, it might however be possible to invoke the tort of inducing breach of contract or interference with contractual relations, as the basis of supporting an injunction. In order to proceed against the puchaser on this ground, it would be necessary to show that the purchaser was aiming at the occupant and intending to deprive him or her of his or her occupation rights under the contract. Alternatively, action may be by means of the tort of conspiracy to injure, where a remedy might be available against either party or both. In *Midland Bank Trust Co.* v. *Green*[78] it was held that an action in the tort of conspiracy would lie if land was sold with the specific intention on the part of both vendor and purchaser of defeating a prior option to purchase. If the conspiracy were detected in advance, an injunction would presumably lie (unless the need to show actual damage prevented a claim in anticipation of that damage being suffered).

E. Licence by Estoppel

In contemporary discussions,[79] this has come to be viewed as the main alternative type of licence which may arise in family relationships. Once again, the term is not without difficulty. As we shall see, an equity or estoppel may frequently arise through time in the course of the conduct of domestic relations. When this happens, it can be confusing to suggest that the equity creates a licence. If a claimant seeks a remedy based on his or her "equity," a licence is not the only, or necessary, possible successful outcome. What rather should be said is that if an occupant successfully establishes an equity, it will often be the result that his or her occupation is protected, for a definite or indefinite period. It should be noted, however, that "licensed" occupation may often precede the events which give rise to the "equity." It is simply that once the "equity" is generated, the licence, even if originally revocable, becomes irrevocable since the legal owner is estopped from asserting his strict legal rights in the courts.

The rise of equitable estoppel has been one of the most remarkable success stories in modern jurisprudence. We now examine the development and consider its application in domestic disputes.

(1) *Introduction*

Recent judges have emphasised that the various species of equitable estoppel which are found in the books—notably *promissory* and *proprietary* estoppel—are merely illustrations of a more general principle of unconscionability, which the courts will invoke in a dispute when they think it proper.[80] On this basis, Scarman L.J. formulated the relevant tests in the following broad terms[81]:

" . . . first there is an equity established . . . secondly, what is the extent of the equity if one is established . . . and thirdly, what is the relief appropriate to satisfy the equity?"

Clearly, the crucial question is the first—what factors or circumstances will "generate" an equity? No clear answer can be given to this question, possibly because the courts have shown reluctance to confine their discretion for the future, or, put differently, have sought to keep the equity inchoate.

The leading cases which have been treated by modern courts and writers as constituting the antecedents of estoppel in the context of land ownership (which, despite the preceding remarks, we shall call "proprietary estoppel") possess the common feature that someone incurred significant expenditure in building upon land belonging to someone else. We examine these before turning to the modern cases.

(2) *The antecedents of proprietary estoppel*

The two most influential cases have been *Dillwyn* v. *Llewellyn*[82] and *Ramsden* v. *Dyson*.[83] In the former, a father invited one of his sons to build a house upon land owned by the father, on the understanding that, if this was done, the father would convey the title to the land to his son. The son acted upon this and spent very large sums building on the land. The father then died and the question arose as to whether the son was entitled to his conveyance. Lord Chancellor King ordered the conveyance to be made.

In *Dillwyn*, there is no readily discernible distinct doctrine of estoppel—the arrangement between father and son was treated as a bargain, and the central problem was one of informality—the arrangement was purely oral. In other words, the basis of the court's intervention in that case is close to or even squarely within what today we would call the equitable doctrine of part performance.[84] Paradoxically, as we shall see, the modern law has developed in such a way that it may be easier to base a successful claim[85] on proprietary estoppel than to invoke the doctrine of part performance in domestic disputes.[86]

Ramsden v. *Dyson* involved a dispute which arose out of the way in which the Ramsden family developed Huddersfield.[87] They adopted the practice of granting informal building leases for the standard term of years, and entering the tenants' names in a book, changing the entry when the "lease" was transferred (operating, in effect, their own private "Land Registry"). At law, therefore, the "tenants" were simply tenants at will. One such tenant built upon his land. The Ramsdens claimed that he was only a tenant at will and gave him notice to quit. He claimed that he had built on the land on the understanding that he was to have a building lease for a term of years, or was to be treated as a tenant for years. The House of Lords split 4:1 on the facts, but the differing ways in which they formulated the applicable law remain of interest.

Lord Cranworth couched the test in terms of mistake and unjust enrichment[88]:

> "If a stranger begins to build on my land supposing it to be his own, and I, perceiving his mistake, abstain from setting him right and leave him to persevere in his error, a Court of equity will not allow me afterwards to assert my title to the land on which he had expended money . . . it considers that, when I saw the mistake into which he had fallen, it was my duty to be active and to state my adverse title; and that it would be dishonest in one to remain wilfully passive on such an occasion, in order afterwards to profit by the mistake which I might have prevented."

But

> " . . . if a stranger builds upon my land knowing it to be mine, there is no principle of equity which would prevent my claiming the land with the benefit of all the expenditure made on it."

By contrast, Lord Kingsdown was much closer to the doctrine of part performance[89]:

> "If a man, under a verbal agreement with a landlord for a certain interest in land, or, what amounts to the same things, under an expectation, created or encouraged by the landlord, that he shall have a certain interest, takes possession of such land, with the consent of the landlord, and upon the faith of such promise or expectation, with the knowledge of the landlord, and without objection by him, lays out money upon the land, a Court of equity will compel

> the landlord to give effect to such promise or expectation."

But

> "If . . . a tenant being in possession of land, and knowing the nature and extent of his interest, lays out money upon it in the hope or expectation of an extended term or an allowance for expenditure, then, if such hope of expectation has not been created or encouraged by the landlord, the tenant has no claim which any Court of law or equity can enforce."

In the landlord-tenant cases of the nineteenth century, where the tenant expended money on the property demised, and a dispute later arose as to whether he should be granted another (or a longer) term or be compensated for improvements, it was often inevitable that the landlord would stand to benefit if the tenant's claim was denied. In other words, a dispute could readily be analysed in terms of whether, if the landlord was allowed to succeed, he would, in consequence, be unjustly enriched. But such cases equally involved factual questions amenable to an analysis which could, without difficulty, be couched in terms of mistake. The question was what kind of term or tenancy the tenant had. Given the pervasiveness of the landlord-tenant relationship in the nineteenth century, many difficulties could obviously arise in striking the balance between formality and informality, or between upholding, on the one hand, the landlord's right to rely upon the documentary evidence of title (or lack of it) and, on the other hand, doing justice to the tenant.

Whether the practice of courts of former times would be acceptable to us today is not especially germane. What is important is to observe how the focus of the modern law is different. The nineteenth century disputes we have discussed are about ownership—in each case, the occupant is seeking a formal document of title. In the modern cases, the focus is upon protecting occupation. Estoppel has become one device for achieving this result. Secondly, following on from this, where the courts find an equity today, a fairly informal solution is often adopted, and it is less common[90] for the courts to require any formal instrument to be prepared.

(3) *Estoppel and the family home: the modern case law*

Two overlapping strands can be discerned in the modern cases: first, where, whether or not expenditure is involved, the reliance gives rise to an equity justifying the award of lifetime occupation; secondly, where expenditure of money and other reliance gives rise to an equity such that occupation is protected until the money expended is repaid (in effect, an equitable lien).

(a) Estoppel and lifetime occupation

In *Inwards* v. *Baker*,[91] a son expended money and labour in building a bungalow near his parents' home on land belonging to his father, on the understanding that he would be able to remain in the bungalow for life. On the death of the father, his widow was held to be estopped from claiming possession of the bungalow from the son. His reliance and expenditure went to protecting occupation for the life of the son. The basis of the decision was the analogy with *Dillwyn* v. *Llewelyn*. By contrast with that case, however, the son acquired no formal title to the bungalow.

In *Greasley* v. *Cooke*,[92] the Court of Appeal went much further in protecting lifetime occupation by means of estoppel. The defendant had been employed by the plaintiffs' family as a maid in 1938. She looked after the householder (Arthur) and his four children. In 1946 she and Kenneth (one of the children) began to live together in the house as man and wife. She remained in the house acting as an unpaid housekeeper/nurse to whoever happened to be there at any time, but particularly, she looked after Kenneth's mentally-ill sister until the sister's death in 1975. Arthur had long since died leaving the house to Kenneth and another brother, Howard, in equal shares. When Kenneth died he left his share to another brother, Hedley, who in turn left his share to his two daughters. Howard and the two daughters then brought possession proceedings against the defendant, and she counter-claimed to be entitled to remain on the property rent-free for the rest of her life. The defendant based her claim on assurances given to her by Kenneth and Hedley after Arthur's death, that she could remain in the house as long as she wished. She claimed this raised an equity in her favour which prevented or estopped the plaintiffs from asserting that she had no right to stay. The plaintiffs, on the other hand, said that the defendant had not acted to her detriment in reliance on those assurances and there-fore no issue of equity arose.

Interpreting the Court of Appeal's decision (which was in favour of the defendant) is made difficult by the unusual course followed at the trial stage. The plaintiffs withdrew their claim, but the judge found against the defendant on the counterclaim, on the basis that she had not spent money on the property or in any other way proved that her conduct subsequent to the assurances constituted a detriment. The Court of Appeal unanimously held that the burden of proof in such cases was on the person making the assurance. Thus it was for the plaintiffs to show that there was no reliance upon their (or their predecessors') assurances.

The decision does not remove the need for a detriment as the basis for estoppel, but determines where, given a *prima facie* case, the burden of proof lies. It also clarifies the question of whether expenditure of money is neces-sary in order to constitute a detriment. Such a limit on the doctrine was rejected. However, the decision does not clarify what the minimum prerequisites of detriment are—in this case, presumably, foregone wages or lost opportunities.

The most extreme case is *Pascoe* v. *Turner*.[93] The plaintiff bought a house in his sole name, in 1965, for himself and his mistress, the defendant, to live in. They lived together in the house as man and wife until 1973 when they separated. During these years the plaintiff had allowed the defendant a housekeeping allowance, but she had paid for all her own personal things. After the relationship broke up the defendant continued to live in the house; she spent some £200 on repairs and decoration on the house in the belief, which the plaintiff encouraged, that the house would be hers. In 1976, however, the plaintiff gave her two months' notice to quit, and subsequently sought an order for possession on her refusal to leave. The Court of Appeal refused the order, holding that an equity arose in favour of the defendant. The basis of this equity appears to have been the expenditure of the defendant's small savings on repairs, in the light of the understanding that she could remain in the house. The Court seems to have assumed that the extent of the equity went to lifetime occupation, but ordered the title to the house to be conveyed to her, since otherwise, her occupation might be at risk if the plaintiff sold to a purchaser without notice. Again, the contrast with *Dillwyn* v. *Llewelyn* should be noted. There, ownership was what was bargained for or at the core of the arrangement; here, ownership is awarded as a means of protecting occupation.

It is clear from these recent decisions that the need for expenditure has been downgraded—even in *Pascoe* v. *Turner*, the sums expended bore little relation to the value of the property in question. Yet, once detriment or reliance are set loose from any narrow criterion like expenditure, and, moreover, are to be extracted from events which occurred over a number of years, it perhaps becomes impossible, in many situations, to discern whether there is detriment or reliance or not. In some fact situations it is possible to point concretely to "lost opportunities"—not taking a job, foregoing wages—

but in many cases this will be a highly speculative exercise.

Moreover, it can perhaps be suggested that there are few discernable traces of traditional concepts of acquisition of property rights in this version of estoppel. Personal exchanges, quite unrelated to the property as such, constitute the justification for protecting occupation.

(i) The Settled Land Act point

Some judges, usually those with a Chancery background, have taken the view that awarding protected lifetime occupation may be to confer upon the occupant a life interest within the reach of the Settled Land Act scheme, on the grounds that the award of a life interest creates a settlement within section 1 of the Settled Land Act 1925.[94] If so, the occupant becomes a tenant for life under the Act, acquires all the statutory powers of a tenant for life, including the power of sale,[95] and must have the legal estate vested in him or her. Thus, in *Bannister* v. *Bannister*,[96] two adjoining cottages were sold at an undervalue to a purchaser, on the understanding that the vendor could remain in one rent-free for her lifetime. The Court of Appeal held that she was entitled to occupy the cottage where she lived after the sale, but that she became a tenant for life within the Settled Land Act. In *Binions* v. *Evans*[97] Lord Denning M.R. held that implied or constructive interests fell outside the Settled Land Act; Stephenson and Megaw L.JJ. felt constrained to follow *Bannister*.[98] Subsequently, Russell L.J. has indicated that, in his view, the Settled Land Act point was "overlooked" in *Inwards* v. *Baker*.[99] As a matter of law, the question turns on whether, on the facts, anything which can be described as a "settlement" can be found. In *Griffiths* v. *Williams*,[1] Goff L.J. suggested that an agreement or contract for lifetime occupation is within section 1 of the Act and that, in the case of estoppel, the court order might be treated as the "settle-ment."[2]

There is perhaps general agreement that most cases should, if possible, be kept out of the Settled Land Act because of the expense and complexities involved.[3] In *Griffiths* v. *Williams*, Goff L.J. went to considerable lengths to achieve this result. A mother was looked after by her daughter for a number of years, the understanding between them being that the daughter would have the house for her life. Subsequently, the mother left the house by will to her granddaughter, and her executors began possession proceedings against the daughter. The Court held that an equity to remain for life was established in favour of the mother. Goff L.J. made an elaborate order to give effect to the equity. The executors were to grant the mother a long lease determinable on her death. The lease was to be non-assignable and at a nominal rent so as to avoid any claim for protection under the Rent Acts by her husband.[4]

(ii) A transferable equity?

The precision of the order made in *Griffiths* v. *Williams* illustrates another feature of this line of estoppel deci-sions. The equity appears to arise in respect of the house where the occupant lives. What if he or she wants to move elsewhere, especially in old age, which is easier to manage or in a more appropriate location? Perhaps paradoxically, invoking the Settled Land Act machinery would give this very choice to the occupant since under the Act he or she would have a statutory power of sale. A simpler way of achieving a fairly similar result would be to create a trust for sale, for the occupant for life, with remainders over. This might be particularly suitable when the owner has died and there is a contest between the occupant and the successors in title. They could be made co-trustees, and a dispute about a proposed sale could be dealt with under the section 30 procedure.

(b) Estoppel as an "equitable lien"

This has a narrower scope than the version of estoppel discussed above. Sometimes an occupant or intending occupant either lends money to the owner or pays for repairs or improvements. One way of giving effect to such a transaction is to interpret it as giving rise to an equity protecting occupation until the loan is repaid or recompense is made for the improvements.

For example, in *Dodsworth* v. *Dodsworth*[5] an elderly woman persuaded her younger brother and his wife to come and live with her. They did so and spent £700 on improvements to her house in the expectation that they would be able to remain in the house as their home, and she encouraged the couple in this belief. Later she grew tired of them and wanted to throw them out of the house. The Court of Appeal accepted the trial judge's view that the circumstances surrounding the original relationship generated an equity such that the defendants were entitled to remain in occupation until they were reimbursed for their expenditure.

Dodsworth discloses some of the particular problems which arise in an occupation dispute between cohabitees.[6] There are practical limits in the viability of trying to protect occupation of one party when the disputants are both living in the family home. Outside of the context of domestic violence, there are no clear guidelines to follow, but ultimately the court may have to order one of the parties to leave.[7]

A similar case was *Hussey* v. *Palmer*,[8] where a mother whose house was compulsorily purchased went to live with her daughter and son-in-law and the money she received was used to build on an extra bedroom. A dispute subsequently arose and the mother left and successfully sought repayment of the money. The Court of Appeal held that on the facts a "resulting or constructive" trust arose in the mother's favour. However, in *Savva* v. *Costa and Harymode Investments*[9] a later Court described the mother's equity as a lien, such that her occupation was protected until the money was repaid. In *Savva*, a man and a woman lived together and she had two children by him. She left him and subsequently bought a flat where she lived with the children. Three years later, she moved to a house belonging to the defendant. Substantial work was done on the house, much of which she paid for. Later, she claimed a beneficial interest in the property. The finding of fact was that there was no agreement between them that she would have such an interest. Moreover, her expenditure was with the knowledge of the defendant, but not at his request, nor was there any representation that she would have an interest in the house. On these facts, the Court of Appeal held that the most which could be justified was an irrevocable licence to occupy protected by a lien. Another example of facts probably best viewed in this way[10] is *Re Sharpe*,[11] when an aunt lent her nephew a large sum to buy a business with accommodation above. Part of the arrangement was that she would be entitled to live there for the rest of her life and be looked after by her nephew and his wife. The judge described the arrangement as a contractual licence to remain until repayment.[12]

This form of estoppel is, no doubt, a convenient way of resolving some intra-familial disputes. It is not easy, however, to give a clear explanation of what kind of right is created. As between the original parties, it usually suffices to say that the owner cannot evict until repayment. Even here, a question arises which led Lord Denning in *Hussey* v. *Palmer* to call the position a trust rather than a loan. If it is a loan, is it repayable on demand? This difficulty could be exaggerated: the courts can probably imply a reasonable period for repayment, from the time the person goes out of occupation. However, practical difficulties may obviously arise. If the legal owner against whom the estoppel is raised has capital other than the family home, or an income earning capacity sufficient to borrow money (secured on the family home if necessary) then reimbursement is a practical possibility. It is more difficult if the legal owner is, for example, a pensioner, who is not in a position to repay a loan. It might be necessary in such cases for the owners to sell the home in oder to repay a loan raised in order to discharge the equity.

A second question is whether the Limitation Act applies in respect of the loan, and, if it does, when time begins to run.[13] As between the original parties, this question seems only to arise after the occupants have left. While they remain in occupation, the equity appears to protect the right to repayment indefinitely. But where third parties are involved, some of whom may not be bound by the equity,[14] it can become important, especially where either party dies[15] or becomes bankrupt.[16]

In the event of a death or bankruptcy, it may also become essential to decide whether the right to repayment makes the occupant a secured or unsecured creditor. For the sake of convenience, we have described this form of estoppel as an equitable lien. This should probably be regarded as shorthand for a more complicated right. A 'lien' at common law is a right to retain goods of another until certain claims are satisfied—for example, a repairer's lien permitting retention (though not use) until payment for the work done. Equitable liens differ in that they normally do not involve physical retention of the property but a charge upon property in possession of another—for example, an unpaid vendor's lien upon property in the possession of the purchaser. It is unclear at present whether this form of estoppel envisages the right to repayment as constituting such a charge or not. If it is a charge, then the occupant presumably has available the remedies of a chargee, which would seem inappropriate.[17] Moreover, as a chargee, the occupant would rank ahead of ordinary creditors in the event of insolvency.[18]

(4) *Permanent and provisional protection*

Finally, it should be noted that, in their different ways, *Pascoe* v. *Turner* and *Dodsworth* v. *Dodsworth* do share the feature that each provides a conclusive resolution of the dispute. By contrast, the other cases leave many issues unsettled as to the ongoing mutual obligations of the parties interested in the property. In this respect, the approach of the courts resembles what we have already seen in some of the contractual licence cases.

Another resemblance is highlighted in the recognition by the court that an 'estoppel solution' to a dispute may be provisional rather than final. It may, for instance, be lost if the conduct of the occupier is such that he loses any claim to equitable protection. *Williams* v. *Staite*[19] contains a clear statement on this point. Protection in this case was nearly lost by the conduct of the occupier after the original equity has arisen. Goff L.J. opined[20]: " ... (W)hen a party raises an equity of this character and it is alleged against him that his own behaviour has been wrong, the court has to decide on the facts whether a sufficient answer to his equity has been made out." And Cumming Bruce L.J. was even more emphatic[21]: "I do not think that in a proper case the rights in equity of the defendants crystallise forever at the time when the equitable rights come into existence."

Notes to pages 80–123

[1] Some reformers were concerned about the lack of security of tenure in short residential leases; here, the focus was upon the injustice of the landlord benefitting from the tenant's improvement of the property: see, for example, Land Enquiry Committee *The Land* Vol. 2 *Urban*, p.424.

[2] See C.S. Kenny, *op. cit.*

[3] Especially as regards children: see the Custody of Infants Act 1873; Guardianship of Infants Act 1886. As regards inheritance see the Intestate's Estates Act 1890.

[4] [1952] 1 All E.R. 1307.

[5] See also *Errington* v. *Errington and Woods* [1952] 1 K.B. 290; [1952] 1 All E.R. 149; *Ferris* v. *Weaven* [1952] 2 All E.R. 233; *Jess B. Woodcock & Sons Ltd.* v. *Hobbs* [1955] 1 W.L.R. 152; [1955] 1 All E.R. 445; *cf. Westminster Bank Ltd.* v. *Lee* [1956] Ch. 7; [1955] 3 W.L.R. 376;

F.R. Crane "The Deserted Wife's Licence" (1955) 19 Conv. (N.S.) 343; R.E. Megarry "The Deserted Wife's Right to Occupy the Matrimonial Home" (1952) 68 L.Q.R. 379.

[6] [1965] A.C. 1175; [1965] 3 W.L.R. 1.

[7] *Lee* v. *Lee* [1952] 2 Q.B. 489; *Halden* v. *Halden* [1966] 3 All E.R. 412.

[8] See *Stewart* v. *Stewart* [1947] 2 All E.R. 813.

[9] *Barnett* v. *Hassett* [1981] 1 W.L.R. 1385; but for the practical consequence of this facility, see *infra.*, p.000.

[10] s. 1(1) Matrimonial Homes Act 1967.

[11] See *infra.*, pp.172–174.

[12] Matrimonial Homes and Property Act 1981, s. 4.

[13] See especially *Wroth* v. *Tyler* [1974] Ch. 30; [1974] 2 W.L.R. 405.

[14] Which does not mean that the volume of registration is insignificant. Thus, in 1977–78, there were 10,687 applications to register Class F land charges and 6,300 (approx.) applications in respect of registered land: see Cretney, *op. cit.* p.214, n.10a.

[15] [1979] Ch. 312; [1979] 2 All E.R. 697, p. 702, (C.A.).

[16] Law Com. No. 86, paras. 1.270–1.292.

[17] See *infra.*, pp. 175–178.

[18] *Strachan* v. *Strachan* [1965] 2 All E.R. 77.

[19] *Cobb* v. *Cobb* [1955] 2 All E.R. 696, 699 *per* Denning L.J.

[20] *Mesher* v. *Mesher* [1980] 1 All E.R. 126 (C.A.) (decided Feb. 1973). See also *Harnett* v. *Harnett* [1974] 1 W.L.R. 219; [1974] 1 All E.R. 764; *Hanlon* v. *Hanlon* [1978] 1 W.L.R. 592; [1978] 2 All E.R. 889; R.C.A. White (1981) M.L.R. 96; J. M. Eekelaar "Some Principles of Finance and Property Adjustment on Divorce" (1979) 95 L.Q.R. 253.

[21] See *Dunford* v. *Dunford* [1980] 1 W.L.R. 5; *Carson* v. *Carson, The Times*, July 7 1981, (1981) 125 S.J. 513.

[22] *Brown* v. *Brown, The Times*, December 11 1981 (C.A.).

[23] See, for example, *Hall* v. *Hall* [1971] 1 W.L.R. 404; [1971] 1 All E.R. 762; *Montgomery* v. *Montgomery* [1965] P. 46; [1964] 2 W.L.R. 1036.

[24] s. 4 Matrimonial Causes Act 1878, which applied only when the husband was convicted of an aggravated assault on his wife. The grounds were broadened by successive statutes—see Bromley, *Family Law* (6th ed., 1981) 5n3.

[24a] To which great importance is attached: see *Richards* v. *Richards, The Times*, December 8, 1982 (C.A.).

[25] Practice Note (Family Division: Injunction; exclusion from Matrimonial Home) [1978] 2 All E.R. 1056, where the President suggests that a period of 3 months is "likely to suffice at least in the first instance." For general discussions of the legal regulation of domestic violence, see M.D.A. Freeman, "Violence Against Women . . . " 7 B.J.L.S. 215 (1980). E. Pizzey, *Scream Quietly or the Neighbours Will Hear* 1974; S. Maidment, "The Law's Response to Marital Violence in England and

the USA" (1977) 26 I.C.L.Q. 403; M.D.A. Freeman, *Violence in the Home—A Socio-Legal Study* (1978).

[26] *Re Power* [1947] Ch. 572; [1947] 2 All E.R. 282.

[27] See especially the litigation surrounding the Ailesbury's Savernake estate, when the fourth Marquess wished to sell and the family tried to prevent him: note the comments of Bowen L.J. [1892] 1 Ch. 506, 539; Fry L.J. at p.542, and, less lyrically, Lord Halsbury L.C. [1892] A.C. p.356, 360.

[28] See generally J.A. Hornby, "Tenancy for Life or Licence" (1977) 93 L.Q.R. 561.

[29] *cf.* Davidson's *Concise Precedents in Conveyancing* (19th ed., 1910), CXLIX and *Re Inn's, Inns* v. *Wallace* [1947] Ch. 576; [1947] 2 All E.R. 308. Marriage settlements might permit residence: Davidson *op. cit.* CXXXIV but *cf.* p. 541n.(a).

[30] See further *infra* Chap. 5.

[31] Administration of Justice Act 1705 (4 & 5 Anne c.3).

[32] See *Henderson* v. *Eason* (1851) 17 Q.B. 701.

[33] For the use of this device, see Jenks, *Modern Land Law* (1899), p.411; Lord St. Leonard's *Handy Book on Property Law* (5th ed., 1858), pp.111–113.

[34] On the meaning of "overreaching", see Chap. 6, p.170.

[35] Jenks *op. cit.* 417 *et seq*; and see further pp. 152–154, *infra*.

[36] See further, Megarry and Wade pp.286–288.

[37] Lightwood, "Trusts for Sale" (1927–29) 3 C.L.J. 59.

[38] [1955] 1 Q.B. 234; [1955] 1 W.L.R. 78.

[39] *Per* Denning L.J. *ibid.* at p.79.

[40] *Ibid.* at p.80.

[41] See especially Ian Saunders, "Right of the Equitable Tenant in Common" 122 S. J. 134 488 (1978). *Cf.* The early case of *Re Landi* [1939] Ch. 828 which treated the introduction of a fiduciary relationship as a substantial change.

[42] *Waller* v. *Waller* [1967] 1 W.L.R. 451; [1967] 1 All E.R. 305.

[43] *Ibid.*

[44] [1970] 2 Q.B. 677; [1970] 3 W.L.R. 82.

[45] [1970] 2 Q.B. 677, p.684 *per* Lord Denning M.R. and the references to *Jones* v. *Challenger* [1961] 1 Q.B. 176 by Lord Denning M.R. and Edmund Davies L.J.

[46] (1673) Vaug. 330, p.351.

[47] *Ibid.* at p.350.

[48] *Ibid.* at p.351.

[49] *Ibid.* at p.351.

[50] "There was no such right created, either at law or in equity, as constitutes any known estate or interest in land" *per* Romer L.J. in *Warr* v. *L.C.C.* [1904] 1 K.B. 713—concerned with the effect of such transactions as to entitlement to compensation under compulsory purchase legislation. See also, *Clore* v. *Theatrical Properties* [1936] 3 All

E.R. 483—concerned with their effect on third parties; *Edwardes* v. *Barrington* (1901) 85 L.T. 650—concerned with their effect upon no-subletting clause in leases.

[51] (1845) 13 M. & W. 838.

[52] [1915] 1 K.B. 1.

[53] *Ibid.* at p.10.

[54] *Cf. Walsh* v. *Lonsdale* (1882) 21 Ch.D. 9; 52 L.J. Ch. 2.

[55] *Wood* v. *Leadbitter* (1845) 13 M. & W. 838, at p. 845.

[56] *Hounslow U.B.C.* v. *Twickenham Garden Developments Ltd.* [1970] 3 All E.R. 326, 334–343.

[57] Hargreaves "Licensed Possessors" (1953) 69 L.Q.R. 466.

[58] It should, however, be noted that some commercial transactions have been couched as licences in order to avoid the Rent Acts—for the chequered fate of "non-exclusive occupation agreements" see Martin Partington, *Landlord and Tenant* (2nd ed., 1980), pp.119–148. For criticism of these developments in policy terms, see also Robson and Watchman, "Sabotaging the Rent Acts" in Robson and Watchman (ed.) *Justice, Lord Denning and the Constitution* (1981) p.187.

[59] [1919] 2 K.B. 571.

[60] [1978] 1 W.L.R. 683; [1978] 2 All E.R. 935.

[61] [1969] 1 W.L.R. 328; [1969] 2 All E.R. 616.

[62] See especially Lord Denning in *Hardwick* v. *Johnson supra.*, n.60.

[63] E. Ellis, "Contractual and Equitable Licences" (1979) 95 L.Q.R. 11; A.A.S. Zuckerman, "Formality and the Family—Reform and the Status Quo" (1980) 96 L.Q.R. 248; J.S. Anderson, (1979) 42 M.L.R. 203.

[64] *Cf.* the more general arguments of P.S. Atiyah, especially in *The Rise and Fall of Freedom of Contract* (1979).

[65] [1978] 1 W.L.R. 683; [1968] 2 All E.R. 935.

[66] See *supra*, pp.85–86.

[67] [1976] 1 W.L.R. 1346; [1975] 3 All E.R. 776.

[68] [1978] 1 W.L.R. 693; [1978] 2 All E.R. 942.

[69] [1978] 2 All E.R. 942, 945.

[70] *Ibid.* at p.947.

[71] [1976] 1 W.L.R. 230; [1976] 1 All E.R. 737.

[72] *Ibid.* at p.236.

[73] [1975] 1 W.L.R. 1338; [1975] 3 All E.R. 786.

[74] [1976] 1 All E.R. 745.

[75] *Ibid.* at pp.745–746.

[76] See especially *Pascoe* v. *Turner* [1979] 1 W.L.R. 431; [1979] 1 W.L.R. 431.

[77] [1977] A.C. 239; [1976] 2 W.L.R. 562.

[78] [1980] Ch. 590; (1980) 125 S.J. 33.

[79] See for example, D.J. Hayton, "The Licensee's Interest", (1972) 36 Conv.S 277; P.V., Baker "The Law is what it ought to be" (1972) 88 L.Q.R. 336; B. Sufrin (1979) 42 M.L.R. 574; J. Martin (1980) Conv.

207; G. Woodman (1980) 96 L.Q.R. 336; F.R. Crane, "Estoppel Interests in Land" (1967) 31 Conv. 332.

[80] *e.g. Taylors Fashions Ltd.* v. *Liverpool Trustees Co.* [1981] 2 W.L.R. 576, 595–596.

[81] *Crabb* v. *Arun District Council* [1975] 3 W.L.R. 847; [1975] 3 All E.R. 876. For two contrasting views of this case see P. Atiyah 92 L.Q.R. 174 (for a contractual approach) and P. Millett 92 L.Q.R. 342 (for an estoppel approach).

[82] (1862) 4 De G.F. & J. 517.

[83] (1866) L.R. 1 HL 129.

[84] See *Maddison* v. *Alderson* (1883) 8 App. Cas. 467 and *Steadman* v. *Steadman* [1974] 3 W.L.R. 56; [1974] 2 All E.R. 977. The change of possession and subsequent building would bring the facts of *Dillwyn* within even the narrow basis formulated in *Maddison*.

[85] We pass over difficulties which have surfaced in some areas of estoppel as to whether it can be used as a "sword'" (*i.e.* the basis of a cause of action) as well as a "shield" (a defence to a claim). There is general agreement that, whether or not the distinction (first raised in *Combe* v. *Combe* [1951] 2 K.B. 215; [1951] 1 All E.R. 767) survives in promissory estoppel, it is not applicable in proprietary estoppel—see *Crabb* v. *Arun* [1975] 3 W.L.R. 847 *per* Lord Denning M.R. and see further *Amalgamated Investment and Property Co. Ltd. (in liquidation)* v. *Texas Commerce International Bank Ltd.* [1981] 2 W.L.R. 554.

[86] See *Re Gonin, Gonin* v. *Garmeson* [1979] Ch. 16; [1977] 3 W.L.R. 379 and *cf. Greaseley* v. *Cooke* [1980] 1 W.L.R. 1306.

[87] For the background, see D.F.E. Sykes, *The History of Huddersfield and its Vicinity* (1898), pp.219–227.

[88] (1866) L.R. 1 H.L. 129, pp.140, 141.

[89] *Ibid.* at p.171.

[90] But *cf.* *Pascoe* v. *Turner* [1979] 1 W.L.R. 431; [1979] 2 All E.R. 945 and especially *Griffiths* v. *Williams* (1977) 248 E.G. 947.

[91] [1965] 2 Q.B. 29; [1965] 2 W.L.R. 212.

[92] [1980] 1 W.L.R. 1306; [1980] 3 All E.R. 710.

[93] [1979] 1 W.L.R. 431; [1979] 2 All E.R. 945.

[94] Presumably within the s. 19(1) definition of tenant for life.

[95] s. 38(1) S.L.A. 1925.

[96] [1948] 2 All E.R. 133.

[97] [1972] Ch. 359.

[98] See further *infra*. Chap. 7, pp.182–186.

[99] *Dodsworth* v. *Dodsworth* (1973) 228 E.G. 115.

[1] (1977) 248 E.G. 947.

[2] *Ibid.* at p.949.

[3] *Cf. Binions* v. *Evans* [1972] 2 All E.R. 70, 78 (*per* Megaw L.J.); *Chandler* v. *Kerley* [1978] 2 All E.R. 942, 946 *per* Lord Scarman.

[4] In particular, a claim to take over the statutory tenancy if his wife died first.

[5] (1973) 228 E.G. 115.

[6] Other problems occur where one party dies (as in *Dodsworth*): see *infra*. Chap. 5.

[7] *Cf. Thompson* v. *Park* [1944] K.B. 408, decided "*quasi in furore*" per Megarry J. in *Hounslow* v. *Twickenham Garden* [1970] 3 All E.R. 326, 339.

[8] [1972] 1 W.L.R. 1286; [1972] 3 All E.R. 744.

[9] [1980] C.A.T. 723, October 9, 1980; 131 New L.J. 1114.

[10] See Jill Martin, "Constructive Trusts and Licences; Re Sharpe" [1980] Conv. 207.

[11] [1980] 1 W.L.R. 219.

[12] See further *infra*, Chap. 8, p. 203.

[13] This presumably depends upon whether the debt is regarded as a contract debt or as an equitable, restitutionary right to reimbursement. If the latter, the doctrine of laches, rather than the Limitation Act, would seem to govern the running of time against the creditor.

[14] Such as mortgagees whose securities take effect before the creditor's occupation began.

[15] See *infra*, Chap. 5, pp. 142–145.

[16] See *infra*, Chap. 8, p. 203.

[17] *Infra*, Chap. 8, pp. 208–212. The term 'lien' is also used in Snell's *Equity* (28th ed., 1982), p. 562.

[18] *Infra*, pp.144; 194–196.

[19] [1979] Ch. 291; [1978] 2 All E.R. 928.

[20] [1978] 2 All E.R. 933.

[21] *Ibid*. at pp.928, 934.

Chapter 5

DEATH

In this chapter, we examine, first, how the death of owners or occupants of the home affects the rights of ownership or occupation considered in the previous two chapters. We then consider, more briefly, claims for ownership or occupation of the home which might arise for the first time after the death of the owner. We introduce this chapter by outlining the ways in which an estate is adminstered on death.

A. THE ADMINISTRATION OF A DECEASED'S ESTATE

Succession on death is primarily determined either by the will of the deceased or by the rules for intestate succession. A combination of both may occur, where some of the deceased's property passes according to his will while the intestacy rules govern the devolution of the rest.

The deceased's property does not go directly to the people entitled, but first vests in the deceased's personal representatives. Personal representatives are either one or more executors normally appointed by the will or, in intestate succession, an administrator appointed by the court.[1] Their duty is to administer the deceased's estate. This involves ascertaining what belonged to the deceased, collecting in his assets and, if necessary, paying the deceased's creditors. After completing the administration of the estate (which may also involved the payment of Capital Transfer Tax) the personal representatives then vest the property in the person(s) entitled under the will or under the rules relating to intestacy.

(1) *Testate succession: procedure*

The executors must first obtain a grant of probate from a probate registry, in order to 'prove' the validity of the will and thereby have the estate vested in them. This is normally a routine matter, but if there is some possibility that the will is not valid, the proceedings may be transferred to a judge before the grant is made.

(2) *Intestate succession: procedure*

Where a person dies without leaving a valid will, the rules relating to intestate succession come into force. In this situation, someone must apply for a grant of letters of administration. This will ofter be the person principally entitled under the intestacy rules. The grant establishes the administrator's title to deal with the estate. The administrator then has the same duties to perform as an executor.

(3) *Application of assets for payment of costs of administration and debts*

The personal representatives must meet all the liabilities[2] of the deceased before distributing the net assets to the beneficiaries. The order in which they meet the liabilities is normally irrelevant where the estate is solvent, but is strictly prescribed by statute where the estate is insolvent and there are insufficient assets to meet all liabilities.[3] In such a case, the beneficiaries are not concerned with which property will be used to meet particular debts, since, by definition, the whole estate must be applied to meet the costs of administration and the payment of debts. By contrast, when the estate is solvent, it does concern the beneficiaries. This operates differently in testate and intestate succession.

(a) Testate succession

The Administration of Estates Act 1925, Sched. 1 Pt. II sets out an order of application which determines which property is to be used in any particular case to pay the debts and expenses, although the testator can stipulate a different order in his will. How this will operate in practice depends on the extent to which, and how, the testator has divided up his assets into specific or "earmarked" gifts of his chattels (bequests) and land (devises) or given specific sums of money to individuals (pecuniary legacies), and whether he has made provision as to the devolution of what is left over (the residue), or stipulated that particular items of property are to be used for the payment of expenses and debts. To simplify somewhat, property included in the residue will be used to pay debts and expenses before pecuniary legacies, and specific bequests and devises will be touched only after all the property in the previous two categories is exhausted.[4]

(b) Intestate succession

Prima facie, all property vests in the personal representatives on trust to sell and convert into money. Personal chattels, however, are not to be sold except for a special reason,[5] and the matrimonial home is not normally to be sold within the first twelve months.[6] These rules form part of the special provisions for spouses on intestacy, which are considered in the next section.

(4) *The mode of distribution of the estate*

(a) Testate succession

After payment of taxes, expenses and debts, the net estate is ready for distribution. In testate succession, freedom of testation is paramount (subject to a partial erosion in favour of surviving spouses, specified relatives and dependants now contained in the Inheritance (Provision for Family and Dependants) Act 1975.[7] Specific bequests (of personalty) and devises (of land) must be satisfied first; residuary legatees and devisees take what is left over.

(b) Intestate succession

The mode of distribution is specified by the Administration of Estates Act 1925 (again, as "tempered" by the 1975 Act). The detailed rules are set out in section 46 of the Administration of Estates Act 1925 as amended by the Intestates' Estates Act 1952 and later statutes.[8] For present purposes, it is important to note that the position of a surviving spouse of an intestate depends upon (a) whether there are children or grandchildren of the intestate (whether legitimate or illegitimate)[9] and (b) whether there are parents, siblings or nephews and nieces of the intestate living at his or her death.

(i)   Where neither (a) or (b) applies, the administrator holds everything on trust for the surviving spouse;

(ii) Where (a) applies, the surviving spouse takes all personal chattels, a first charge of £40,000[10] (sometimes called the "statutory legacy"). Subject to that, the estate is held on trust as to half for the surviving spouse for life, remainder to the issue, and as to the other half, on trust for the issue absolutely[11]

(iii) When there are no issue but (b) applies, the surviving spouse takes a larger part of the estate – the personal chattels, a statutory legacy of £80,000, and the rest is held, as to half, on trust for the spouse absolutely, and as to the other half, on trust for a surviving parent or parents of the deceased absolutely, or, if neither survive, on trust for siblings.[12]

The effect of this statutory order of distribution is that for the majority of families, the surviving spouse will take most or all of the property of the deceased, to the exclusion of children or relatives. Only in relatively wealthy families will the elaborate formulae outlined above come into play. This means that children or relatives who wish to make a claim upon the deceased's estate will have to do so under the court's statutory jurisdiction to make provision for children and dependants, which is examined below.[13] Surviving spouses will only need to resort to this jurisdiction where the deceased makes a will disinheriting them.

(5) *Intestacy and the right to claim the home*

Although, on intestacy, all the property is held on trust for sale, personal chattels, which the surviving spouse takes, are not to be sold except for a special reason. The trust for sale is further modified in practice by the Intestates' Estates Act 1952 Sched. 2, which confers certain rights in respect of the matrimonial home. In this context, "matrimonial home" has an extended meaning and includes the intestate's interest in a dwelling house in which the surviving spouse was resident when the intestate died; there is no requirement that the deceased spouse should have also been resident at that address.[14] First, the house cannot be sold within twelve months of the intestate's death without the surviving spouse's permission unless it is required for the payment of debts and liabilities owing to the lack of other assets.[15] Secondly, the surviving spouse can require the personal representatives to appropriate any interest of the deceased in the matrimonial home "in or towards the satisfaction of any absolute interest" which, under the intestacy rules, the surviving spouse acquires in the estate.[16] Thus, if the deceased was sole beneficial owner of a home worth £45,000, and leaves issue, the surviving spouse can first require the statutory legacy of £40,000 to be met out of the home. Secondly, he or she can require the life interest in half the residue to be capitalised[17] and add its value to the £40,000. If this leaves a shortfall, the survivor will need to find the difference in order to keep the house. If, by contrast, there are no issue, the larger statutory legacy will, if the survivor invokes this procedure, enable him or her to keep the house.

(a) Mortgaged property

Most debts of the deceased are payable out of property which has been specifically set aside for that purpose by the testator, or in accordance with a statutory list of priority of assets for the payment of debts laid out in the Administration of Estates Act 1925, Sched. 1, Pt. II. Different rules apply, however, in relation to mortgage debts. Section 35 of the Administration of Estates Act 1925 provides that where any debt is charged[18] on specific property of the deceased, that property is itself primarily liable for the payment of the debt. The deceased can alter this statutory rule by specific direction in his will to the contrary.[19] This is, by definition, inapplicable on intestacy.

The effect of section 35 is to place the liability upon the property, not to make the person who takes it personally liable for the debt. This means first, that where, on death, there is an outstanding mortgage, the person entitled to the house cannot make the personal representatives pay off the mortgage from the rest of the estate. Secondly, the mortgagee can seek his usual remedies but cannot compel the successors in title to pay, though, if they wish to resist sale or foreclosure by the mortgagee, they may seek to arrange to take over the mortgage themselves.[20] The most convenient way, however, to anticipate the difficulties created by outstanding mortgages on death is for the owner to obtain appropriate life insurance policies.

(b) Capital Transfer Tax

Capital Transfer Tax is normally payable in respect of estates valued at over £50,000.[21] One exception is where the property is left to a surviving spouse.[22] Apart from this exception, the Finance Act 1975 provides that Capital Transfer Tax on property other than personal estate in the U.K. is payable by the property itself and must be borne by the recipient of the gift.[22a] The testator can, however, provide by will that the gift should be free of tax, such that it is payable out of the estate generally. Personal estate in the U.K. does not bear its own C.T.T.; the tax is payable out of the estate as an administration expense. So if the home is leasehold property, it would not be subject to a charge to C.T.T.

B. The Impact of Death on Pre-existing Legal Relationships

(1) *Co-ownership*

In previous chapters, we have examined the legal issues which arise when the ownership of the equity in the home is shared. If one of the equitable co-owners dies, a particular problem can arise. Was the equity held by the parties as joint tenants or tenants in common? The answer determines the devolution of the deceased co-owner's "share."

(a) Joint tenancy and tenancy in common

If A and B are joint tenants of property, and A dies, B becomes absolutely entitled to the property by virtue of the *ius accrescendi* or the right of survivorship. In other words, an integral feature of the joint tenancy is the opportunity of surviving the other joint tenants or the right to take the interest of the other on that person's death. In this situation, neither party will be able to dispose of his "share" or interest on death; it will pass automatically to the surviving joint tenant by operation of the *ius accrescendi*. The position will be different if the joint tenancy has been "converted" into a tenancy in common before the relevant death. (This process of conversion is called "severance" and its main features are outlined below).

By contrast, if A and B are tenants in common of property, they have undivided "shares" or, in the context of the family home, respective percentages of the equity. These shares are not affected by the operation of survivorship and will devolve on the death of the tenant in common in accordance with that person's will or by virtue of the intestacy rules discussed above.

Finally, it should be recalled that the 1925 code abolished the legal tenancy in common. Consequently, all co-owned legal estates must be held jointly, and will be governed by the *ius accrescendi*. Severance and the tenancy in common can, after 1925 only exist in equity, behind a trust.

We now examine these distinctions with reference to modern home ownership.

(i) *Where the home is in joint names*

Two situations can be distinguished. First, when the legal estate is expressed to be taken jointly on trust for the parties as joint tenants or tenants in common. Here, the instrument governs the position in equity. If the instrument specifies joint tenancies, they may be converted to tenancies in equity in common through the subsequent conduct of the parties. This involves special rules of severance which are discussed in the next section.

The second situation is when the legal title is held jointly but the position in equity is not expressly stated in the instrument. At this point, traditional equitable presumptions come into play to determine whether the parties are equitable joint tenants or tenants in common. "Equity leans against joint tenancy" and so in certain situations, an equitable tenancy in common is presumed in the absence of evidence of contrary intention. These situations are: (1) unequal contribution to the purchase price; (2) partnership property; (3) joint mortgagees. If a case falls within these categories, equity presumes that the *ius accrescendi* does not apply, on the grounds that a joint tenancy could not have been intended. The application of (1) in the context of home purchase is straightforward. (2) could be an important role, if "partnership" were broadened so as to cover those situations where a home is bought by couples or friends contributing equally.

(ii) Where the legal estate is vested in one person with the beneficial interests in two or more people

Normally, this situation will come above through the operation of an implied trust, but it is possible that such a trust may be created expressly. In the latter case, the instrument creating the trust may, and normally should, specify whether the beneficial interests are held jointly or in common. By contrast, where the trust arises by implication, it will be necessary to ascertain whether there is a joint tenancy or tenancy in common in equity. This is to be done by applying the equitable presumptions considered above, though in principle they should give way to any manifest intention of the parties.

(b) Severance

The simplest method of severance under the post-1925 law is the service of a notice in writing by a tenant wishing to sever upon the other joint tenants under section 36(2) of the Law of Property Act 1925. Section 36(2) also provides, however, that a severance will take place if a joint tenant does" . . . such other acts or things as would, in the case of personal estate, have been effectual to sever the joint tenancy in equity."

These methods were set out in *Williams* v. *Hensman*[23]:

(1) actual agreement; (2) a course of dealings between the joint tenants indicating a mutual intention to sever; and (3) where a joint tenant alienates his interest, which automatically effects a severance.[24]

It is not always easy to apply these tests in the context of the family home. The main difficulty is that the dealings between the parties may often take place in ignorance of the consequences of the legal distinction between joint tenancy and tenancy in common. Perhaps the best that can be done is to look at these dealings and ask whether the parties are behaving as if they have distinct shares in the home. This could be inferred if, for example, they are negotiating to wind up their affairs, with one party buying out the other. In this situation, the question is how far such dealings have to go before they can be treated as effecting a severance. In *Neilsen-Jones* v. *Fedden*,[25] Walton J. held that the parties must have reached a point of no return or done some irrevocable act (for example, concluded a binding or specifically enforceable contract); but this was overruled by the Court of Appeal in *Burgess* v. *Rawnsley*.[26] In this latter case, an oral agreement between the joint tenants whereby one would buy out the other, though unenforceable for lack of writing, was held to be sufficient to constitute a severance by actual agreement or course of dealings.[27]

If the equitable joint tenancy is severed, the survivor will hold the legal estate on trust for him or herself and those entitled under the will of the deceased or on his intestacy. The personal representatives of the deceased will be entitled to call for that share of the property so that they can distribute it in accordance with the will or as required in the event of intestacy. This may of course require a sale of the home; this is discussed in the next section.

If no severance takes place during the lifetime of both parties, the *ius accrescendi* will operate on the death of one joint tenant, and the property will vest automatically in the survivors. Where, prior to death, there is a joint tenancy at law as well as in equity, this can have conveyancing implications, since a purchaser from the survivor may not be sure whether a severance took place in equity prior to the death of the other joint tenant on the title.[28]

(c) Sale

When one of the equitable co-owners dies and the other co-owner does not take by survivorship or inherit the share of the deceased, the question arises as to whether the surviving co-owner will be able to remain in occupation or whether a sale will be ordered. The survivor may seek to buy out the claims of those entitled by virtue of inheritance; but if this is not possible, the personal representatives of the deceased may apply to the court for an order for sale under the section 30 jurisdiction.

There is no reason why the guidelines considered earlier for the exercise of the section 30 discretion should not apply with equal force here. Thus, if the purpose for which the house was acquired was to be a family home, and that purpose subsists, a sale may be refused. One difficulty which does arise is to what extent, if a sale is refused, are the interests of the inheritors secure? They could best be protected if the court could order the appointment of a co-trustee (say one of the personal representatives) so that it could be guaranteed that, in a sale, the proceeds would be duly distributed.

Apart from the continuation of the purpose, a sale might be refused if the trust is complemented by an estoppel. For example, in *Jones* v. *Jones*,[29] the legal owner encouraged his son to give up his job and home in London in order to live in Suffolk and be near his father. The father provided a house in Suffolk towards which the son paid £1,000. The son was led to believe by his father that he would be able to live in the house for as long as he wished. A dispute arose after the father died. The Court of Appeal held that the son had a quarter share in the property, but that, in the circumstances, his widow (who inherited his share) was estopped from evicting the son and obtaining a sale.

(2) *Licences*

(a) Death of licensor/legal owner

If the licence is not contractual, nor protected by any equity, the death of the licensor will normally revoke the licence and his personal representatives will be entitled to a possession order.[30] Thus in *Horrocks* v. *Forray*[31] an order for possession was made against a mistress who failed to establish anything more than a bare licence to occupy the home which her deceased lover had bought her to live in.

Where the licence is contractual, matters are less straightforward. Implicit in the Court of Appeal's approach in *Horrocks* v. *Forray* is the suggestion that no order for possession would have been made if the mistress had succeeded in establishing that she occcupied her home by virtue of a contractual licence. But since the Court did not have to confront the point squarely (since it rejected a contractual analysis of the facts) the question must be regarded as open.

The effect of the death of the owner upon a contractual licence must turn primarily upon the construction of the contract. This presents (relatively) little difficulty if the licence is formalised, but the effect of death will necessarily be less predictable if the courts have to infer a contract from the circumstantial evidence.

If a contract is found, the question of construction turns on whether the licence was personal or not; whether, in other words, it was envisaged that it would automatically terminate on the death of the owner. If the contract is taken to contemplate occupation until the children of the relationship between licensor and licensee are of school-leaving age (as in *Tanner* v. *Tanner*)[32] or envisages life-time occupation by the licensee, then such a contract will bind the personal representatives of the licensor (who stand in the shoes of the deceased). Clearly this presents practical difficulties for the personal representatives, who may well seek to negotiate a release of the licensee's claims if they have such freedom to manoeuvre. Otherwise, in order to administer the estate, they will have to vest title to the home in those entitled by way of succession, but (presumably) subject to the licence. Finally, it should be mentioned that where the occupant lives in the home under a contractual arrangement whereby he or she is buying the equity from the owner, this arrangement will bind the personal representatives and successors in title.[33]

Somewhat analogous is the case where the occupant provides services for the owner during his or her lifetime under an arrangement whereby the occupant is to have the house (either absolutely or for life) on the death of the owner. Such arrangements potentially bind the personal representatives and successors in title. However, unless they are formalized, there may be problems both of proof and of enforceability. Since they are contracts for the disposition of an interest in land, they require written evidence (s.40(1) L.P.A. 1925). In the absence of this, the contract will only be enforceable if the occupant can successfully invoke the doctrine of part performance, which may be difficult.[34] It may, however, be easier to ground a successful claim in estoppel rather than contract.[35] This possibility is considered in the next section.

(b) Death of the licensee

A bare licence will automatically terminate on the death of the licensee. If the licence is contractual, it will first be necessary to construe the contract or interpret the relationship in order to determine whether the right to occupy was to terminate on the death of the licensee. If, as a matter of interpretation, the intention of the parties was that the licensee and his or her family (relatives, dependants, etc.) are entitled to occupy, the legal consequences of the licensee's death are not altogether straightforward. If the arrangement is under seal, then all the parties to the covenant or deed can enforce it irrespective of whether any consideration moves from them. When the arrangement is informal, the obligation will in principle only be enforceable by those who have given consideration for the promise.[36] The personal representatives of the deceased would however be able to enforce the contract.[37]

(3) *Estoppel*

(a) Death of the owner

In many situations, the personal representatives of and successors in title to the deceased will be bound by the equity. We have already seen that the mode of satisfaction of the equity can vary considerably—and so the precise implications of the death of the owner will depend upon the circumstances. Thus, in the older form of estoppel, if the equity required a transfer of the fee simple, this will bind the personal representatives.[38] In the modern context, if the estoppel protects life-time occupation, the personal representatives and successors in title will not be able to obtain possession of the property.[39] Equally, if the estoppel takes the form of a "lien,"[40] a possession order will be refused until the debt has been discharged. This could cause particular difficulties, since the personal representatives may require vacant possession of the property in order to administer the estate.

The main situations should be distinguished.

(i) Where the estate is solvent

The personal representatives must apply the assets of the estate in satisfaction of debts and to discharge expenses in the order specified in the Administration of Estates Act 1925, Sched. I, Pt. II, subject to any contrary provisions in the will. This order of application is designed to specify which beneficiaries (in testate succession) should bear the cost of expenses and debts. Thus residuary estate is to be applied in payment of debt before specific bequests and devises.[41] In the case of intestacy, all the personal and real estate is held on trust to sell and convert into money, initially for payment of debts and expenses, and then for distribution under section 46 of the Administration of Estates Act (outlined above). In each case, the creditors are not concerned with the order of application of assets for debt repayment, since, *ex hypothesi*, all debts will be repaid in full.

This means that the personal representatives can discharge the equity by paying the debt to the occupant. The precise mechanisms will depend on the circumstances. When there is insufficient personal estate, or where the house is primarily liable for payment of debts (for example, if it is residuary estate, where there is an intestacy and the house is the only asset, or where it has been charged for payment of debts and insufficient prior assets are available) it may be necessary for the personal representatives to raise money on security of the house in order to discharge the equity and sell the house with vacant possession to repay the other debts and meet the costs of administration. They have such powers prior to distribution to the beneficiaries under section 39(1)(i) of the Administration of Estates Act 1925.

(ii) Where the estate is insolvent

Special difficulties arise here, since all the assets of the estate must be realised in order to discharge the liabilities. In this situation, the personal representatives are required by the Administration of Estates Act, Sched. I, Pt. I to apply the assets in a specified order. First, they must discharge the general and testamentary expenses and costs of administration. Then, the residue is to be applied in the same way as on bankruptcy—to secured creditors who have proved their debts, then to preferential creditors, with the surplus being shared *pari passu* by ordinary creditors, and anything remaining going to meet deferred debts.[42] If the personal representatives disregard this mandatory order, they may be liable for any shortfall.[43]

The personal representatives will want to sell the house with vacant possession, but will probably be refused a possession order since the equity protects occupation until (presumably) full payment.[44] Secondly, if there are funds at their disposal or they borrow further money, there are difficulties as to whether they can apply this in repayment of the debt so as to sell with vacant possession.

If this course of action is adopted, it may be a breach of the statutory duty to apply the assets in the specified order. Here, it is necessary to recall the open question as to whether the equitable "lien" takes effect as a charge or merely as an ordinary debt coupled with an equity protecting occupation pending repayment. If the former, then the occupant will rank much higher in the order of distribution. As an ordinary creditor, unless the occupant agrees to accept partial payment in full satisfaction, it will often be unlikely that the debt can be discharged.[45] Thus if the "lien" does not operate as a charge, it will be hazardous for the personal representatives to use funds to repay the debt before meeting all prior claims. They should rather apply to the Court for directions as to how to proceed with the administration.

Finally, it should be noted that all these possessory claims which bind the personal representatives will be overridden by secured creditors without notice or creditors whose security was created prior to the *generation* of the equity.[46] Thus, for example, to take the simplest case, a legal mortgagee not bound by the equity should be able to obtain possession and, exercising his power of sale,[47] sell with vacant possession, paying any surplus to the personal representatives after subtracting the principal and interest owed. It is to be noted that this would enable the mortgagee to "jump ahead" of the statutory order of application of assets by recouping his debt ahead of the discharge of administration expenses.

(b) Death of the occupant

The question which arises here is whether the estoppel is transmissible on the death of the person in whose favour the equity arises. The answer will depend upon the kind of equity which can be established. If the equity is satisfied by means of protected lifetime occupation (in whatever form), then nothing is transmissible to the successors in title of the person so protected. An equity of the lien variety will probably be extinguished on death of the creditor, leaving only the debt to be collected in by the personal representatives (unless the operation of Limitation Act, if applicable, has rendered the debt statute-barred).[48] On the other hand, an equity which extends to the award of a legal estate, as in *Pascoe* v. *Turner*,[49] may be capable of being claimed by the personal representatives on behalf of the estate. It may be doubted, however, that *Pascoe* v. *Turner* would have been decided in the same way if the occupant had died and the claim had been made by her personal representatives.

4. *The Inheritance (Provision for Family and Dependants) Act 1975*

English law contains no mandatory provision whereby a fixed portion of the deceased's estate must be set aside for the surviving spouse and children. Thus if, for example, in a quasi-marital relationship, a man buys a house in his sole name for the woman to live in, and he dies without making provision for her in his will, his death will prima facie put her occupation at risk, unless she can establish a pre-existing legal relationship between them—such as a contractual licence or an estoppel—which is capable of binding his personal representatives. If none can be established, the 1975 Act may provide an alternative remedy. Under the Act, the woman can apply to the court for provision to be made for her from the deceased's estate. One possible outcome of a successful application would be the transfer to her of the home by order of the court.

(a) Background

Before the 1975 Act came into force the court had a rather narrower power conferred by the Inheritance (Family Provision) Act 1938 in respect of the deceased's spouse and children and by sections 27–28A of the Matrimonial Causes Act 1965 in respect of an application by a former spouse. The categories of possible applicant were strictly limited and defined, as was the kind of financial provision which could actually be ordered by the court. The 1975 Act was passed after a Law Commission Report[50] which recommended that both the categories of applicant and the type of financial provision which could be ordered be broadened.

(b) Eligible applicants

(a) Deceased's wife or husband[51]

(b) Deceased's former wife or husband who has not remarried. Contracting out with the approval of the court is permitted.[52]

(c) A child of the deceased, irrespective of age or marital status[53]

(d) A person treated by the deceased as a child of the family[54]

(e) A dependant of the deceased, *i.e.* someone not included in any of the preceding categories "who immediately before the death of the deceased was being maintained, either wholly or partly, by the deceased."

This last category constituted the main innovation of

the 1975 Act and it seems the Law Commission intended it to apply primarily in quasi-marital relationships, where previously the survivor had no right to claim any part of the deceased's estate even if the couple had lived together as man and wife for many years. It should be noted, though, that the meaning of dependant has been interpreted as being exhaustively defined by section 1(3), which provides that a person is to be treated as being maintained if the deceased was making substantial contribution in money or money's worth toward the reasonable needs of the claimant, 'otherwise than for full valuable consideration'.[55]

(c) The requirement of reasonable financial provision

Before making an order the court must decide that "reasonable financial provision" has not already been made for the applicant. The Act contains two separate standards. The first standard of reasonable financial provision is that which applies to *spouses* and is defined as:

" . . . such financial provision as it would be reasonable in all the circumstances of the case for a husband or wife to receive, whether or not that provision is required for his or her maintenance."[56]

The second standard applies to all other applicants and is defined as:

" . . . such financial provision as it would be reasonable in all the circumstances of the case for the applicant to receive for his maintenance."[57]

In each case, the court is directed to consider a broad range of factors set out in section 3 of the Act. If the Court concludes that reasonable financial provision has not been made by the deceased's will or on his intestacy, then the court is obliged to consider these same factors set out in section 3 in order to assess what kind of provision should be ordered.

(d) The Range of Orders

Section 2 of the Act empowers the Court, *inter alia*, to
make an order for the transfer to an applicant of specific
property in the estate,[58] or for the making of a
settlement.[59] Thus the Court has the power to order the
home to be vested in a claimant, or could direct a
settlement on trust. This latter would be a convenient way
of giving protected lifetime occupation.[60] The Court is
empowered to make orders out of the deceased's net
estate. By section 9 property which is subject to a joint
tenancy may, by order of the Court, form part of this net
estate. This might mean that the deceased's "half-share"
in a jointly-owned matrimonial home could be used to
make financial provision for an applicant. This in turn
might mean the surviving spouse having to sell the
property or borrow money in order to provide the money
for the deceased's estate.

(e) Anti-Avoidance Provisions

The deceased might also attempt to evade possible
claims for financial provision being made after his or her
death by transferring property before death and thereby
reducing the value of the estate. Consequently, the Act
contains certain anti-avoidance provisions. By section 10,
the Court can order the donee to provide a sum of money
or property which he has received from the deceased. This
is subject to a number of limitations. First, the power only
applies in respect of gifts made within six years of death
and made with the intention of defeating a claim under the
Act.[61] Secondly, it is inapplicable if the recipient or any
other person has given full valuable consideration for the
initial transfer. Thirdly, the claimant must show that an
exercise of the section 10 power would facilitate the
making of financial provision. The recipient's liability is
confined to the amount of money received or the value of

the property transferred at the date of death or at the time when the recipient disposed of it.

Notes to pages 129–149

[1] s.55(1)(i) and (ii) A.E.A. 1925.

[2] See *Re Tankard* [1942] Ch.69, 72.

[3] Sched. I, Pt. I A.E.A. 1925.

[4] The actual order has 7 categories of gift, the residue is in the second category, pecuniary legacies in the fifth, and specific gifts in the sixth. See further, n.41 *post.*

[5] s.33(1) A.E.A. 1925. Personal chattels are defined in s.55(1) (x) A.E.A. 1925.

[6] Sched. 2 para. 4(1), (3) and (5) Intestates Estates Act 1952.

[7] For the background to the 1938 Act, see Dainow, "Limitations on Testamentary Freedom in England" (1940) 25 Cornell L.Q. 337.

[8] Also Family Provision Act 1966; Family Law Reform Act 1969.

[9] s.14 Family Law Reform Act 1969.

[10] As amended by the Family Provision (Intestate Succession) Order 1981 (S.I. 1981 No. 82 No. 255).

[11] s.46 (2) A.E.A. 1925.

[12] s.46 (3) A.E.A. 1925

[13] pp.145 *et seq.*

[14] Sched. 2, para. 1(1).

[15] Sched. 2, para. 4(1)(3) and (5).

[16] This includes the fixed net sum of the statutory legacy and also the capital value of life interest which a surviving spouse may elect to redeem under s.47A A.E.A., Sched. 2 para. 1 (4).

[17] s.47A A.E.A. 1925.

[18] "Whether by way of legal mortgage, equitable charge or otherwise . . . ." It is not confined to acts of the parties, but extends to the Inland Revenue's charge for C.T.T., an equitable mortgage by deposit of title deeds, and a vendor's lien.

[19] s.35(1) and (2) A.E.A. 1925.

[20] s.36 Administration of Justice Act 1970; this is normal building society practice where possible in any event. For the distinction between a charge on the property and personal liability, see *Syer* v. *Gladstone* (1885) 30 Ch. D. 614.

[21] s.37(3) F.A. 1975 and s. 92(1)(*a*) and Sched. 13 F.A. 1981. It was suggested that the bands for CTT should be fixed in accordance with the rate of inflation in the 1982 Budget; this is to begin in April 1983: s.91 F.A. 1982.

[22] Sched. 6. para. 1(1) F.A. 1975 as amended by s.94, F.A. 1976.

[22a] But *cf. Re Dougall* (1981) S.T.C. 514.

[23] *Williams* v. *Hensman* (1861) 1 J. & H. 564.

[24] Megarry and Wade, pp. 393–396. This last method also operated *at law* pre–1926 as well as in equity.

[25] *Nielsen-Jones* v. *Fedden* [1975] Ch. 222; [1974] 3 W.L.R. 583; [1974] 3 All E.R. 38.

[26] *Burgess* v. *Rawnsley* [1975] Ch. 429 [1975] 3 W.L.R. 99.

[27] (1976) 35 C.L.J. 20 (D.J. Hayton); (1977) 41 Conv. (N.S.) 243 (S. Bandali.)

[28] But see now *Re Cook* [1948] Ch. 212; [1948] 1 All E.R. 231; Law of Property (Joint Tenants) Act 1964.

[29] *Jones* v. *Jones* [1977] 1 W.L.R. 438; (1976) 33 P. & C.R. 147.

[30] *Per* Lord Devlin in *Terrunanse* v. *Terrunanse* [1968] A.C. 1086; [1968] 1 All E.R. 651.

[31] *Horrocks* v. *Forray* [1976] 1 W.L.R. 230; [1976] 1 All E.R. 737.

[32] *Tanner* v. *Tanner* [1975] 1 W.L.R. 1346; [1976] 3 All E.R. 776.

[33] *Errington* v. *Errington & Woods* [1952] 1 K.B. 290; [1952] 1 All E.R. 149.

[34] *Re Gonin* [1979] Ch. 16; [1977] 3 W.L.R. 379; [1977] 2 All E.R. 720.

[35] *Greasley* v. *Cooke* [1980] 1 W.L.R. 1306; [1980] 3 All E.R. 710.

[36] Even if the arrangement is under seal damages are the only remedy on the grounds that "equity will not assist a volunteer."

[37] *Beswick* v. *Beswick* [1968] A.C. 58; [1967] 3 W.L.R. 932; [1967] 2 All E.R. 1197.

[38] *Dillwyn* v. *Llewelyn* (1862) 4 De G.F. & J. 517.

[39] *Griffiths* v. *Williams* (1977) 248 E.G. 947.

[40] *Dodsworth* v. *Dodsworth* (1973) 228 E.G. 115.

[41] For the full list, see Parry and Clark, *The Law of Succession* (7th ed., 1977) pp.258 *et seq.*; Williams, Mortimer and Sunnuck's *Executors, Administrators and Probate*, (1982) pp.560 *et seq.*

[42] s.130 Bankruptcy Act 1914.

[43] s.25 and 34(1) A.E.A. 1925, and s. 9 A.E.A. 1971. The Personal Representative would commit a breach of duty or devastavit, see Parry and Clark, *op. cit.* pp. 382–386.

[44] See *Dodsworth* v. *Dodsworth* (*supra.*), n.40, *post.*

[45] In accordance with what normally happens in bankruptcy, see further *infra*, Chap. 8, p.195.

[46] *Cf. Lloyds Bank* v. *O's Trustee* [1953] 1 W.L.R. 1460.

[47] By virtue of s.103 L.P.A. 1925 and see *infra*, pp.212–213.

[48] In which case the Personal Representative commits a breach of duty if he pays it. For the Limitation Act, see *supra*, p.128, n.13.

[49] *Pascoe* v. *Turner* [1979] 1 W.L.R. 431; [1979] 2 All E.R. 945.

[50] Law Com. No. 61.

[51] s.1(1)(*a*). This may include a person who has entered into a void marriage in good faith.

[52] By s.1(1)(*b*). By s.15 of the 1975 Act, on a divorce, the court may make an order barring a former wife or husband from applying under the 1975 Act, if both parties agree to the making of such an order.

[53] s.1(1)(*c*). See *Re Coventry* [1980] Ch. 461 and *Re Christie* 1979] Ch. 168. Such applications by adult children were not permitted under the previous legislation.

[54] s.1(1)(*d*).

[55] *Cf. Re Wilkinson* [1977] 3 W.L.R. 514; [1979] 1 All E.R. 221.

[56] s.1(2)(*a*) 1975 Act.

[57] s.1(2)(*b*) 1975 Act.

[58] s.2(1)(*c*) 1975 Act.

[59] s.2(1)(*e*) 1975 Act.

[60] By creating an equitable life interest taking effect either under the S.L.A. 1925 or on trust for sale under L.P.A. 1925.

[61] s.10(2)(*a*) 1975 Act.

Chapter 6

PRIORITIES: TRUSTS

In this chapter we examine the relative positions of beneficiaries behind a trust and purchasers or mortgagees of the home. We are concerned here solely with the question of ascertaining priorities. We consider below the mechanisms through which third parties can enforce their claims and occupants resist them.

A. INTRODUCTION

1. *Trusts and Purchasers; The Old Régime*

In the nineteenth century, the basic rule was that where trustees held a legal estate in land under a simple trust for a group of beneficiaries, the trustees had no power to sell the land without the consent of those entitled in equity.[1] A purchaser dealing with such trustees would therefore be put to the inconvenience of obtaining these consents before he could obtain a good title. The trustees had to have either a power of sale or hold under a trust to sell before a purchaser could safely take a conveyance of title without the concurrence of the beneficiaries. Hence, it was necessary for the purchaser to ensure that the terms of the trust or power were strictly followed. Thirdly, having paid the purchase price and obtained a receipt, the purchaser was required to ensure that the trustees duly applied the proceeds in accordance with the terms of the trust, unless, under the trust, he was exonerated from such an obligation. Without such exoneration, the purchaser was liable to pay the money again, if the trustees defaulted. This last requirement was relaxed by the Conveyancing Act 1881 as reproduced in the Trustee Act 1893, which permitted the purchaser to rely upon receiving a receipt in due form from (all) the trustees.[2] It is presently contained in section 14 of the Trustee Act 1925 in modified form.

This position meant that it was somewhat hazardous for purchasers to deal with trustees, and consequently, in some contexts, it became the practice to keep trusts off the title, in the strong sense that the property would be vested in trustees as beneficial owners.[3] This was common when the subject-matter of the trust was a mortgage. Here it was particularly desirable that the mortgage could readily be sold since the borrower would often have difficulty in redeeming the mortgage at short notice. Although it was normal to assume that joint mortgagees were in fact trustees, the courts upheld the attempts of conveyancers to prevent the complexities of trusts from obstructing the buying and selling of such mortgages.[4] If, however, in the course of his inquiries, the purchaser obtained some concrete reason (that went beyond the form of his vendor's title) to suspect that a trust existed, he then had to ensure either that the trustees had the requisite powers or obtain the concurrence of the beneficiaries.[5]

To summarise, nineteenth century conveyancing practice involved two distinct problems for purchasers dealing with trusts. First, where a purchaser knew he was dealing with a trust, he had to ensure that the trustees acted in accordance with the terms of the trust. Secondly, where he was dealing with vendors who were, on the face of the title, beneficial owners, he might be put on inquiry to the effect that his vendors were really trustees.

2. *Trusts and the Doctrine of Notice*

From the foregoing, it should be clear that, in the majority of cases, purchasers had actual notice of the existence of a trust. Apart from the example of the mortgage held on trust, questions of constructive notice arose most commonly, so far as trusts were concerned, where agents,

especially solicitors, dealt fraudulently with trust property, and the issue was whether their actual notice could be
imputed to the purchasers for whom they acted.[6]

When purchasers dealt with trustees, they acquired
most of their information about the state of the title from
inspecting the documentary evidence of title and the
replies received to their inquiries. The practitioners'
manuals very rarely mention inspection of the land itself
as likely to be relevant to the discovery of a trust, except
in the context of partnership property. If one or two
partners held the title to land on trust for a partnership
firm, a purchaser would be put on inquiry if the firm
occupied the land, and would be obliged to insist that all
the partners concurred in the conveyance in order to get a
good title.[7] Normally, however, inspection of the land was
undertaken to ascertain either, if sale was with vacant
possession, whether there were occupiers, or, if the sale
was subject to tenancies, to check that the tenants were
paying rent to the vendor.[8] The position of the purchaser
here was formulated in what came to be called "the rule in
Hunt v. *Luck*."[9]

3. *Trusts, Occupation and the 1925 Code*

Against this background, it is perhaps easy to see why
little explicit provision was made in the 1925 code for the
modern form in which a dispute between beneficiaries and
purchasers can often arise—when the home is vested in
one party as sole beneficial owner, and another occupant
has acquired a share of the equity behind an implied trust
in one of the ways previously considered.

First, as we have seen, the 1925 code was largely silent
about implied trusts, although they have, for the most
part, been brought within the scheme of the statutory trust
for sale by judicial decision.[10] Secondly, the code retained, with some modifications, which we consider
below, the rule in *Hunt* v. *Luck*, but presumably on the
assumption that it had little bearing upon trusts. Trusts of

land would thenceforth take effect either under the Settled Land Act or by means of an express or statutory trust for sale under the Law of Property Act. Therefore, in the case of most trusts of land, there would be a power of sale or a trust to sell, the safeguard for the beneficiaries being in each case that a purchaser had to obtain a receipt from at least two trustees.[11]

We examine below how the 1925 scheme has been interpreted to accommodate modern trusts of the family home. We conclude this historical introduction by asking how the modern conveyancing problem—where the home is vested in a sole trustee—might have been treated had it arisen for decision in 1925. This is of course a speculative procedure, but it serves to highlight precisely what is difficult about applying the 1925 scheme in modern conditions.

How then, would the position of a purchaser from a sole trustee have been conceived in the light of the conveyancing principles upon which the 1925 scheme was predicated? A purchaser from a sole beneficial owner who is in fact holding subject to an implied trust can prima facie rely upon the recital of title, and, after exchange of contracts, the vendor would be able to compel the purchaser to complete. If the sale is to be with vacant possession, however, the purchaser will be expected to inspect the land, which might lead him to discover the beneficiary in occupation. This would give him notice of the existence of a trust.

The question at this point is what kind of trust is discovered. If it is a statutory trust for sale, then the purchaser can presumably require the appointment of a second trustee in order to make title under the Law of Property Act, and can rely upon a receipt from both in order to exonerate him from liability to see to the application of the proceeds. This assumes that the right to give vacant possession is with the trustees, which is fundamental to the 1925 scheme. Under the Law of Property Act, a beneficiary can only obstruct a sale where there is an express trust for sale, if his or her consent is made requisite to a sale.[12] Where, as in our example, the trust for sale is statutory, the beneficiary has only a right to be consulted under section 26(3) of the Law of Property Act and it is expressly provided that a purchaser is not to be concerned to see that this duty has been performed.

How would the scheme apply if the purchaser, on notice of the trust, went ahead and took a conveyance from the sole trustee? Lord Denning has suggested[13] that in this situation vacant possession cannot be delivered. It is not clear that this answer would have been given in 1925, but perhaps, through judicial interpretation, the law has changed. We have already examined the view that, under the modern law, the right to possession of the home is with the beneficiaries, not the trustees,[14] and if this view is maintained when purchasers are involved, it follows that the purchasers will not obtain vacant possession. In 1925, however, the answer would probably have been different. Under section 14 of the Trustee Act 1925, a purchaser is only exonerated from seeing to the due application of the purchase moneys of land held on trust for sale if he obtains a receipt from at least two trustees for sale. Therefore, if the vendor-trustee defaulted, the purchaser would have to pay the purchase price again or more precisely recompense the beneficiary to the extent of the value of his or her interest in the proceeds. Title, in other words, would be obtained, but at an added cost.[15]

It is even more difficult to speculate as to how the problem would have been dealt with under the Land Registration Act. The register would indicate that the vendor was the registered proprietor, and *ex hypothesi* no restriction on his ability to sell would be revealed by a search. Section 74 of the Act provides that a purchaser " . . . shall [not] be affected with notice of a trust express implied or constructive . . . " It is unclear whether this is an administrative provision[16] directing that, beyond the entry of a restriction, details of trusts are to be excluded from the register, or a substantive provision excluding the doctrine of notice in favour of purchasers of trust property. It can probably be safely asserted that no-one in 1925 would have considered interests behind trusts to be capable of protection as overriding interests.[17] This leaves, however, the problem of relating section 74 of the Land Registration Act (if intended to have substantive effect) to section 14 of the Trustee Act. The answer may be that section 74 was intended to ensure that the purchaser would obtain *title* while section 14 meant that the purchaser had to pay again. The difficulty with this is that section 14 would seem only to apply where a purchaser has actual or constructive notice of the existence of a trust.

It is perhaps not surprising that some of these questions are unanswerable. The different statutes which make up the code had different antecendents, affected different interests and, no doubt, not every strand was tied together. But the difficulties today are as much the product of the radical rupture with the assumptions underpinning the code which has been effected by modern judicial decision. As we have indicated, the key to the change is the recognition that, in many cases,[18] beneficiaries have the right to occupy the home. We examine the impact of this shift in the succeeding sections as we discuss how the conveyancing framework of 1925 has been reshaped by judicial decision.

B. The Sole Trustee: Registered Conveyancing

1. *Where Beneficial Interest Protected by Registration*

(1) *All beneficiaries*

The primary registration mechanism envisaged under the Land Registration Act scheme for trusts for sale is the registration of a restriction. If a restriction is entered, for example when the house is bought, the terms of the restriction specifying that the purchase price must be paid to at least two trustees for sale, then under the registered conveyancing scheme, the beneficiary would be adequately protected. Where there is only one trustee, and no restriction has been entered, it is possible to enter a notice, though, since resort to the register is likely to take place during a breakdown of the relationship, a caution against dealings (the "hostile" entry) would be more usual.[19] To enter a caution, the applicant must complete a form 14 statutory declaration indicating the nature of his or her interest. This may, of course, give rise to difficulties as to what kind of interest is to be claimed. Once a caution against dealings has been entered, the cautioner will be notified of any proposed dealings with the land and the "warning-off" procedure will come into operation at that time. In *Williams & Glyn's Bank* v. *Boland*[20] (C.A.), Ormrod L.J. made comments which may mean that, where there is a sole trustee, a beneficiary does not have a minor interest that can be protected in the ways here described. This, it is suggested, is clearly contrary to the tenor of section 49(2) of the Land Registration Act 1925 and is based upon a misconstruction of section 3(xv)(*a*) of the same Act. One view of Lord Roskill's brief comments in *Boland*[21] (H.L.) is that he was repudiating Ormrod L.J.'s observations on this point and thus reaffirming that a beneficiary behind a trust can always make use of the minor interests machinery to protect his or her rights.[22]

(2) *Special procedure for spouses*

Since the enactment of the Matrimonial Homes Act 1967 (as amended by s.4 of the Matrimonial Homes and Property Act 1981) spouses can register their statutory rights of occupation by way of a notice. The procedure for such registration is cheaper and simpler than the general procedure outlined above. Registration of the right of occupation is not equivalent to registration of the beneficial interest; but it can serve, for most purposes, to provide the same protection in terms of notification of dealings which the more expensive and cumbersome general procedure ensures.[23] Therefore, spouses who wish to protect their rights through registration would probably employ the Matrimonial Homes Act method. The Law Commission has proposed more extensive registrable rights for spouses, which are discussed below in the context of general reform of this area of the law.

2. *Where Beneficial Interest Not Protected by Registration*

(1) *Where claimant is in occupation*

The House of Lords held in *Williams & Glyn's Bank* v. *Boland*[24] that the beneficiary can rely on section $70(1)(g)$ of the Land Registration Act 1925 and claim that the beneficial interest is an overriding interest subject to which any purchaser automatically takes. The paragraph provides that a purchaser will take subject to "the rights of every person in actual occupation of the land or in receipt of the rents and profits therefore, save where enquiry is made of such person and the rights are not disclosed." The beneficiary must therefore establish that he or she is in "actual occupation" or "in receipt of the rents and profits." However, a proviso is appended which provides that a purchaser may defeat such a claim if he can prove that he made enquiries and the rights were not disclosed. Although it is not explicitly provided, a purchaser may also be able to defeat a claim if the beneficiary actually consents to the proposed transaction. These points will be examined in turn.

(a) "Actual occupation"

In *Bird* v. *Syme-Thomson*[25] Templeman J., following the reasoning in the unregistered conveyancing case of *Caunce* v. *Caunce*,[26] had formulated a test whereby an occupant whose occupation was consistent with the title offered by the vendor would not be treated as falling within the paragraph. This approach was overruled by the Court of Appeal in *Boland*.[27] Following the doubts earlier expressed about *Caunce* in *Hodgson* v. *Marks*,[28] the Court of Appeal held that the proper approach was to ask whether, as a *question of fact*, the beneficiary was in actual occupation. This approach was affirmed in the House of Lords, where it was emphasised that the status of the occupant was not relevant and that any person in physical occupation who had proprietary rights fell within the paragraph. It was irrelevant that in *Boland* the parties were married. The position would be identical for unmarried couples or if the occupants were of the same sex. It would therefore seem that children are potentially included if they possess the right kinds of rights.[29]

Clearly, this gives rise to a number of practical problems, and there is some uncertainty as to exactly what kind of occupation is to count for the purposes of the paragraph. First, are there any requirements as to the duration of occupation? For example, is a beneficiary who happens to be staying as a house guest in actual occupation? Is someone staying in the home on a temporary basis? (This is to leave on one side the question of the relevant time for occupation which is dealt with below). Equally is someone on holiday or in hospital in actual occupation? Is the crucial question whether someone is *normally* in actual occupation of the home? Equally, there are practical problems for purchasers seeking to ascertain the existence of someone in actual occupation. For example, in a case like *Hodgson* v. *Marks*, the purchasers could easily have been unaware of the existence of the person with the equitable title who was in actual occupation.

(b) In receipt of rent or profits

There are also practical difficulties in this area. Consider the following examples. First, where the house is in the name of A but B has a half share under a resulting trust. Neither A nor B are in occupation, and tenants or licensees are paying rent to A. Can B in this situation be said to be "in receipt of rents and profits"? Secondly, where A's name is on the title but B has an equitable share (and neither is in occupation) but the tenants or licensees instead of paying *rent* to A or B, are paying the rates and utility bills. This example is closer to *Strand Securities* v. *Caswell*[30] where there was a rent-free occupation licence granted by a non-resident licensor, and it was held neither the licensor nor the licensee was within the paragraph.

(c) The relevant time

In registered conveyancing, title is transferred not by conveyance but by entry of the new proprietor on the register. Since *Re Boyle's Claim*,[31] it appears to be settled that the relevant time for overriding interests to affect purchasers is the moment at which title passes, namely entry in the register. Consequently, the person claiming an overriding interest must be in actual occupation at the time of the applicable registration. This requires a careful differentiation of the kinds of purchasers and mortgagees who may be affected by overriding interests. Consider the following example.

On November 1, 1980, V and P exchange contracts to complete on January 1, 1981. After the due searches etc., a deed of transfer is exchanged on January 1, 1981, along with the land certificate or the charge certificate and discharge documentation. The purchase money (a bankers' draft from P's building society) is handed over to V's solicitors, and P and his family move in the same day. A mortgage deed has already been drawn up between the Building Society and P. P's solicitor forwards the land or charge certificate, the transfer deed and the mortgage deed to the Land Registry duly stamped. One month later P is entered on the register as the new registered proprietor, V's building society's charge is removed from the register and P's building society charge is duly entered. The land certificate is retained in the Land Registry, and a new charge certificate is forwarded to P's building society.

(i) V's wife

We assume that, prior to the sale, V's wife had a half-share behind an implied trust. Since V's wife moves out before title is passed (that is before the relevant time) she cannot assert an overrding interest within section 70(1)(*g*) which would affect either P or his building society.

(ii) P's wife

Again, assume for the moment that she acquires a share of the equity. Does this affect the building society as first mortgagee? If the trust arises at the moment of acquisition, then P's wife will be in actual occupation at the time that the building society's charge is registered. Even if the trust only arises when P is registered as the new proprietor, it would seem that the trust will bite on the title a moment in time before the charge takes effect as a legal estate. How serious this consequence is will depend upon the valuation of the wife's share. If, for example, her share arises by virtue of a contribution to the deposit and is strictly quantified so as to give her only a *pro rata* share of the equity, the building society's security will only be at risk if the value of the house falls appreciably before much capital repayment has been achieved. Alternatively, as we suggested in Chapter 3, if the beneficiary's claims are confined to the value of the equity of redemption, a first mortgagee's security is not normally at risk. But if the share of the equity is assessed on a broader basis, the first mortgagee may have to argue that the trust should be set aside insofar as it is a settlement, normally in the course of bankruptcy proceedings.[32]

(d) The proviso: "Save where enquiry . . . "

If the purchaser inquires of a beneficiary whether he or she possesses rights and that person fails to disclose the rights, the purchaser will take free of the potentially overriding interest. Obviously this could give rise to difficulties of proof; as Jill Martin has observed,[33] a purchaser would be well advised to have written evidence of the inquiry and the answers given if he sought to rely upon this proviso to section 70(1)(g). There are further difficulties involved in this question of disclosure: in particular, what kind of disclosure can be expected?

The problem is, first, what degree of precision can be expected, and secondly, to what extent is the occupant bound for the future, so far as the purchaser is concerned, by the answer given? It is one thing to suggest that a negative reply to an enquiry should suffice so far as the purchaser is concerned (though even here, problems of undue influence could arise); but to what extent, if a positive answer of some kind, asserting some form of rights, is given, will the occupant be held to that statement in the future, even though a court might subsequently feel that the answer did not "truly" reflect the legal position? However, these questions are perhaps academic, since a purchaser, on encountering an occupant making some claim or another, is likely, after *Boland*, to seek to have that person joined as a party to the transaction or at least to obtain his or her consent (see further below).

(2) *Where claimants not in occupation*

A beneficiary who is not in actual occupation nor in receipt of rents and profits (see above) will not be able to claim an overriding interest within section 70(1)(g). The normal method of protection in this situation for the beneficiary would be some entry on the register (see above). Without this, there will normally be no protection against a purchaser.[34]

C. THE SOLE TRUSTEE: UNREGISTERED CONVEYANCING

1. *Where Beneficial Interest Protected by Registration*

By contrast with the position under the scheme of registered conveyancing there are few registration procedures available here.

(1) *All beneficiaries*

In very limited circumstances, beneficiaries may be able to make a *lis pendens* registration in the register of pending land actions. A *lis pendens* is "any action or proceeding pending in court relating to land or any interest in or charge on land" (s.17(1) Land Charges Act 1972). It is therefore important to establish where a beneficiary under a trust for sale has such an interest in the land. In *Taylor* v. *Taylor*[35] it was held that a claim to a share in the proceeds of sale of land held on trust for sale was *not* covered by section 17(1). However, this rather formalistic resort to the doctrine of conversion may not have survived *Boland*. It is therefore possible that a beneficiary may be able to make a registration in the register of pending land actions. By section 1(6) of the Land Charges Act 1972 the court has a wide jurisdiction to order the removal of an unjustified entry. The effect of such a registration is to ensure that a new owner will be bound by the claim.

(2) *Spouses*

Spouses may enter a class F land charge protecting their right of occupation under the Matrimonial Homes Act (as amended).

2. *Where Beneficial Interest not Protected by Registration*

(1) *Where claimant is in occupation*

The position here was, prior to *Boland*, broadly defined in the case of *Caunce* v. *Caunce*,[36] where Stamp J. held that a beneficiary who was jointly occupying the property with the vendor trustee did not put a purchaser on enquiry (at least if that beneficiary was the wife of the vendor trustee) and consequently the purchaser took free from the interest of the beneficiary as a bona fide purchaser of the legal estate without notice. The test as formulated by Stamp J. was whether the presence of the occupant was consistent with the title offered by the mortgagor. Joint occupation by a husband and wife was not inconsistent with the idea that he was sole beneficial owner and did not put a purchaser on enquiry as to the wife's claims. Whether a beneficiary in sole occupation would necessarily put a purchaser on notice was left open. This decision, which was doubted *obiter* in *Hodgson* v. *Marks*,[37] has probably not survived the House of Lords' decision in *Boland*. Although Lord Scarman treated the future of *Caunce* as still open, the contrast between Lord Wilberforce's dictum in *Boland* concerning the "easygoing practice of dispensing with enquiries as to occupation"[38] and Stamp J.'s emphasis in *Caunce* upon the need to respect conveyancing practice and to avoid (quoting Lord Upjohn)[39] "embarrassing enquiries,"[40] is such as to suggest that the present approach leans in favour of more stringent enquiries and therefore towards a broader scope for the doctrine of notice. As a strict matter of law, however, the question must still be treated as unresolved.

(2) *Relevant time and transfer of title*

In unregistered conveyancing title passes on completion by virtue of a conveyance of the title deeds. Consequently, if we return to the example we used in registered conveyancing, we can see that as between the parties involved in a sale/purchase and mortgage transaction, the question of priorities is somewhat different. If we assume that the vendor's family moves out and the purchaser's family moves in at some point after title has passed (be it only a matter of hours or minutes) then the following principles will apply–

1. The purchaser may take subject to the claims of any beneficiary behind a trust affecting the vendor, at least if those beneficiaries had been in occupation prior to completion and their presence was such as to put the purchaser on notice. As we have seen, in registered conveyancing the position would normally be different.

2. The purchaser's building society will be in the same position as the purchaser *vis-à-vis* those claiming through the vendor. As regards claims through the purchaser, the building society will only take subject to the claims of those who contribute to the deposit or of those who contribute to the mortgage payments if the society has actual or constructive notice of the existence of a trust in favour of, for example, the purchaser's wife. In the absence of actual notice, it is difficult to predict what standards of enquiry will be required of building societies so as to put them on constructive notice. In this respect, another element of the decision in *Caunce* should be noted. Stamp J. held that the existence of a joint bank account did not put the mortgagee bank on constructive notice of the wife's claim. This would still appear, despite *Boland,* to be good law.

(3) *Where claimant not in occupation*

We have already seen that there is little room for registration of interests behind trusts under the Land Charges Act. A purchaser who has actual notice of the existence of a trust will be bound even though the claimant is not in occupation. But there seems little likelihood of a purchaser being affected by a constructive notice where a claimant is *not* in occupation.

D. THE PRACTICAL CONSEQUENCES OF BOLAND

1. *The Position of Home Buyers*

For home buyers, the main threat to acquiring a good title occurs in unregistered conveyancing, especially if *Caunce* v. *Caunce* is no longer good law. Here, there is the possibility (though surely a rare one) of taking subject to the claims of a beneficiary of whom they have constructive notice. The consequences of this could be that in unregistered conveyancing solicitors might endeavour, wherever possible, to secure the appointment of a co-trustee by the vendor. On the assumption that the two-trustees rule has survived intact, this would, in nearly every case, ensure that any claims were overridden on the sale. As we have seen, in registered conveyancing this manoeuvre would normally be otiose, since the beneficiaries claiming through the vendor would have given up occupation at the time the title passes.

2. *Building Societies and Other First Mortgagees*

In unregistered conveyancing, first mortgagees are in a similar position to home buyers so far as people claiming through the vendor are concerned, and overreaching is equally desirable for them. In registered conveyancing, and perhaps in unregistered conveyancing, lenders face an additional problem after *Boland* in that the value of their security may be diminished because of superior claims coming from those claiming through the purchaser. The main way around this is to obtain in some form the consent of interested parties, although, if the mortgage is executed by two trustees, overreaching would normally apply. There are however difficulties about the ground rules for obtaining valid consents. These are discussed below.

3. *Second Mortgagees*

In both systems of conveyancing second mortgagees are particularly vulnerable to claims from beneficiaries behind a trust imposed on borrowers. The best protection is again to obtain the consents of the beneficiaries, in order to preclude a subsequent claim. It may also be possible to override possible claims through the appointment of a second trustee, but there are particular problems here which have not yet been fully explored concerning the purposes for which the borrower arranges the loan.[41]

4. *Obtaining Consents*

Many of the difficulties involved with land transactions can at first sight be overcome by obtaining the consent of potential claimants to the particular transaction. There are a number of different ways in which this could be done. We now consider some of these.

(a) Occupants can be joined as parties to the deed of transfer or conveyance or to the mortgage deed. In accordance with general principles of conveyancing, this would preclude the party from subsequently asserting a claim against the purchaser or mortgagee. (This is subject however to the possibility that the occupant might challenge the validity of the consent). Occupants joined as parties to the mortgage deed could or could not be made jointly or severally liable for the mortgage repayments. In the case of a deed of transfer or conveyance of title, the vendor could be required, at contract stage, to obtain the participation of the occupant in the deed of transfer or conveyance, and failure to do so could consequently be a ground for the purchaser refusing to complete.

(b) As far as mortgages are concerned, it is open to mortgagees to insist, as a condition of the loan, that the occupant consents to the transaction. This could take a number of different forms. First, an assignment of all rights and claims; secondly, a general waiver. The consideration for such waiver could be found in the granting of a loan to the borrower. Alternatively, the occupant could be required to undertake to indemnify the lender for any loss the lender might suffer as a result of adverse claims subsequently being made.

(c) Even if no formal consent has been obtained for the transaction, it is possible that the acquiescence of the occupant might estop that person from subsequently claiming priority over a purchaser or mortgagees.[42]

5. *Impugning Consents*

The next question is whether such consents or acquiescence can later be impugned by the occupant, which we must now consider. The main basis for impugning consents is the decision of the Court of Appeal in *Lloyds Bank* v. *Bundy*[43] where the Court refused to allow the Bank to evict Mr. Bundy, who had provided his house as security to the Bank for further overdraft facilities for his son's company. Unfortunately, the rule in this case is not clear. On the one hand Lord Denning M.R. formulated a broad principle of protecting weaker parties in cases of unequal bargaining power; on the other Sir Eric Sachs appeared to rest his decision on the fact that Mr. Bundy was a client of the Bank and therefore the Bank owed him a fiduciary duty since they knew that he relied upon them and the advice they gave. The best precaution for lenders is to ensure that potential claimants receive independent legal advice before consenting in one of the ways already discussed to the transaction.

Before leaving the question of *Boland's* practical consequences, it is important to emphasise that these prophylactic measures open to purchasers and mortgagees may well be employed in respect of most adult occupants. We have seen from the earlier chapters of this book that it is by no means always clear in advance how a court would classify an occupant's rights in a particular case. Therefore, the practical effects of *Boland* could be quite far-reaching, insofar as the concurrence of most occupants may become established conveyancing practice in many of the transactions outlined in this chapter.

E. Two or More Trustees: Unregistered Conveyancing

The position where there are two trustees is in principle more straightforwarded in unregistered conveyancing, and so we begin with it. The basic rules are set out in section 14 of the Trustee Act 1925 and section 27 of the Law of Property Act 1925. A purchaser who pays the purchase money to two or more trustees and obtains a receipt for that money from them can resist any claim from beneficiaries. This is commonly said to be because the interests of the beneficiaries are, by virtue of section 27, overreached, *i.e.* converted into interests in the proceeds of sale. This leaves the beneficiaries with remedies only against their trustees.

This is a convenient shorthand description of the "two-trustee" rule but it is not quite correct to describe the interests of the beneficiaries as being overreached. What seems to have been envisaged, in 1925, as we have seen, is that where land is held on an express or statutory trust for sale, the trustees are empowered to sell and a purchaser can obtain title without the concurrence of the beneficiaries. The presence of two trustees for sale means that the purchaser is not liable to see to the application of the proceeds, that is, he does not run the risk of having to pay the purchase price again.

Whichever way the two-trustee rule is formulated, it remains to ask whether there are any exceptions to (or loopholes in) this general rule. The main question which is posed by section 27 concerns the conduct of the purchaser and vendor *vis-à-vis* the beneficiary. In what circumstances, if any, might the court hold that a purchaser or mortgagee does not come within the protection of the section?

1. *Money or Money's Worth*

The *general* definition of purchaser, for the purposes of the Law of Property Act 1925, is contained in section 205(1)(xxi) and provides as follows:

> " 'Purchaser' means a purchaser in good faith for valuable consideration . . . except that in Part I of the Act . . . 'purchaser' only means a person who acquires an interest in or charge on property for money or money's worth . . . and 'valuable consideration', includes marriage but does not include a nominal consideration in money."

A question arises as to whether a transaction can be attacked (and the two-trustee rule displaced) by claiming the inadequate consideration has been given. Without direct authority on the point, it may be possible to treat *Midland Bank Trust Co.* v. *Green*[44] (a decision on the Land Charges Act 1972) as analogous. In this case, a father granted a son an option to buy some freehold land for £22,500. The son failed to register the option. Later the father discovered the option has not been registered and conveyed the land (now worth £40,000) to his wife for a consideration of £500. The son argued on two fronts; first, that the conveyance was in bad faith, and secondly, that the wife was not a purchaser for money or money's worth within section 4(6) of the Land Charges Act 1972. Although the son succeeded in the Court of Appeal, the House of Lords unanimously reversed their decision holding that the wife had been a "purchaser of a legal estate for money or money's worth." The court refused to consider the adequacy or otherwise of the consideration, even though by the time the case was heard the land was worth £400,000.

The question was left open, to some extent, as to

whether "money or money's worth" included nominal consideration, but, whatever the answer, nominal consideration was given a narrow meaning and firmly distinguished from inadequate consideration.

2. *Good Faith*

The next question is whether good faith is thereby excluded from section 27. The difficulty is that the scope of the cut down definition of purchaser which by section 205(1)(xxi) is to apply in Part I of the Law of Property Act 1925 (which includes section 27) is ambiguous. The reduction could refer simply to the requisite consideration (*i.e.* money or money's worth rather than value). Alternatively, the reduction could involve a complete substitution of a special definition for the general definition, and the omission of any requirement to act in good faith. If the latter view is taken there would seem to be little scope for ousting the operation of the two-trustee rule wherever the purchaser has a receipt from two trustees, even if all the parties consciously intended to defeat the beneficiaries' claims. *Green* is also interesting because the House was insistent that the different statutes which comprise the 1925 code would often have to be interpreted separately from each other. A broader, code-based, approach was rejected. Thus, it may therefore be that *Green* (on the Land Charges Act) is of limited assistance in drawing the boundaries of the two-trustee rule as contained in the Trustee Act and Law of Property Act. In particular, while *Green* does appear to provide a definitive interpretation of "money or money's worth" which presumably is applicable throughout the code, the question of good faith (outside the Land Charges Act) must be regarded as open.

3. *Fraud and the Two-Trustee Rule*

Transactions have sometimes been attacked on the basis of being shams,[45] or general equitable principles have been applied to override express statutory provisions.[46] Such cases have been doubted in the past[47] and the recent decision of the House of Lords in *Green* suggest that courts should be slow to modify the requirements of the conveyancing statutes.[48] But what about a clear case of fraud?

For example, consider the position where the house is in the joint names but one party persuades another person to be co-signatory to a proposed transaction, leading the purchaser or mortgagee to suppose that he is dealing with both the legal owners (in circumstances which occur behind the back of the other, innocent, joint tenant). This is not a totally fanciful situation, especially when, on a breakdown of the relationship, one of the parties wishes to raise money quickly on the security of the home. The legal consequences of such a fraudulent transaction were considered in *Cedar Holdings Ltd.* v. *Green*.[49] A man sought an overdraft from his bank, offering as security the former matrimonial home, which was still vested jointly in him and his former wife. A document executing a legal charge was signed by the man and a woman who was represented to the bank as the former wife. A dispute subsequently arose between the bank and the wife, who had in no sense participated in the fraud, as to the legal effect of the transaction.

The bank conceded that the wife's beneficial share was not affected, but claimed that the husband had charged his beneficial interest in the home. This claim was based in part upon section 63(1) of the Law of Property Act 1975, which provides:

> "Every conveyance is effectual to pass all estate, right, title, interest, claim, and demand which the conveyancing parties respectively have, in, to, or on the property conveyed, or expressed or intended so to be . . . "

The Court of Appeal, held *inter alia*, that section 63 was not effective to charge a beneficial interest behind a trust for sale, since the section operated only upon interests in land, and not upon interests in the proceeds of sale. This meant that the bank's security was wholly ineffective, and the bank was thus left to its personal remedies against the husband, and would only be able to reach his share in the home through one of the methods outlined in Chapter 8. A dictum by Lord Wilberforce in *Boland*,[50] in the context of a discussion of the doctrine of conversion, suggests that the Court of Appeal erred in excluding interests behind trusts for sale from section 63; if so, such a transaction will after all operate to charge the beneficial interest.[50a]

F. Two Trustees: Registered Conveyancing

It would be natural to assume, with regard to a matter so central to the 1925 code, that the position would be the same in registered conveyancing. One difficulty is the lack of any explicit incorporation of the two-trustee rule into the registered conveyancing system. The registered conveyancing system contains mechanisms and procedures which would make overreaching operate—in particular, the availability of a restriction which, if duly entered, would ensure that the purchase price was paid to two trustees, and which would consequently "overreach" the interests of beneficiaries into the proceeds of sale. The difficulty, however, is whether, when a beneficiary has a claim to have an overriding interest of the *Boland* type under section 70(1)(*g*), the two-trustee rule takes priority, or whether, notwithstanding that there are two trustees, the overriding interest will prevail. One obvious explanation for the silence of the Land Registration Act 1925 on this point is that the draftsmen of the Act probably assumed that interests behind trusts for sale would not fall within the reach of section 70(1)(*g*). In other words, it was perhaps assumed that trusts for sale would be protected as minor interests in the same way as settled land, see section 3(xv) of the Land Registration Act 1925. By section 86(2) of the Land Registration Act 1925, interests taking effect under a Settled Land Act settlement can *only* be protected as minor interests. It is only the omission of a similar provision regarding trusts for sale which made the *Boland* decision possible.

After *Boland*, what is the position of overreaching versus the overriding interest? It is surely desirable that the two conveyancing systems should be in accordance on this point, but some commentators have voiced doubts as to whether this is so. Colin Sydenham[51] suggests that a "wide view" of section 70(1)(*g*) can be formulated by studying some of Lord Roskill's dicta in *Boland*. This "wide view" of section 70(1)(*g*) can be briefly summarised as follows: a beneficiary in actual occupation can assert an overriding interest against a purchaser or mortgagee even where there is a proper sale or mortgage by two trustees, the overreaching machinery not functioning at all. By contrast, Jill Martin[52] supports a "narrow view" whereby the overreaching machinery must prevail over the overriding interest where there is a proper sale by two trustees. It seems unlikely that Lord Roskill's very brief remarks in *Boland* were intended to support the so-called "wide view," and an alternative reading has been suggested above.

If the narrow view is correct then overreaching takes precedence over section 70(1)(*g*) and the position in registered conveyancing, where there are two trustees (and whether or not there is a restriction on the register) will be the same as in unregistered land, and the same questions arise as to when, if at all, the courts will mitigate the operation of section 27 of the Law of Property Act.

G. REFORM

The Law Commission has now recommended the introduction of new legislation to circumvent what it considers to be the unacceptable consequences of *Boland*.[53] First, it has recommended[54] that all "co-ownership interests" (that is, equitable interests arising behind a trust, whether express, implied, or statutory[55]) must be registered in order to bind purchasers or mortgagees. Thus in unregistered conveyancing, purchasers would be unaffected by actual or constructive notice of such claims, and in registered conveyancing, interests behind such trusts would cease to take effect as overriding interests.

Secondly, the Law Commission's new proposals draw a distinction between the co-ownership interests of spouses and all others (unmarried couples, parents and children, etc.) For the latter group, the general law of property relating to acquisition of interests and the rights of beneficiaries *vis-à-vis* their trustees is retained. For spouses, the Law Commission proposes that its Third Report on Family Property be reactivated and the scheme of statutory co-ownership be implemented. This involves first, the introduction of a "consent requirement."[56] This means that any disposition of the home by the spouse who is legal owner without the consent of the other spouse will be a breach of trust. Secondly, the Law Commission recommends compulsory statutory co-ownership by way of equitable joint tenancy of the matrimonial home,[57] subject to certain exceptions which have been considered earlier.[58] Both rights can only be asserted against purchasers or mortgagees if the rights have been duly registered.

Under these proposals, registration has two effects.[59] First, a purchaser will be bound by the interest unless the two-trustee rule is complied with. Secondly, when the consent requirement applies, registration means that a disposition to a purchaser will be of no effect unless the spouse's consent is obtained. Failure to register will enable a sole trustee to overreach the interest of the spouse, and a purchaser is not to be affected by notice of any such interest. Finally, it should be noted that whether or not the parties are spouses, the Law Commission recommends that the two-trustee rule be retained.[60]

How satisfactory is the centrality of registration? It is, of course, convenient from the conveyancing point of view, and consistent with the overreaching—registration framework embedded in the 1925 scheme.[61] But it may be doubted whether such a scheme provides much serious protection in practice. The experience of the Matrimonial Homes Act 1967 has been that it is normally only employed in marital breakdown, and is not effective to protect spouses' occupation rights prior to such an event. Indeed, if the 1967 Act "worked," it is questionable whether, in many cases, any further rights for spouses would in practice be needed.[62] Against this, it could be said that it may become common practice for solicitors on transfer to advise appropriate registration under the proposed scheme.

Again, in practical terms, this may beg the question. The problem of the sole trustee will normally only arise when a solicitors' client, at the time of purchase, was the sole trustee and not his or her spouse. Thus while solicitors may, as a common practice, inform their client about the impact of these proposals (if implemented) it is not obvious that they would inform the other spouse of the availability and importance of registration. Moreover, it remains a nice question whether solicitors should be under any such duty of care in this situation, however foreseeable the loss, in some circumstances, to the other spouse might be.[63]

So far as spouses are concerned, the Law Commission argues that the advisers of husbands would in practice ascertain whether the requirement existed and, if it did, would ensure that it was complied with.[64] Our criticisms are of course predicated upon the assumption that many people will be unaware of the registration facility, at least until it is too late. It may be, therefore, if these proposals become law, that "a determined campaign of education and publicity"[65] will prove to be essential.

The final question, which can only be raised here, is whether the differential treatment of spousal and non-spousal relationships is justifiable. It does not accord unambiguously with the developments traced elsewhere in this book. Moreover, this raises a question about how adequately the problems identified by the Law Commisison are dealt with by these proposals. Many non-marital disputes have centred around arguments couched in terms of licence or estoppel. If these are treated as binding purchasers or mortgagees without registration, it may be that conveyancing remains hazardous, albeit to a lesser extent. This is examined in the next chapter.

Notes to pages 152–178

[1] See Williams on *Vendor and Purchaser* (3rd ed., 1923) Vol. I, p. 241.

[2] s.36 Conveyancing Act 1881; s.20 Trustee Act 1893. For the approach of Equity before the legislation, see *Webb* v. *Ledsam* (1855) 1 K. & J. 385; *cf. Wilkinson* v. *Hartley* (1852) 13 Beav. 183.

[3] See especially S. J. Bailey "Trusts and Titles" 8 C.L.J. 36 (1942–44).

[4] See especially *Re Harman and Uxbridge and Rickmansworth Ry. Co.* (1883) XXIV Ch. D. 720; *Re Chafter and Randall's Contract* [1916] 2 Ch. 8.

[5] See the extended discussion of this problem in Williams, *op. cit.* pp.224–231.

[6] *Ibid.* at p.233–239.

[7] *Ibid.* at p.443.

[8] *Ibid.* at p.574.

[9] *Hunt* v. *Luck* [1902] 1 Ch. 428; 71 L.J. Ch. 239. Mere knowledge that the rents were paid to an estate agent did not put the purchaser on inquiry as to the quality of the vendor's reversion.

[10] *Bull* v. *Bull* [1955] 1 Q.B. 234; [1955] 2 W.L.R. 78 and see *supra.,* pp.91–96.

[11] s.14 Trustee Act 1925.

[12] s.26(1) L.P.A. 1925.

[13] *Bull* v. *Bull* [1955] 1 Q.B. 234, 237.

[14] See *supra,* pp.94–96.

[15] For the distinction between obtaining title and being liable to pay again, see *Balfour* v. *Welland* (1809) 16 Ves. Jun. 151.

[16] The view adopted in *Williams and Glyn's Bank* v. *Boland* [1979] 2 All E.R. 697; [1979] Ch. 312; [1979] 2 W.L.R. (C.A.).

[17] Brickdale and Stewart-Wallace merely comment that "it would apparently include the rights of a person in occupation of an underground space . . . " *Land Registration Act 1925* (4th ed., 1939) p.193.

18 See the discussion in *Barclays* v. *Barclay* [1970] 2 Q.B. 677; [1979] 3 W.L.R. 82; [1979] 1 All E.R. 676, *supra*, pp.95–96.

19 *Elias* v. *Mitchell* [1972] Ch. 652; [1972] 2 W.L.R. 740; [1972] 2 All E.R. 153.

20 *Boland* (C.A.) [1979] Ch. 312, 337.

21 *Boland* (H.L.) [1981] A.C. 487, 512. For the same point see Murphy (1979) 42 M.L.R. 567, 570.

22 For an alternative discussion of these dicta, see *infra*, n.51 and n.52, p.180.

23 *Barnett* v. *Hassett* [1981] 1 W.L.R 1385. The effect of this decision is that spouses in occupation can, in a practical sense, use the Matrimonial Homes Act procedures to protect their interests, but those out of occupation with no intention to occupy cannot.

24 [1980] 3 W.L.R. 138; [1980] 2 All E.R. 408.

25 [1979] 1 W.L.R. 440.

26 [1969] 1 W.L.R. 286; [1969] 1 All E.R. 722.

27 *Boland* (C.A.) [1979] Ch. 312; [1979] 2 W.L.R. 550; [1979] 2 All E.R. 697.

28 [1971] Ch. 892.

29 *Boland per* Wilberforce, p.144.

30 *Strand Securities* v. *Caswell* [1965] Ch. 958; [1965] 2 W.L.R. 958; [1965] 1 All E.R. 820.

31 [1961] 1 W.L.R. 339.

32 See *infra*, pp.205–207.

33 Jill Martin [1980] Conv. 361.

34 But *cf. Peffer* v. *Rigg* [1977] 1 W.L.R. 285; [1978] 3 All E.R. 745.

35 *Taylor* v. *Taylor* [1968] 1 W.L.R. 378; [1968] 1 All E.R. 843.

36 *Caunce* v. *Caunce* [1969] 1 W.L.R. 286; [1969] 1 All E.R. 722.

37 [1971] Ch. 892; [1971] 2 W.L.R. 1263; [1971] 2 All E.R. 682.

38 [1981] A.C. 487, 508–509.

39 [1965] A.C. 1175, 1233.

40 [1969] 1 W.L.R. 286, 292.

41 See Clayton, "Void Mortgages?" [1981] Conv. 19.

42 See *Wroth* v. *Tyler* [1974] Ch. 30; [1973] 2 W.L.R. 405; [1973] 1 All E.R. 897; *Spiro* v. *Lintern* [1973] 1 W.L.R. 1002; [1973] 2 All E.R. 319; *Taylors Fashions Ltd.* v. *Liverpool Victoria Trustees Co. Ltd.* [1981] 2 W.L.R. 576; [1981] 1 All E.R. 897.

43 *Lloyds Bank Ltd.* v. *Bundy* [1974] 3 W.L.R. 501.

44 *Midland Bank Trust Co.* v. *Green* [1981] A.C. 513.

45 *Ferris* v. *Weaven* [1952] 2 All E.R. 233 which " . . . may possibly be justified on its own facts." *National Provincial Bank* v. *Ainsworth* [1965] A.C. 1175, 1240, *per* Lord Upjohn.

46 *Ives (E.R. Investment)* v. *High* [1967] 2 Q.B. 379.

47 *Miles* v. *Bull* [1968] 3 All E.R. 632.

48 [1981] A.C. 513, 530–531.

49 [1981] Ch. 129.

[50] [1981] A.C. 487, 507.

[50a] This approach is adopted in *First National Securities Ltd.* v. *Hegarty*, *The Times*, November 2, 1982 (Q.B.).

[51] C. Sydenham [1980] Conv. 427.

[52] Jill Martin [1981] Conv. 219.

[53] Law Com. No. 115 (1982). For the consequences, see paras. 27–43.

[54] *Ibid.* para. 83.

[55] *i.e.* an interest arising under the statutory co-ownership proposals contained in Law Com. No. 86.

[56] Law Com. No. 115, paras. 95 and 97.

[57] para. 115; and see *supra*, Chaps. 3 and 4, pp.47; 84–85.

[58] See p.47.

[59] Law Com. No. 86, paras. 1.320 and 1.321; cl.21(5).

[60] Law Com. No. 115, paras. 87, 89–91.

[61] The conventional generalisation is that the overreaching—registration polarity is co-terminous with the distinction between the treatment of "family" and "commercial" interests. The Matrimonial Homes Act 1967 marked the first significant breach of this previously neat framework. In this respect, the Law Commission's proposals represent a further erosion of the 1925 system. But it must be remembered that the design of the registered conveyancing system always laid greater emphasis upon registration, even, apparently, (see *supra*, n.51 and n.52) as a means of ensuring overreaching.

[62] Because it will effectively freeze dealings with the home. For the main limitation upon using the Matrimonial Homes Act in this way, see *supra*, n.23.

[63] *cf. Ross* v. *Caunters* [1980] Ch. 297, 322.

[64] Law Com. No. 115, para. 100.

[65] Law Com. No. 115, para. 78.

Chapter 7

PRIORITIES: LICENCES AND ESTOPPEL

A. Licences: The General Position

In both systems of conveyancing, a fundamental distinction is drawn between the effect of personal and proprietary rights upon purchasers and mortgagees. Proprietary rights potentially bind third parties, but personal rights do not. This distinction lay at the core of the House of Lords' decision in *National Provincial Bank* v. *Ainsworth*.[1] It can, of course, be difficult, with regard to some of the rights discussed in this book, to classify a particular right as proprietary or personal, but if we overcome this problem of classification, the path is, thenceforth, straightforward.

In the case of unregistered conveyancing, this general principle applies automatically. Equitable interests (of a proprietary kind) will bind purchasers with notice either actual or by virtue of registration, but subject to that, the bona fide purchaser of a legal estate for value without notice will take free. Personal rights however cannot be asserted against purchasers with or without notice. Thus, for example, in *Clore* v. *Theatrical Properties*,[2] the owner of a theatre purported to "grant" front of house rights to the plaintiff for a specified period of time. The theatre was sold before that time had expired, but it was held that the "grant," which could only take effect as a licence,[3] did not bind the purchasers of the theatre, and, that any remedy would therefore only lie against the licensor. In registered conveyancing, in the context of the family home, the issue, for present purposes, will normally arise in terms of whether those with personal rights against the owner of the house have overriding interests within section 70(1)(g) of the Land Registration Act 1925 which can be asserted against the purchasers. After *Ainsworth*, the answer is that such rights are not overriding interests, on the grounds that "rights" in section 70(1)(*g*) means proprietary rights. Equally, as a matter of principle, those who have personal rights do not have the appropriate kind of right to protect their position by registration as a minor interest—(see *Pritchard* v. *Briggs*).[4] Although this principle has been firmly asserted in the House of Lords, some dicta in the Court of Appeal in recent years have suggested an alternative view.[5] It is therefore necessary to examine the position in more detail.

B. LICENCES WITHOUT AN ESTOPPEL ELEMENT

Such licences, whether bare or contractual, confer only personal rights and duties between licensor and licensee. Thus, the licence in *Hardwick* v. *Johnson*,[6] if classified as contractual, would not affect a third party who, for example, bought the house from the mother. The purchaser would be able to claim vacant possession of the house, and the daughter's remedy, if any, would be against the mother for breach of contract. In a number of Lord Denning's decisions, however, this principle has been blurred through the intrusion of the equitable remedy of the injunction. As we have already seen, these contracts can be and have been (in effect) specifically enforced against the licensor directly[7] or indirectly, by refusing the licensor an order for possession. Such remedies do no more than specifically enforce agreements between the original parties. The availability of such an equitable remedy does not, as Lord Denning has suggested,[8] in itself convert the relationship into a proprietary one. From this it should follow that mere knowledge by the third party of the existence of the licence should not, without more, affect the position of the third party *vis-à-vis* the licensee.

These difficulties are illustrated sharply in *Binions* v.

Evans.[9] Mrs. Evans was the widow of a former employee of Tredegar Estates, and lived in her cottage under a written agreement which was called a "tenancy agreement." Under this agreement, Tredegar Estates permitted her lifetime rent-free occupation, and she was required to maintain the cottage and garden in good repair. Tredegar Estates subsequently sold the cottage to the Binions's, at an undervalue, and expressly subject to Mrs. Evans' tenancy (in other words, they did not undertake to deliver vacant possession to the purchasers). The Binionses subsequently sought, unsuccessfully, to evict her from the premises.

The Court of Appeal presented different grounds for refusing an order for possession. Lord Denning offered two grounds. First, he suggested that the licence amounted to an equitable interest so that a purchaser with notice was bound. This view, though supported to some extent by his earlier decision in *Errington* v. *Errington*, seems incompatible with the *obiter dicta* in *Ainsworth.*[10] His alternative ground was that if the licence was not itself an equitable interest, the circumstances of the sale gave rise to the constructive trust which prevented the purchasers from evicting her. The basis of this constructive trust was twofold: first that the Binionses bought at an undervalue, and secondly, that they expressly undertook in the contract of sale not to evict her. The low price, taking into account the licence, invites comparison with *Bannister* v. *Bannister*[11] and suggests that the basis of the trust might be unjust enrichment. It remains unclear whether Lord Denning was suggesting that the stipulation in the contract was in itself a sufficient ground for imposing a constructive trust.

The other views of the case were quite different. Stephenson L.J. appeared to think that by virtue of her arrangement with Tredegar Estates (the original owners of the cottage) Mrs. Evans was entitled, as of right, to remain in the property for life and that such entitlement amounted to a tenancy for life. Both Megaw and

Stephenson L.JJ. suggested that the trust, if there was one, arose prior to the appearance of the Binionses on the scene. By analogy with *Bannister* v. *Bannister*, he further held that she was a tenant for life within the Settled Land Act (a view which Lord Denning rejected on the basis that interests arising under constructive trusts were not within the scope of the Settled Land Act). Megaw L.J. had difficulty in seeing how the Settled Land Act was applicable, but also assumed that a tenancy for life arose here and that, following *Bannister*, the Settled Land Act applied.

The invocation of the Settled Land Act leads to rather extreme results; if Mrs. Evans was a tenant for life within the Settled Land Act, then the legal estate, held by the Binionses at the time of the litigation, would have to be vested in her, and, further, she would have, by virtue of the Settled Land Act, a power of sale over the property.[12]

It is difficult to provide an acceptable analytical foundation to support a common sense view of what the Court considered to be the appropriate result. Tredegar Estates had promised lifetime occupation, and there was enough of a *quid pro quo* to support a contractual analysis at that stage. Equally, when Tredegar Estates exchanged contracts with the Binionses, the transaction was underscored by (and made expressly subject to) Mrs. Evans's right to lifetime occupation. The *right* result thus seems evident on the facts. Yet each arrangement, so analysed, involves privity of contract, which did not exist between Mrs. Evans and the Binionses.

Sometimes, where a relationship cannot be interpreted as contractual, it is possible to invoke some species of equitable estoppel. Again, there are obstacles given the particular facts of *Binionses*. First, there were no apparent dealings between the Binionses and Mrs. Evans and, therefore, no representations as such by the Binionses to Mrs. Evans. Secondly, it is difficult to see any reliance or detriment in Mrs. Evans's conduct or circumstances. At most, one might suggest that she had assumed that by

virtue of the agreement her occupation would be protected for her life. It is difficult to see that there was any
further reliance in the case.

Evidence of reliance or of direct dealings between the
Binionses and Mrs. Evans would have been irrelevant if it
had been possible to view the arrangement as a tenancy.
There are, however, special difficulties in analysing a
transaction designed to protect lifetime occupation as a
tenancy, which flow from the way in which the 1925 code
dealt with interests limited to the duration of a life.

We have already suggested that the conveyancing
reforms of 1925 were, in large measure aimed at simplifying the consequences for land transfer of relatively
formalised family and commercial transactions. So far as
life interests were concerned, there were two classic
instances—the lease for life or lives[13] and the tenancy for
life in a strict settlement. In each case, the 1925 code
instituted a statutory regime intended to rationalise the
position. Leases for a life or successive lives were to take
effect as leases for a fixed term of 90 years, determinable
on one month's notice after the dropping of the last
relevant life. But this would only apply if the lease was
granted for a rent.[14] So far as settlements were concerned
legal life estates were abolished and such interests
permitted thenceforth to subsist only in equity, behind a
trust. In this context, the elaborate scheme of the Settled
Land Act 1925 was devised, one aspect of which was to
ensure that the fragmentation of title which the old strict
settlement had involved was replaced by a series of
imperative requirements which meant (in the present
context) that the person with the life interest in possession
would be vested with the legal estate in the settled
property.

The arrangement in *Binions* v. *Evans* was rather like a
tenancy. Even though no rent as such was due, occupation
was conditional upon Mrs. Evans maintaining the property. Moreover, the transaction between Tredegar Estates
and the Binionses is intelligible in the light of the

assumption (on each side) that vacant possession of the cottage could not be delivered since the purchase was subject to a prior occupancy. However, this "tenancy" could not neatly be transposed into the framework of the 1925 code. Quite apart from questions of intention it could not amount to a 90 year determinable lease because no rent was payable under the arrangement.

The only other route to secure lifetime protected occupancy within the 1925 framework was thus to resort to the Settled Land Act. As we have seen, the majority in the case seemed to incline in this direction. The intention of the original parties was to secure lifetime occupation; the transaction could not amount to a lease for life and therefore was a tenancy for life (*i.e.* an equitable life interest). Between the original parties such an analogy would have been unneccessary (as we have seen, contract would have sufficed); as between the occupant and a stranger, a contractual view would have been inadequate, unless a contractual licence was to be treated as an equitable interest as such, outside the legislative framework and dependent, in accordance with the general rule of equity, upon the doctrine of notice.

Lord Denning M.R. held that the Settled Land Act was inapplicable in that it only applied to settlements when interests were "limited" (*i.e.* expressly settled) by way of succession. In other words, the Settled Land Act scheme was not designed to cater for interests arising otherwise than by virtue of an express settlement. On this basis, *Banninster* v. *Bannister* was wrong. But his alternative solution is hardly more satisfactory. The original relationship is contractual, but because of the circumstances surrounding the purchase, an equity arises such that the purchaser becomes a constructive trustee. Although the decision has subsequently been followed[15] the question remains—in what circumstances, and for what reasons, is it proper to move the analysis from a contractual basis to a proprietary one when a transfer of title or mortgage is executed?

C. ESTOPPEL

If we assume that the term "proprietary estoppel" designates that the equity is proprietary in character, it follows that such estoppels will potentially bind purchasers and mortgagees. Where, as will be usual in the context of the family home, the equities are occupation-related, purchasers will be bound (a) in unregistered conveyancing, if they have notice; (b) in registered conveyancing, by virtue of section 70(1)(g) of the Land Registration Act 1925.

This position is assumed, for example, in *Pascoe* v. *Turner*. In this case, the Court appears to have thought that the equity went to protected lifetime occupation, but ordered the owner to transfer the fee simple to the occupant on the basis that otherwise, with simply a licence for life, she would have been liable to be ousted by a purchaser for value without notice.[16]

1. *The Settled Land Act Problem*

We have seen above that some judges have taken the view that an equity extending to lifetime occupation may constitute a settlement within the Settled Land Act 1925, thereby making the person in whose favour the equity arises a tenant for life within that Act. We now sketch the conveyancing consequences of invoking the Settled Land Act in this context.

The first point is that the Settled Land Act requires the legal estate to be vested in the tenant for life. This will, no doubt, rarely take place because of the informality of the relationship in which these equities arise and because of the parties' ignorance of the applicable statutory law. The rule which applies where the legal estate has not been duly vested in the tenant for life is contained in section 13 of the Settled Land Act 1925, by which any conveyance or transfer by the legal owner will operate only as a contract to convey and will not transfer the title except

when it is made in favour of a purchaser of the legal estate
for value without notice of the settlement. In unregistered
conveyancing, this is the only applicable provision, and
therefore, in relation to estoppel interests, whether or not
the Settled Land Act applies, the position of a purchaser
or mortgagee *vis-à-vis* someone protected by an estoppel
will turn upon notice. In practical terms, in each case, a
purchaser with actual or constructive notice will take
subject to the rights of lifetime occupation.

In registered conveyancing, the position may be more
complex, because of the interaction of section 13 of the
Settled Land Act 1925 with section 86(2) of the Land
Registration Act 1925. Section 86(2) provides that " . . .
interests created by or arising under a settlement shall . . .
take effect as minor interests and not otherwise . . . "
This appears to mean that interests under Settled Land
Act settlements cannot be protected as overriding interests
within section 70(1)(g). However, it is not clear whether
this applies in a situation when the legal estate is not
vested, as required, in the tenant for life (*i.e.* when the
person in whose favour the equity arises has not been
entered as registered proprietor on the Register).

2. Special Cases

We have assumed that it is possible to draw a distinction
between the position of a person in occupation by virtue
of a contract and a person whose occupation is protected
by an estoppel which assumes a proprietary form.
Sometimes, however, the position may be further complicated by additional elements arising in the original
two-party relationship. The clearest example of this is
Errington v. *Errington*[17] which has given rise to considerable confusion about the scope of contractual licences.
The licence in that case was of a very particular kind; the
licensee was in occupation by virtue of a unilateral
contract for the sale of the house. Initially, the father

bought a house for his son and daughter-in-law to live in, and obtained a mortgage in his own name. The terms of the arrangement were that if they paid him monthly sums equivalent to the mortgage repayments, he would transfer the title to them when the equity was fully redeemed. This gave rise to an equity on the border line of the doctrine of part performance, in the sense that the periodic mortgage repayments made by the licensee were generating in a contingent way a right to specific performance. Whether or not it was clear at the time *Errington* was decided that these payments were sufficient acts of part performance (though it was so assumed in the case), it is now fairly certain, following *Steadman* v. *Steadman*,[18] that payments of this kind can fall within that equitable doctrine. In such a case the occupant will have a proprietary interest not dissimilar to that of the person protected by means of proprietary estoppel. An important distinction may perhaps be drawn, however, between an estoppel and an oral contract supported by acts of part perfomance. The former case clearly (subject to the Settled Land Act problem) falls outside the registration framework of the 1925 code; in the latter case the position is more difficult.

The basic approach of the 1925 code to the enforceability of estate contracts against purchasers was to make it hinge upon registration (as a Class C(iv) land charge or by means of the minor interests machinery). The question is whether contracts enforceable by virtue of the doctrine of part performance are caught by the registration requirements.

Authority on the question is slender. In *Mens* v. *Wilson*[19] registration of a contract which was not evidenced in writing was vacated, but the question of the basis of registrability was not fully discussed. As to principle, there is no clear answer, and this is partly because of the ambiguity inherent in the doctrine of part performance. If the acts of part performance are viewed primarily as proving or evidencing the *existence* of a contract, they can be treated as on all fours with written evidence complying with section 40 of the Law of Property Act. If this strong analogy is drawn, it can then be argued that to draw a distinction so far as registration is concerned cannot be justified. An alternative view of the doctrine is to hold that the defendant is "charged upon the equities" resulting from the acts of part performance. Presented in an extreme form, it could be argued that this means that the remedy follows from the equity which arises from reliance upon the contract. The contract can then be used to establish what remedy should be ordered (and on what terms). Formulated in this way, the doctrine becomes virtually indistinguishable from proprietary estoppel, which might justify excluding part performance from the registration requirements. Indeed, it might be suggested that the common origin of part performance and proprietary estoppel itself constitutes a good reason for excluding registration.

There is perhaps also a practical objection to registration. Would the contract only be registrable when there were *sufficient* acts of part performance and therefore the right to specific performance of the oral contract? If so, it would be difficult to tell when the right accrued, and it would inevitably mean additionally that unenforceable contracts would be entered on the register.

If, despite these points, it was held that oral contracts are registrable, it would follow that in the unregistered system, failure to enter a Class C(iv) charge would make the contract void against a purchaser of the legal estate for money or money's worth, unless some overriding equity permitted the plea that the statute should not be used as an instrument of fraud.[20] Paradoxically, the registration requirement will be less severe in the registered system. If the claimant is in actual occupation, his rights will be protected by that occupation without need for registration. Even if occupation did not originally begin under the contract, section 70(1)(*g*) potentially applies[21] though in such a case the absence of any change of possession following the making of the oral contract may make it more difficult to establish that there are sufficient acts of part performance.

In conclusion, a practical complication in this type of case should be noted. Suppose the "licensor" sold the fee simple to the home. Such a transaction would quite easily take place without the knowledge of the occupant, if, for example, he or she was on holiday when the purchaser looked at the house. In such a case, as part of the transaction of sale and purchase, the building society mortgage would normally be discharged. The purchaser might pay cash, or raise the purchase price by means of a loan from another building society. The difficulty which arises after such a transaction is what would be the position of the instalment—paying occupant, since there would no longer be a mortgagee or a relevant building society to whom those payments could be made. The occupant would have made some payments (and in broad terms, partly acquired the equity to the property) but would no longer be able to continue to make such payments. Since the right to specific performance of the contract would apparently only accrue when the total repayments have been made, (which is why we have so far described that right as contingent) it is not at all clear that the occupant could obtain specific performance. (In *Errington* itself, this problem does not arise because the house had simply passed by way of succession to the widow of the original licensor, who was not in any event a purchaser for value.)

3. *Conclusion*

The preceding discussion was based around the idea that a clear analytical distinction could be drawn between contractual interests and equitable estoppel interests. One can further generalise by suggesting that it is *only* with regard to a dispute involving a third party that the distinction becomes of great significance. Enough has gone before to demonstrate that, for example, a specifically enforceable contractual licence for life and an estoppel for life can lead to similar practical results in a dispute between the original parties. But we have also suggested in earlier chapters that, in many cases, the analytical distinction between promise and reliance is artificial when applied to the facts of domestic disputes. While some cases have a more promise-based flavour (*e.g. Hardwick* v. *Johnson*[22]) other cases are more ambiguous (*e.g. Tanner* v. *Tanner*[23] and *Chandler* v. *Kerley*[24]). The very artificiality of maintaining this distinction in the two-party context may be one reason for suggesting that, when purchasers are involved, it may be unsatisfactory, if analytically sound, to retain the rigid personal—proprietary division as we have done in this chapter. This could be put differently, by suggesting that maintaining this division permits the courts to tailor the analysis of the original two-party relationship in order to fit their appreciation of the merits of the dispute as between the occupant and stranger. This is, after all, one way of looking at the decision in *Horrocks* v. *Forray*[25] where there was in a practical sense a conflict of interest between the occupant (the mistress) and a third party (the wife) of a kind where the Court may well have thought that the merits lay more significantly on the side of the wife. Whether such flexibility is desirable or not, it should at least be noted that under the guise of analytical purity, a rigid distinction between contract and estoppel permits an ad hoc and discretionary approach to domestic disputes involving purchasers and mortgagees.

Notes to pages 181–192

[1] [1965] A.C. 1175; [1965] 3 W.L.R. 1; [1965] 2 All E.R. 472.
[2] [1936] 3 All E.R. 483.
[3] See *supra*, p.101.
[4] [1980] Ch. 338; [1979] 3 W.L.R. 868; [1980] 1 All E.R. 294.
[5] Stemming largely from *Errington* v. *Errington and Woods* [1952] 1 K.B. 290.

[6] *Hardwick* v. *Johnson* [1978] 1 W.L.R. 683; [1978] 2 All E.R. 935.

[7] *Verrall* v. *Gt. Yarmouth B.C.* [1981] Q.B. 202.

[8] Opaquely in *Errington* v. *Errington* see *supra*, n.5; see also *Binions* v. *Evans infra*.

[9] [1972] Ch. 359; [1972] 2 W.L.R. 729; [1972] 2 All E.R. 70.

[10] [1965] A.C. 1175, 1251–1252 (Lord Wilberforce).

[11] [1948] 2 All E.R. 133; 92 S.J. 377.

[12] s.38(1) S.L.A. 1925.

[13] Commonly found when the landlord was the Church of England or an Oxbridge college and also where copyhold was leased.

[14] s.149(6) L.P.A. 1925.

[15] *D.H.N. Food Distributors* v. *Tower Hamlets L.B.C.* [1976] 1 W.L.R. 852 (C.A.).

[16] [1979] 1 W.L.R. 431, 439.

[17] [1952] 1 K.B. 290; [1952] 1 All E.R. 149.

[18] [1974] 3 W.L.R. 56; [1964] 2 All E.R. 977.

[19] (1973) 231 E.G. 843.

[20] *Cf. Ives* v. *High* [1967] 2 Q.B. 379 (C.A.).

[21] *Cf. Webb* v. *Pollmount* [1966] Ch. 584.

[22] [1978] 1 W.L.R. 683.

[23] [1975] 1 W.L.R. 1346; [1975] 3 All E.R. 776.

[24] [1978] 1 W.L.R. 693; [1978] 2 All E.R. 942.

[25] [1976] 1 W.L.R. 230; [1976] 1 All E.R. 737.

Chapter 8

BANKRUPTCY, DEBT AND MORTGAGE
ARREARS

When the home owner or occupants of the home are in debt, the home may often be the focus of attempts by creditors to recoup what is owed to them, since, especially when the burden of debt is heavy, the home may be the most valuable asset owned by the debtor. Secondly, the process of home purchase on mortgage means that for many people the mortgage debt itself is the main source of indebtedness. If the mortgage repayments fall into arrears, the lender may wish to take steps to recover what is owed. In this chapter, we examine the legal aspects of these questions. Questions of procedure are particularly prominent here, and are therefore given greater emphasis than elsewhere in this book.

A. BANKRUPTCY

Bankruptcy may be defined as the compulsory administration of a person's estate by the court for the benefit of his creditors generally.

When a person is insolvent(*i.e.* unable to pay his debts as and when they fall due) either he or his creditors may petition for the court to take over the administration of his estate within the terms of the Bankruptcy Act 1914 (as amended).[1] The procedure is quite complex; the following are the main stages.

(1) The Debtor or a creditor or mortgagee presents the petition to the relevant court, asking that a receiving order may be made in respect of the debtor's estate.

(2) The court grants a receiving order (in proper cases). The order vests control and possession of the debtor's

property in an officer of the court called an Official Receiver. It is an interim stage, preserving the status quo until the adjudication order.

(3) The debtor must then undergo a preliminary examination by the Official Receiver and prepare a full statement of his assets and liabilities. A copy of this statement should then be sent to each of the creditors.

(4) The Official Receiver will convene a "first meeting" of the creditors; at this stage, any proposals for re-scheduling the debts can be considered. The creditors may, alternatively, accept a reduced payment or settlement of their respective debts.

(5) On the basis of information obtained both at this meeting and from the debtor's statement, the Official Receiver may recommend that a public examination be held at a duly convened sitting of the Court, where the debtor will be on oath.

(6) The court may then make an adjudication order and it is not until this stage that a debtor becomes bankrupt. This order vests the title to the property of the debtor in either the Official Receiver or a trustee in bankruptcy (hereinafter, "the Trustee").

(7) All the bankrupt's property must then be realised. Secured creditors must then be paid in order of priority.[2] All costs incurred must be paid.[3] Then preferential debts[4] must be paid, and finally, dividends are paid to those unsecured creditors who have "proved" their debt to the satisfaction of the Trustee.[5] Certain debts must be deferred (notably, debts between husband and wife). They can only be paid after the claims of unsecured creditors are met. The debtor is entitled to any surplus remaining.

(8) The final stage is where the bankrupt applies for an order of discharge. Prior to this order, all property acquired by the bankrupt vests in the Trustee, and many disabilities are imposed upon the bankrupt. The order of discharge relieves the bankrupt from these disabilities, and allows all subsequently acquired property to vest in

him. The order frees the bankrupt from the debts existing at the date of the adjudication order, but does not relieve him from any after acquired debts.[6]

1. *The Role of the Trustee in Bankruptcy*

Section 18 of the Bankruptcy Act 1914 requires the Trustee to take control of the debtor's property as soon as possible and administer it so as to maximise the return upon realisation. By section 62(1) of the 1914 Act, the trustee must "with all convenient speed declare and distribute dividends among those creditors who have proved their debts." His primary role is to act on behalf of the unsecured creditors, who, once bankruptcy proceedings are in hand, have no recourse against the debtor except (usually futile) remedies in contract.[7] Normally, the Trustee does not act on behalf of secured creditors, but their claims in respect of secured property must be met before anything is available for unsecured creditors. However, a secured creditor may opt to surrender his security and prove to the full extent of his debt as an unsecured creditor. This would normally only occur when the value of the security is negligible or much diminished. It probably has little application if the creditor's security is a house, unless, because of the rules as to priorities discussed in the two preceding chapters, the security is rendered virtually worthless through subsequently discovered interests binding the secured creditor.[8]

2. *Bankruptcy and the Family Home*

Here, we are concerned with stages (6) and (7) of the bankruptcy procedure. First we consider the position where the legal owner of a house is made bankrupt; secondly, we examine the position where a beneficiary, licensee, etc. is declared a bankrupt.

(1) *Bankruptcy of the legal owner*

Since bankruptcy involves the realisation of the bankrupt's assets, it may affect not only the legal owner himself but also those in occupation of the home. We examine these in turn.

(a) Position of the legal owner *vis-à-vis* the Trustee in bankruptcy

The Trustee is often described as standing in the bankrupt's shoes. This is not quite accurate since not all of the bankrupt's obligations bind him. But he does take over all the rights and assets of the bankrupt.[9]

Where the home is vested in the bankrupt as sole beneficial owner, the legal title vests in the Trustee who can then sell the property, and give a good title to a purchaser, using the proceeds to discharge the bankrupt's liabilities in the order required by statute. The Trustee will need to sell with vacant possession if he is to obtain the best price for the house. Therefore, he may need to obtain a possession order from the courts if occupants refuse to quit. We examine the chances of succeeding below.

Where the property is in joint names, the bankrupt's joint tenancy vests in the Trustee. In this situation, the Trustee requires the co-operation of the other joint tenant to effect a sale. If the other legal owner refuses to join in, the Trustee must apply to the court under section 30 of the Law of Property Act 1925 for an order for sale. Similarly, where the bankrupt is holding the title subject to an implied trust, and the beneficiary refuses to quit, the Trustee must use the section 30 procedure if he wishes to sell with vacant possession.

(b) Position of the Trustee in bankruptcy *vis-à-vis* beneficiaries under a trust for sale

It is immaterial in a section 30 application by the Trustee whether the house is in joint names or not, or whether the trust is express or implied. But the question of whether a sale will be ordered must be distinguished from the question of whether, if one is, the beneficiary will be able to claim his or her share of the proceeds in priority to the creditors. This latter question requires discussion of the "trust avoidance" machinery in bankruptcy law, and is considered below.[10] Here, we consider the criteria for ordering or refusing a sale.

On an application for sale, the court has to weigh the competing claims of beneficiaries such as the bankrupt's wife to stay in the home against the interests of the creditors in being paid. Although, as we have seen earlier, the court has a wide discretion under section 30, the reported cases lean firmly in the direction of sale, the courts emphasising the Trustee's statutory duty to realise the assets of the bankrupt's estate.[11] For example, in *Re Bailey*[12] a matrimonial home was jointly owned by a husband and wife. The couple divorced and the husband went bankrupt. The wife was still living in the former matrimonial home with their sixteen year old son. The Trustee applied for a sale of the property. The wife sought a postponement of sale until the son had completed his "A" level examinations. The court refused a postponement of sale for this purpose, and indeed Sir Robert Megarry V.C. hinted that bankruptcy altered the whole nature of a section 30 application. It was no longer a family dispute but a bankruptcy case. "Bankruptcy" stated the Vice Chancellor, "has, in relation to the matrimonial home, its own claim to protection."[13]

Re Holliday[14] is a conspicious departure from this practice. Here, sale was postponed for five years. An ex-wife was still living in the former matrimonial home with three children of the marriage. The ex-husband was adjudicated bankrupt on his own petition (there was a distinct suggestion that he regarded bankruptcy as a way of avoiding provision for his ex-wife) and the Trustee sought to sell the house. The outstanding debts of the bankrupt were not vast, amounting to around £6,000. The

Court of Appeal held that it would be unfair to the wife to grant a sale in the circumstances. Subsequently in *Re Lowrie*[15] a Divisional Court of the Chancery Division has treated *Re Holliday* as exceptional, since the petition for bankruptcy was a tactical move by the husband, where no creditors were pressing and where the husband could, without difficulty, meet his debts out of his income.

To conclude, a sale will normally be ordered at the request of the Trustee, although a short postponement of up to a year may be permitted to avoid hardship (for example, changes of school in the midst of important exams.)[16] Only in exceptional circumstances will a postponement for a more substantial period be granted.

(c) Position of the Trustee in respect of contractual licensees

Where the occupant of a house is a tenant of the bankrupt, the Trustee takes subject to the term held by the tenant and the attendant rights and duties as contained in or implied into the lease, in exactly the same position as the bankrupt prior to the vesting of his estate in the Trustee.[17] Following the development of statutory control of residential tenancies, the courts have held that the rights of statutory tenants constitute "equities" which bind the Trustee, who, for these purposes, stands in the shoes of the bankrupt.[18] Thus the Trustee must sell subject to the rights of a sitting tenant, unless he can succeed in persuading the tenant to quit so that he can sell with vacant possession.

In practical terms, the Trustee may be similarly placed if the occupant of the home (whether exclusive of or jointly with the bankrupt) is there by virtue of a contractual licence. In fulfilment of his duty to realise the assets of the bankrupt, the Trustee will seek to sell the house, either with vacant possession, or subject to the subsisting occupancy. In most cases, no doubt, he will seek to sell with vacant possession so as to realise the best price; he may therefore seek to terminate the licence to occupy by serving a notice to quit upon the licensee. If the licensee refuses to go, the Trustee will have to apply to the court for an order for possession. The difficult question is whether such an order will be made.

The starting point must be that all the contractual obligations of the bankrupt pass to the Trustee, save for limited exceptions, notably where the performance of the contract requires the exercise of personal skill on the part of the bankrupt,[19] an exception which has little bearing on the present question. Bankruptcy may mean that fewer remedies are available to the other party to the contract. Thus specific performance of a contract to purchase land will not be granted against an unwilling Trustee.[20] But if the licensee is in occupation, the question is not one of the licensee seeking specific performance of the contract from the courts, but of the Trustee seeking the assistance of the court to enable him to break the contract which binds him. In principle, therefore, it would seem that such applications for possession by the Trustee should fail.

The position is complicated somewhat by the rise and fall of the "deserted wife's equity." In *Bendall* v. *McWhirter*[21] the Court of Appeal held that the right to occupy the matrimonial home was an equity which arose in favour of a deserted wife, upon desertion by the husband, which bound the Trustee and purchasers from the husband. The position of most mortgagees was subsequently distinguished by a differently constituted Court on the ground that such rights arose prior to the wife's equity (*i.e.* prior to desertion).[22] *Bendall* was subsequently overruled by the House of Lords in *NPB* v. *Ainsworth*.[23] That latter case however concerned the question of whether the equity bound purchasers and mortgagees from the husband irrespective of whether their rights arose before or after the desertion. The House held that the equity was personal to the husband and wife and did not bind purchasers. The question is whether this applies in the case of contractual licences. It seems from *Ainsworth* that the wife's equity would not bind a Trustee on the grounds that the duty is personal to the husband and therefore is not one of the liabilities which passes to the Trustee: "*Bendall* v. *McWhirter* was itself wrongly decided, for a trustee in bankruptcy succeeds only to the property of the bankrupt in its then plight and condition and is not concerned with personal rights that do not affect that property."[24] In this respect, a contractual licence seems to be different in kind from such a personal equity.[25] We have argued above[26] that while the right to occupy under such licences would seem to be personal to the licensee (and thus not assignable or transmissible), the contractual duty to permit occupation is not personal; it is capable of binding executors and successors in title on death, and, by analogy, capable of binding the Trustee in bankruptcy.

On this view of the question, the Trustee is affected by the licence as a matter of contract, not property. He is bound not because the licence is an encumbrance on the property (a view which would be inconsistent with the *obiter dicta* in *Ainsworth*[27]) but because he takes on the contractual liabilities of the bankrupt.[28]

Three related paradoxes seem to flow from suggesting that the Trustee may be refused a possession order. First, as we have said, he will not be able to sell with vacant possession but only with the licensee in occupation. Inevitably, therefore, he will have to sell at a lower price than if the premises were vacant. In practical terms therefore, the licence operates as an encumbrance, even though we have taken care to avoid such an analysis above. Secondly, what, is the position of the purchaser from the Trustee after such a sale? On the one hand, contractual licenses do not bind purchasers. On this analysis, the purchaser should be able to obtain possession from the licensee and thus obtain vacant possession which the Trustee himself could not deliver. On the other hand, the purchaser will usually have paid a lower price in full knowledge of the licensee's existence (though he may not have stipulated with the Trustee to permit continued occupation after the sale). If the purchaser seeks possession, the licensee might resist the claim by arguing that the purchaser would be unjustly "enriched" if he obtained possession, seeking to bring himself within *Binions* v. *Evans*.[29]

Thirdly, if the Trustee is denied possession, a licensee wishing to remain in the home would seem to be better placed than a beneficiary behind a trust. In commonsense terms, this would seem perverse. It could be argued that the difference is that a beneficiary will obtain his or her share of the proceeds whereas a licensee who is evicted will at most be an unsecured creditor in respect of whatever damages are awarded for loss of occupation. But, as we indicate below, a beneficiary's share of the proceeds may often be assailable if it takes effect under a voluntary settlement.[30] If a beneficiary is, save in exceptional circumstances, forced to leave the home it seems difficult to justify according a greater privilege to a licensee.

These factors may justify the granting of possession orders to Trustees. If this is done, the courts may either imply a term into the licence such that it is determinable on the bankruptcy of the licensor, or award damages for loss of occupation, leaving the licensee to prove his debt as an unsecured creditor.

(d) Estoppel or licences coupled with an "equity"

Here, it seems more likely that the Trustee will fail to obtain possession. We have seen that an estoppel interest can bind purchasers and personal representatives; it seems to follow that the Trustee too is bound. We have employed above a distinction between an equity protecting lifetime occupation, and an equity operating as a lien protecting occupation until repayment.[31] In each case, it would seem, the equity will bind the Trustee. The closest authority is *Re Sharpe,*[32] which may be regarded as involving an equitable lien.[33]

S. had acquired the lease of a shop and maisonette, much of the purchase price being contributed by S.'s elderly aunt, J. J. had sold her own home in order to contribute to S.'s purchase, and she did so on the understanding that she would move in with S. and his wife and they would look after her for the rest of her days. S. eventually became bankrupt. S.'s trustee in bankruptcy contracted to sell the premises to P. with vacant possession, and then sought a possession order against J. in order to perform his contract with P. In some respects, the relationship between S. and J. resembled a loan; indeed, J. had obtained from S. a promissory note for £15,700 after S. had been made bankrupt. Browne-Wilkinson J. however held that J. had something more than a mere contractual right to be repaid—she had a right to stay on the premises until the money she had provided for acquisition had been repaid to her[34]:

" . . . (I)t is now established that, if the parties have proceeded on a common assumption that the plaintiff is to enjoy a right to reside in a particular property and in reliance on that assumption the plaintiff has expended money or otherwise acted to his detriment the defendant will not be allowed to go back on that common assumption and the court will imply an irrevocable licence on trust which will give effect to that common assumption."

J.'s rights apparently amounted to a "contractual or equitable licence" which conferred "some interest in the property under a constructive trust"[35] which bound the Trustee in bankruptcy and prevented him from obtaining possession. In this situation, the Trustee then faces identical obstacles to those which confront personal representatives in the administration of an insolvent estate.[36]

(e) Conclusion

The position on bankruptcy with regard to contractual licences and estoppel is far from clear. It may be that the "problem" does not arise frequently in practice. The occcupant's claim for a licence or estoppel will often arise for the first time when the Trustee seeks possession, and it may be that on such occasions the courts adopt a more robust attitude towards inferring such occupation rights. It is, however, to be noted that all these possessory claims may be defeated by a mortgagee with a power of sale where the security takes priority over the claims of the occupant such that the mortgagee can obtain possession and sell with vacant possession.[37] This would leave the surplus available to the Trustee for distribution.

(2) *Bankruptcy of a beneficiary under a trust for sale, or a licensee, or an occupant protected by estoppel*

Where the legal owner remains solvent but another party entitled in some way to the family home goes bankrupt, what is the position?

(a) Bankruptcy of a beneficiary

The situation here is exactly the same as where the legal owner goes bankrupt. The Trustee in bankruptcy is under a statutory duty to realise the assets of the bankrupt and therefore he will seek to realise the family home in which the beneficiary has a share. This will involve a section 30 application and the same principles discussed earlier will apply.

(b) Bankruptcy of a contractual licensee

If the contract merely confers a right of occupancy upon the licensee, which is not assignable or transmissible, it would seem that the licence will not pass to the Trustee. If a transmissible right is contemplated by the parties, this could constitute a valuable asset in the hands of the Trustee which (in principle at least) could be sold.

(c) Bankruptcy of an occupant protected by estoppel

The position here is also rather unclear. Where the equity constitutes a right to remain in the home (albeit *potentially* binding third parties) it would seem that it cannot constitute a valuable asset capable of passing to the Trustee. Where, however, the equity results in a tangible ownership right (as in some of the old cases[38] and in *Pascoe* v. *Turner*[39]), this right would seem to be something which the Trustee can claim and sell.

When the estoppel takes the form of an equitable lien, the position is once again difficult. If the bankrupt is still in occupation, the Trustee may be unable to compel repayment of the debt by the owner. Equally, it is unclear whether the Trustee can compel the bankrupt to give up occupation so as to render the debt repayable. Thirdly, it is unclear whether the right takes effect as an ordinary debt or a charge, and relatedly, which period of limitation, if any, applies to the debt, and when time begins to run.[40]

(3) *Avoidance*

Two statutory provisions must now be outlined which confer powers upon the court to set aside transfers of property made by the bankrupt before the bankruptcy proceedings so that the property can be reached by the Trustee or creditors.

(a) *Section 42 of the Bankruptcy Act 1914*

Section 42 provides that, in specified circumstances, voluntary settlements made by the bankrupt may be avoided by the Trustee. "Settlement" has a wide meaning, including any conveyance or transfer of property, and includes implied trusts.[41] A settlement or transfer of property effected under the Matrimonial Causes Act is also a settlement within section 42.[42] Voidable settlements are those made by the bankrupt within two years before the bankruptcy if the settlor was then solvent, or within ten years if he was insolvent. This jurisdiction is excluded if the settlement was made (i) in consideration of marriage or (ii) in favour of a purchaser in good faith and for valuable consideration.

(i) In consideration of marriage

To come within this exception, the settlement must (a) be made on the occasion of the marriage; (b) be conditioned only to take effect on the marriage taking place; and (c) be made by a person for the purposes of or with a view to encouraging or facilitating the marriage.[43] In the modern context, a gift of a house by a parent to a child on his or her marriage comes most clearly within this definition. Another example would be when the home was taken in the joint names of husband and wife on marriage, where one party was solely responsible for the deposit and mortgage repayments.

(ii) Purchaser in good faith for valuable consideration

This has been interpreted as operating in favour of a purchaser who is a "buyer in the commercial sense."[44] Thus express or implied trusts of the home will not be voidable to the extent that each beneficiary has made financial contributions to the purchase of the home. For example, in *Re Densham*,[45] it was held that a trust based on the actual common intention of the parties arose to the effect that the husband and wife were joint owners in equity. On the bankruptcy of the husband, however, this was treated as a voluntary settlement by him within section 42, except to the extent that the wife could show actual acquisition-related payments moving from her, so that she could only claim a share, as against the Trustee in bankruptcy, which reflected her financial contribution.

(b) Section 172 of the Law of Property Act 1925

This provides that any conveyance made "with intent to defraud creditors" can be set aside "at the instance of any person thereby prejudiced." Intent can be presumed from the circumstances. Unlike section 42, no time limits restrict the operation of this section. Section 172 will not apply in respect of a conveyance for valuable consideration made in good faith to a person without notice, at the time of the conveyance, of the intent to defraud.

(4) *Reform*

The Cork Report[46] has recommended certain changes in the treatment of insolvency and the family home.[47] These proposals would require the Trustee to apply to the Insolvency Court in most cases[48] where there are dependent children or parents living in the home, and the Court is to be given a broad discretion as to whether a sale should be ordered. In exercising its discretion the Court is to "give primary consideration to the welfare of dependent children, to the circumstances of the wife, and to the situation of dependent parents who are resident in the family dwelling."[49] "In considering the welfare of dependent children the Court will also have regard to their ages and needs, the desirability of avoiding unnecessary emotional damage or interruption of their schooling, and to the interests of the community in keeping the family together in suitable accommodation."[50]

B. Debt: Charging Orders and Appointment of Receivers

Initiating bankruptcy proceedings is a drastic and relatively complex step for a creditor to take. In many cases, a creditor may prefer to pursue one of the courses of action outlined in this section. First, he may seek to have the debt secured on property belonging to the debtor, and, for present purposes, on the home in particular. This can be sought through the procedure for obtaining "charging orders." Alternatively, a creditor may apply for appointment of a receiver and recoup his money in that way.

1. *Charging Orders*

Where a final judgment or order has been obtained requiring the payment of a definite sum of money to a creditor, the creditor can proceed to apply to the Court for a charging order to be imposed on the property of the debtor. The scope of this procedure was limited prior to 1979 by the decision of *Irani Finance* v. *Singh*[51] but has been broadened by the Charging Orders Act 1979.

(1) *The nature of a charging order*

A charging order is not a direct mode of enforcement of the debt. If obtained, the creditor does not immediately recover the money owed. Rather, a charging order first gives the creditor a secured charge over the property of the debtor. Secondly, by becoming a secured creditor, the creditor obtains additional remedies which he can use in order to recover the debt—in particular, the ability to apply for a sale of the property and satisfaction of the debt from the proceeds.

(2) *Property on which a charging order can be imposed*

Section 2 of the 1979 Act specifies which property of the debtor can be made the subject-matter of a charging order. For present purposes, a beneficial interest behind a trust can be charged under section 2(1)(*a*)(ii) of the Act and the legal estate can be charged where there is a sole beneficial owner (section 2(1)(*b*)(ii)) or where the legal owners jointly share the same debt in respect of the same creditor (section 2(1)(*b*)(iii)).[52] A charging order cannot be obtained upon a jointly held legal estate where only one legal owner is endebted to the creditor or where, even if both legal joint tenants owe debts to the creditor, the debts arose separately. In this situation, the creditor must seek his charging order against the several beneficial interests of the debtors.

Thus, in the context of the family home, charging orders may be obtained against beneficial owners, and presumably those with estoppel interests which are satisfied by the imposition of a constructive trust. They cannot be imposed upon contractual licences or other forms of estoppel interests, which, whatever their nature, are not within the definition of property in section 2 of the Act.

(3) *The Procedure*

There is a two stage procedure for obtaining charging orders. First, application is made for a charging order *nisi* (usually before a Master or Registrar). This usually takes place *ex parte*, which means that the debtor only finds out after the order has been granted. An order *nisi* may be coupled with a temporary injunction prohibiting the debtor from disposing of the property charged while the order remains in effect.

One important underlying consideration is whether making a charging order would unduly prejudice other creditors. If the debtor is almost insolvent, the order will usually be refused. In addition, after making the order *nisi*, occupants of the home may be permitted to appear on the grounds that an order absolute may prejudice their rights. At a later stage, the order may be made absolute by the Court. Before this is done, the debtor must make a full disclosure of the relevant circumstances, and directions will be given requiring copies of the order *nisi* and the creditor's affidavit in support to be served on any interested person. This primarily means other creditors, but the procedure can be used to notify spouses or, presumably cohabitees.[53] Such persons are also entitled to appear subsequently before the Master or Judge and thus be given an opportunity to state their case before the order is made absolute.

The court has a wide discretion in determining whether to make the order absolute or discharge it. No order absolute will be made if it would be inequitable to do so.[54] If the debt is small in relation to the value of the property, the order may be refused,[55] similarly if other unsecured creditors would be prejudiced.[56]

(4) *Effect of a charging order*

An order absolute operates as an equitable charge under hand.[57] This means that the creditor can apply to the court for an order for sale of the property charged[58] so that he can recoup the debt out of the net proceeds of sale (after any prior charges have been satisfied). The practical effect of such an order will vary depending upon whether the charge is imposed upon the legal estate or the beneficial interest only.

(a) Charge on the legal estate

In unregistered conveyancing, such a charge is registrable as an order affecting land under section 6 of the Land Charges Act 1972, or by means of a notice under section 49 of the Land Registration Act 1925 as amended by section 3(3) of the 1979 Act. The charge will be subject to prior charges affecting the land, but registration means that further dealings with the land will take place subject to the claims of the creditor.

(b) Charge on the beneficial interest

This provides a less satisfactory security. Following the making of such an order, the creditor should give notice of the charge to the trustee(s). He does not have a registrable interest, so that his security depends upon the trustee(s) performing the obligation to discharge the debt on a sale of the property. If one of the trustees is also the judgment debtor, there is obviously a danger that, on a sale, he might abscond with the proceeds.

(c) Sale

In each of the above cases, the creditor can, subsequent to the order absolute, apply to the court for a sale of the property charged.[58] While this is practicable where the charge is on the legal estate, it will often be pointless to seek a sale of the beneficial interest alone (unless it is to another equitable co-owner). In this latter case, a creditor whose charge is secured on the beneficial interest alone may apply to the Court under section 30 of the Law of Property Act 1925 as a "person interested" for a sale of the property itself. It is, however, probable that it will be more difficult for a creditor to succeed here than in the case of a Trustee in bankruptcy outlined above.

2. *Equitable Execution by Appointment of Receiver*

An alternative method of enforcing judgment debts (which, after *Irani Finance* v. *Singh*,[59] was often necessary before the 1979 Act when the debtor's main asset was the home) is for the creditor to apply to the Court to have a receiver appointed over the interest of the debtor in the home. Such an appointment can be coupled with an injunction restraining the debtor from dealing with the property. Appointment of a receiver does not create a charge upon the property, but prevents the debtor from receiving the income from the property. " . . . It confers on the judgment creditor purely personal rights and gives him no right over rents and profits themselves in rem."[60]

Appointment of a receiver serves a purpose where the property in question yields an income. The receiver will take that income due to the debtor with a view to reducing or discharging the debt. But unless there are occupants paying rent to the debtor, this function of receivership will be redundant. Alternatively, the receiver may seek an order for sale, which, if there is co-ownership of the home, must be under section 30 of the Law of Property Act 1925. It used to be thought that a receiver had no *locus standi* to make such an application since he was not a 'person interested' within that section.[61] This has now been doubted, and a receiver who applies in the due form[62] will be able to seek an order for sale. The criteria to be applied by the court will presumably be similar to those employed when a sale of the home is sought under section 30 pursuant to a charging order on a beneficial interest.

3. *Mortgage Arrears*

Where a borrower defaults on his mortgage repayments, the mortgagee will usually want to realise his security by recouping the outstanding capital advanced and any unpaid interest on the loan. To achieve this result, where the borrower's only substantial asset is the home, the mortgagee will normally wish to sell the property with vacant possession.

(1) *The mortgagee's power of sale*

When the mortgage is made by deed the mortgagee acquires a power of sale over the mortgaged property which arises when the mortgage money becomes due (s. 101(1)(i) L.P.A. 1925). Since it is common practice for the legal redemption period to be short, the power of sale will have arisen in most home purchase mortgages.

By section 103 of the Law of Property Act, the mortgagee's power of sale can only be exercised if one of three pre-conditions applies. First, where, following service of a notice requiring repayment, default has subsequently been made for at least three months; secondly, where mortgage interest payments are at least two months overdue; thirdly, where breach of a term in the mortgage has occurred other than breach of a covenant for payment of capital or interest.

(2) *The mortgagee's right to possession*

Apart from these restrictions upon the exercise of the power of sale, the mortgagee may need to evict the borrower and his family from the home if he is to sell with vacant possession. A legal mortgagee has the right to possession of the mortgaged property even if there has been no default on the part of the mortgagor, unless the mortgage provides otherwise. In the case of a home purchase mortgage, it is normal practice for the building society or other lender to grant to the borrower the right to possession of the mortgaged property.

Certain restrictions have been placed on the mortgagee's ability to obtain possession of the home. Mortgagees are subject to the general statutory requirement that a possession order must be obtained from a court before possession can be obtained of a dwelling house.[63] Where such an application is made, the court, originally under an inherent jurisdiction of the Chancery Division and now by statute, can adjourn the proceedings or postpone the giving of possession in certain circumstances. By section 36(1) of the Administration of Justice Act 1970, the court has a discretion exercisable in any claim for possession of residential property where, "it appears to the court that in the event of its exercising the power the mortgagor[64] is likely to be able within a reasonable period to pay any sums due under the mortgage or to remedy a default consisting of a breach of any obligation arising under or by virtue of the mortgage."

It soon became clear that there was a serious defect in the terms of section 36, since in most instalment mortgages, the whole of the capital sum becomes due when there is just one instalment in arrear. The court could only exercise its discretion under section 36 where it was likely that the mortgagor could pay "any sums due under the mortgage." Only in rare cases would a mortgagor be able to pay back all the capital sums due under the mortgage. The 1970 Act was therefore amended by section 8(1) of the Administration of Justice Act 1973, which provides that "sums due" means instalments in arrears.[65]

How likely the possibility of remedying a default or paying back the arrears has to be before the discretion will be exercised is a difficult question. It seems that the discretion cannot be exercised if the mortgagor cannot provide *any* evidence of ability to pay, as was the case in *Boland*.[66] If, for example, the arrears have arisen because of the unemployment of the mortgagor, who has subsequently found work, this may constitute sufficient evidence for the court to exercise its discretion in favour of the mortgagor. The court cannot however give the mortgagor unlimited time to pay, although it seems that fairly long periods (12–18 months) may be granted in particular circumstances.

A further point which arises under these Acts is whether the discretion is applicable where there is no default as such under the terms of the mortgage. In *Western Bank* v. *Schindler*,[67] the mortgagor borrowed £32,000 from the plaintiff mortgagee. It was an endowment-type mortgage and under its terms no capital or interest was payable for 10 years. The mortgagor was supposed to keep up the instalments on a large insurance policy which was the additional security required by the Bank. The mortgagor failed to keep up the insurance policy and the Bank sought possession. There was no actual default on the terms of the mortgage which apparently did not refer to the insurance policy. The Court of Appeal upheld the mortgagee's claim to possession but it is unclear whether this was because a mortgagee always has a right of possession and no statutory discretion applied or whether the statutory discretion had been considered but there was no reasonable likelihood of the mortgagor being able to remedy the default. On a strict reading of section 36 it would appear that the court only has a discretion to postpone possession if there has been some default. This would however lead to the logical conclusion that a mortgagor who has defaulted is actually in a better position than one who has not; in the former case the court has a discretion whether or not to grant an immediate order and in the latter it has no discretion at all.

(3) *Spouses and mortgage arrears*

One defect of the previous law relating to such enforcement proceedings has now been remedied by the Matrimonial Homes and Property Act 1981. Although, since 1967, a spouse has had the right, under section 1(5) of the Matrimonial Homes Act, to pay off the mortgage where the other spouse was in arrears, and the mortgagee is obliged to accept these payments, it was often the case that he or she did not know that instalments were in arrears and that possession proceedings were being brought. Under the 1981 Act a spouse who has registered a class F land charge (or its equivalent in registered land) must be notified by a mortgagee of his intention to seek possession. The spouse can then exercise his or her right to be joined in the proceedings. The section 36 discretion may be exercised in favour of the spouse if it is likely that he or she may be able to pay off the arrears.

Although this is an improvement in the previous law, it still leaves large gaps in the protection of occupation. The 1981 Act only applies to spouses who have registered their right of occupation. Other occupants have no similar right to apply to make good the arrears.

(4) *Other occupants*

In order to obtain vacant possession, the mortgagee may need to proceed additionally against other occupants.[68] In the two preceding chapters, we discussed the substantive law concerning priorities as between occupants and mortgagees. We now consider how this translates into practice when a mortgagee is seeking to sell with vacant possession.

(a) Beneficiaries behind a trust

Where the mortgagee "takes subject to" the interest of a beneficiary, it may be difficult to obtain an order for possession. Since *Bull* v. *Bull*[69] the courts have held that, in many circumstances,[70] equitable co-owners have the right to occupy the trust property. Therefore, a mortgagee who takes subject to the interest presumably takes subject to the right of occupation which has become an incident of the interest. In this event, the mortgagee will have to apply to the court under section 30 of the Law of Property Act 1925 as a "person interested" in the trust property for an order for sale. A court order under this section has the effect of overriding the occupation rights of beneficiaries. These are dicta in *Boland* which suggest that such an order may be refused,[71] in which case the mortgagee's only alternative is to initiate bankruptcy proceedings, where, as we have seen, a more robust approach to sale is adopted. In any event, a mortgagee might prefer to initiate a bankruptcy since this might make it possible to avoid the share of the beneficiary under the section 42 jurisdiction.

Equitable rights operate *in personam*. Therefore, it follows that where the mortgagee takes free from the beneficial interest, the right of occupation cannot be asserted by the beneficiary against the mortgagee. Therefore, such a mortgagee should succeed in possession proceedings.

(b) Contractual licensees

Since the rights of such licensees to remain in the home rest in contract, they will not, in principle, affect mortgagees, who will be able to evict them. It should be noted, however, that recently the Court of Appeal seems to have assumed that a contractual licensee could resist a claim for possession by a mortgagee who had constructive notice of the licensee's rights.[72] The point of principle does not, however, seem to have been addressed.

(c) Estoppel interests

Where these bind the mortgagee, it would seem that possession will be refused, since, as we have seen, the content of the equity, in most cases, is protected occupation. In this situation, the mortgagee might be forced to sell at an undervalue subject to the occupancy. Where estoppel protects occupation pending repayment, the mortgagee might pay the debt himself and obtain possession, recouping the payment from the proceeds of sale.

Notes to pages 194–217

[1] The conditions on which a creditor may petition are set out in s.4 Bankruptcy Act 1914.

[2] See Megarry and Wade, pp. 958–985.

[3] s.33(3) Bankruptcy Act 1914.

[4] s.33(1)(*a*) and (*b*) as amended, especially by ss.121–127 Employment Protection (Consolidation) Act 1978. Put generally, this category includes rates, taxes, and, subject to statutory limits, wages due to employees. See further Williams and Muir Hunter, *Bankruptcy* (18th ed., 1979), pp. 205 *et seq.*

[5] For the rules as to proof, see Sched. II Bankruptcy Act, Williams and Muir Hunter, *op cit.* pp.523 *et. seq.*

[6] For example, an undischarged bankrupt cannot be a company director (s.187 Companies Act 1948). Some disqualifications normally extend beyond the discharge—thus a bankrupt is barred from public office for five years following the discharge (s.26(4) Bankruptcy Act 1914). See further Williams and Muir Hunter, *op. cit.* p.133.

[7] Since even if a creditor obtains judgment for his debt, he will still be unsecured.

[8] See *supra*, Chap. 6.

[9] ss. 18(1) and 38 Bankruptcy Act 1914; see the discussion in *Bendall* v. *McWhirter* [1952] 2 Q.B. 466, 486–487.

[10] See *infra*, pp. 205–207.

[11] *Re Solomon* [1967] Ch. 573; *Re Turner* [1974] 1 W.L.R. 1556; *Re Bailey* [1977] 1 W.L.R. 278; *Re McCarthy* [1975] 1 W.L.R. 807; *Re Densham* [1975] 1 W.L.R. 1519.

[12] *Re Bailey* [1977] 1 W.L.R. 278.

[13] *Ibid.* at p. 282.

[14] *Holliday* [1980] 3 All E.R. 385.

[15] *Lowrie* [1981] 3 All E.R. 353.

[16] *Ibid.* at p. 356, *per* Walton J.

[17] Except that the Trustee may be able to disclaim an onerous reversion under s.54 Bankruptcy Act 1914.

[18] *Bradley-Hole* v. *Cusen* [1953] 1 All E.R. 87; *cf.* Williams and Muir Hunter, *op. cit.* p.199.

[19] See Williams and Muir Hunter, *op. cit.* p.289 and the cases cited therein.

[20] *Holloway* v. *York* (1877) 25 W.R. 627; *cf. Re Gough* (1927) 96 L.J. Ch. 239; *Jenning's Trustee* v. *King* [1952] Ch. 899.

[21] *Bendall* v. *McWhirter* [1952] 2 Q.B. 466; [1952] 1 All E.R. 1307.

[22] *Lloyd's Bank* v. *O's Trustee* [1953] 1 W.L.R. 1460: [1953] 2 All E.R. 1443.

[23] *National Provincial Bank* v. *Ainsworth* [1965] A.C. 1175.

[24] *Ibid.* at p.1240 *per* Lord Upjohn.

[25] *Ibid.* at pp. 1239–1240 *per* Lord Upjohn.

[26] *Supra*, Chap. 5, pp.140–142.

[27] See especially n.25 and *National Provincial Bank* v. *Ainsworth supra*, at p.1256 *per* Lord Wilberforce.

[28] For this reason, another argument which might be canvassed, at least in registered land, would seem to be irrelevant. Section 43 of the Land Registration Act 1925 provides, *inter alia*, that the trustee " . . . shall in all respects and in particular as respects any registered dealings with (the) land . . . be in the same position as if he had taken such land . . . under a transfer for valuable consideration." Whatever the effect of this section (and it is rather obscure) it does not seem to bear on the present question since it is concerned with the effect of encumbrances on the land and not the contractual engagements of the bankrupt.

[29] *Binions* v. *Evans* [1972] Ch. 359; [1972] 2 W.L.R. 729; [1972] 2 All E.R. 70; see *supra*, pp.183–186.

[30] See pp.205–207.

[31] See *supra*, Chap. 4, pp.115 *et seq.*

[32] *Re Sharpe* [1980] 1 W.L.R. 219; [1980] 1 All E.R. 198.

[33] *Supra*, p.121.

[34] *Re Sharpe* [1980] 1 W.L.R. 219, 223.

[35] *Ibid.* at p.225.

[36] See *supra*, Chap. 5, pp.142–145.

[37] See Chaps. 6 and 7.

[38] *Dillwyn* v. *Llewellyn* (1862) 4 De G.F. & J. 517; 31 L.J. Ch. 658; *Ramsden* v. *Dyson* (1866) L.R. 1 H.L. 129; 14 W.R. 926.

[39] *Pascoe* v. *Turner* [1979] 1 W.L.R. 431; [1979] 2 All E.R. 945.

[40] See *supra*, p.128 n.13.

[41] *Re Densham* [1975] 1 W.L.R. 1319; [1975] 3 All E.R. 726.

[42] s.39 Matrimonial Causes Act 1973.

[43] Adopted by Goff J. in *Re Densham, supra*, n.41 from *IRC* v. *Rennell* [1964] A.C. 173, 202, 208.

[44] *Re Windle* [1975] 1 W.L.R. 1628; [1975] 3 All E.R. 987.

[45] *Densham* [1975] 1 W.L.R. 1519; [1975] 3 All E.R. 726.

[46] *Insolvency Law and Practice* CMND. 8558 (1982).

[47] Which is defined in paras. 1124–1125. Unmarried couples are included within the definition.

[48] For the exceptions, see para. 1127.

[49] Para. 1129.

[50] Para. 1130.

[51] *Irani Finance* v. *Singh* [1971] Ch. 59; [1970] 3 All E.R. 199.

[52] Confirming, in effect, *National Westminster Bank.* v. *Allen* [1971] 2 Q.B. 718; [1971] 3 W.L.R. 495.

[53] *Supreme Court Practice 1982*, para. 50/1–9/15.

[54] *Burston Finance Ltd.* v. *Godfrey* [1976] 1 W.L.R. 719. *Cf. Roberts Petroleum Ltd.* v. *Bernard Kenny Ltd, The Times*, February 15, 1983 (H.L.)

[55] *Robinson* v. *Bailey* [1942] Ch. 268, 271.

[56] *Rainbow* v. *Moorgate Properties Ltd.* [1975] 1 W.L.R. 788.

[57] s.3(4) Charging Orders Act 1979.

[58] *Tennant* v. *Trenchard* L.R. 4 Ch. App. 537.

[59] [1971] Ch. 59; [1970] 3 All E.R. 199.

[60] *Stephens* v. *Hutchinson* [1953] 1 All E.R. 699, 701.

[61] *Ibid.*

[62] *Levermore* v. *Levermore* [1979] 1 W.L.R. 1277; [1980] 1 All E.R. 1.

[63] Under RSC, Ord. 88.

[64] Including those deriving title under him: s.39(1) Administration of Justice Act 1970

[65] For a general discussion, see *Cetrax Trustees* v. *Ross* [1979] 2 All E.R. 952.

[66] [1980] 3 W.L.R. 138; [1980] 2 All E.R. 408.

[67] [1977] Ch. 1; (1976) 32 P. & C.R. 352.

[68] For the notification of such occupants and guidelines as to who should be joined as defendants, see *Supreme Court Practice 1982*, para. 88/2–8/3.

[69] [1955] 1 Q.B. 234; [1955] 2 W.L.R. 78.

[70] See *supra*, pp. 93–96.

[71] [1979] 2 W.L.R. 550, 554, 555, 556, 561 *per* Lord Denning M.R.

[72] *Midland Bank* v. *Farmpride Hatcheries* (1981) 260 E.G. 493.

INDEX

Advancement. *See* Presumption of Advancement.

Annuities, 12, 34

Bankrupt,
discharge of, 196

Bankruptcy, 28, 58, 67, 144, 216
intention to defraud creditors and, 207
legal owner, of,
trustee in bankruptcy and, 197
procedure, 194, 195, 196
purchasers for valuable consideration and, 206, 207
reform of, 207
voidable transactions, 51, 163, 198, 202, 205, 206, 207

Beneficial Interests,
lis pendens registration, 164
not registered, 159–61, 163
occupation rights and, 46, 87
overriding interests, as, 157, 159, 161, 162, 175, 177
protection by registration, 157, 158, 164

Building Lease, 2, 4, 112, 113

Building Societies, 1, 6, 48, 49, 51
See also Mortgages *and* Mortgagees.
charges of,
registration of, 162, 163
credit controls, exemptions from, 10
encouragement of owner-occupation, 4, 5, 6, 11
failures of, 5
government intervention and, 4, 5, 9, 10

Building Societies—*cont.*
growth and consolidation of, 4, 6, 19
history of, 4
interest rates, fluctuations in, and, 7, 8, 10, 55
lending policy, 7, 10
position in finance market, 6, 7, 10
tax advantages of, 10

Building Societies Association–Government Joint Advisory Committee, 10, 11

Capital Gains Tax,
owner-occupier's exemptions from, 9

Capital Transfer Tax, 129, 135

Charging Orders, 208, 209
beneficial interest, on, effect of, 210, 211
legal estate, on, effect of, 210
procedure, 209, 210
property, on which, can be made, 208, 209
sale, 211

Children,
custody on divorce, 22
domestic violence, protection from, 86
family home and, 22, 85, 86
husband's right of guardianship over, 81
juvenile justice, 22
presumption of advancement and, 33, 34
revocability of licences and, 103

Children—*cont.*
  state intervention and
    protection of, 21, 22
  trusts for sale and interests of,
    65, 68
  welfare of, 22
  bankruptcy, and, 207
Community of Property. *See*
  Co-ownership.
Constructive Trust, 41, 42, 120,
  183, 184, 186
  common intention and, 46
  "contemplation of marriage",
    and, 45, 46, 59
  detrimental reliance, 42, 45, 46
  equity of redemption, of, 58,
    59
  "joint ventures," 45
  remedy, as a, 46
  unconscionability, 44, 45, 46
  valuation of shares under, 59
Contract,
  breach of, 182
  disposition of interest in land,
    for, 141, 189
  registration of, 189–91
  estoppel and, 102, 141
  implied, 104
  intention to create legal
    relations,
    family relationships, 102, 106
  mistake, 113
  specific performance, 100, 189,
    191
Contractual Licence. *See*
  Contract, Licence.
Conversion, 91, 92, 164, 174
Co-ownership,
  matrimonial home,
    Law Commission
      recommendations, 26,
      47, 84–5
Copyhold,
  presumption of advancement
    and, 31, 32
Cork Report, 207

Covenants,
  to settle after acquired
    property, 51n.
Creditors, 28
  See also Bankruptcy,
    Mortgagees.
  family home and, 23
  judgment, 211
  preferential, 144, 195
  secured, 144, 195, 196, 202, 208

Debts,
  See also Bankruptcy, Charging
    Orders.
  deferred, 144
  intestate succession, 130, 131
  testate succession, 130, 131
Declaration of Trust. *See* Express
  Trust—declaration of trust.
Deserted Wife's Equity, 81, 82,
  200, 201
Divorce,
  custody of children on. *See*
    Children—custody on
    divorce.
  grounds for, controversy
    concerning, 20, 22
  increase in, 20, 21, 34
  jurisdiction over domestic
    violence on, 86
  maintenance, 20, 21, 26
    clean break, 20n.
    remaining in home and, 85
  property adjustment on, 20, 35,
    54, 61
    co-ownership orders, 27
    deferred charges, 27
    discretion in, 26, 29, 85
    home as only asset, 21
    owner-occupation and, 21
    postponement of sale, 27, 65
    practice of the Courts in, 27
      property law questions, 27,
      28
    protection of occupation in,
      85, 86

Divorce—*cont.*
  property adjustment on—*cont.*
    settlement of matrimonial
      assets, 27
    statutory co-ownership and,
      47
Domestic Violence,
  exclusion injunctions, 86

Easements, 98, 99, 100
Endowment Mortgages 8, 9, 55,
  214
  tax and, 9
  valuation of trust shares and, 57
Entails, 16, 17
Equitable Accounting, 68–71
Equitable "lien" 144, 202, 203
  See also Estoppel.
  bankruptcy of person holding,
    205
Equity of Redemption, 50, 51, 58,
  162, 212
  constructive trust of, 58
  declaration of trust of, 51, 52
Equity to a Settlement,
  wife's, 33n.
Estate Duty, 4
Estoppel, 40, 43, 80, 104, 139,
  145, 178
  bankruptcy of legal owner and,
    202, 203
  constructive trust and, 44
  contract and, 102, 103
  detriment, 116
  equitable, 111, 184
  "equitable lien", as, 120, 121,
    122, 123, 142
  expenditure of money and, 116
  family arrangements, in, 110
  lifetime occupation, 115, 117
    settlement, as, 118–19, 187–8
  loan and, 121
  personal representatives,
    where estate insolvent, 143,
      144, 145
    where estate solvent, 142, 143

Estoppel—*cont.*
  promissory, 111
  proprietary, 111, 112
  protecting occupation by, 114,
    120
  transferability, 119
  transmissibility on death, 145
Executors,
  duties of, 130
  See also Personal
    Representatives, Testate
    Succession.
Express Trusts, 28, 43, 44
  declaration of, 41, 42, 43, 47,
    50
    equity of redemption, of, 51,
      52
    third parties and, 28
    valuation of shares, 51
    writing, evidenced in, 28, 51
  fixed shares under, 28, 29, 68
  joint power of revocation, 29
  right to specific performance of
    contract for sale of land, 50
  valuation of shares, 47, 49, 51
  house in joint names, 50

Families,
  state intervention and, 22
Family Allowances, 22
Family Home 6, 96, 115
  See also Matrimonial Home.
  domestic violence jurisdiction,
    86
  occupation and ownership
    rights, 87
Family Law, 20
  ideology of modern, 22
  Property Law and, 22, 23

Gift, 51n.
  See also Presumption of
    Advancement.
Grant,
  licence and, 98
Ground Rent, 2, 14

Home-ownership. *See*
  Owner-Occupation.
House Building,
  government support of, 5
  local authorities, by, 5
  renting, for, 1
  sale, for, 3

Implied Trusts, 44, 137, 154, 206
  See also Constructive Trusts *and*
    Resulting Trusts.
Income Tax,
  mortgage repayments and, 9
Inheritance,
  statutory protection of
    dependents' occupation, 148
  statutory provision for, 81n.,
    145–148
Insolvency, 194, 209
  See also Bankruptcy.
Instalment Mortgage, 1, 8, 35, 48,
    55
  importance of, 12
  tax and, 9
Insurance Companies,
  loan finance, and, 6
Intestate Succession. *See* Debt,
    Inheritance—statutory
    provision for *and* Personal
    Representatives.
  chattels, 131–3
  "matrimonial home," 133, 134
  mortgage debts, 134
  procedure, 129, 130
  realty/personalty distinction, 18,
    92
  rules of distribution, 131, 132,
    133, 136
  spouses rights on, 132, 133
Ius accrescendi. See Joint
    Tenancy—right of
    survivorship.

Joint Bank Accounts, 166
Joint Tenancies, 28, 88
  See also Trust for Sale.

Joint Tenancies—*cont*.
  equitable, 47
  implied trusts and, 137
  occupation rents, 71
  receipts for rents and profits, 89
  right of survivorship, 135–9
  severance, 67, 136–9
Judicature Acts, 81, 100

Land Law Reform,
  family home, and, 14, 16
  objectives of, 16, 18
  political controversy, 16, 17
  settlements and, 16, 17, 185
  solicitors' conveyancing
    monopoly, 17
  tenancy in common, and, 16,
    17, 18
Landlord and Tenant, 113, 114
  See also Lease.
Landownership,
  private,
    attacks on, through fiscal
      policy, 17
    political power, and, 17
Law Commission,
  co-ownership proposals, 26, 47,
    84
  registration proposals, 84, 85,
    175, 176, 177
Lawyers,
  "drudgery relief," 19
Lease, 99
  short term, 2
Leasehold,
  Capital Transfer Tax and, 135
Legal Aid,
  divorce, for, 21
Licences, 80, 96, 97, 178
  ancillary to grant,
    revocability of, 99, 100
  bare, 100, 105, 140
  contractual, 98, 99, 103, 106,
    145, 184, 188
    bankruptcy of legal owner
      and, 199, 201

Licences—*cont.*
  contractual—*cont.*
    consideration, 107, 142
    death of licensor, effect of,
      140, 141
    duration of, 103, 104
    exclusive possession, 101, 102
  effect of death of licensee, 141
  equitable,
    bankruptcy of legal owner
      and, 202
  equitable interest, as, 183
  estoppel, by, 110
  family arrangements, and, 101,
    106, 107, 110
  grant, and, 97, 98, 99, 100
  importance of contract/property
    distinction, 191, 192
  intention to create legal
    relations, 102
  mere. *See* Licence—bare.
  remedy, as a, 97, 101, 104
  revocability, 99, 100, 101
  seal, under, 100, 101
  traditional view of, 96, 97
Licensee,
  contractual,
    bankruptcy of, 204
    protection of occupation of,
      104
    control over dealings, 108
    injunctions against licensor,
      109, 181
    remedies against purchaser,
      110
  death of bare, 141
  death of contractual, 141, 142
  proprietary interest of, 99, 105
  protection of occupation of,
    doctrine of notice and, 185,
      186
  remedies against licensor,
    injunction and, 182
Licensor,
  death of, 140–141
Life Insurance, 134

Life Interest,
  protection of occupation by, 87,
    88, 183

Magistrates' Courts,
  domestic violence jurisdiction,
    restricted to spouses, 86
  matrimonial jurisdiction,
    maintenance, 22, 88
Marriage Settlements, 33n.
  divorce and, 20
Married Women,
  property rights in the nineteenth
    century, 26, 34n.
Matrimonial Home, 131
  co-ownership, proposals for, 84, 85
    control over dealing in, 84, 85
    third parties, 84, 85, 176
  duty of husband to provide, 81
  intestacy, 130
  occupation rights. *See* Beneficial
    Interests, Deserted Wife's
    Equity, Family Home.
    bankruptcy and, 84
    common law, under, 80
    marriage, during, 82
    protection after divorce, 85
    protection by registration, 83,
      84, 158, 159
Mortgage Arrears, 212, 213, 214
  spouses and, 215
Mortgagees, 28
  See also Creditors.
  Building Societies as, valuation
    of trust shares and, 51
  charge of, 49
    priorities between beneficial
      interest and, 51, 52, 159,
      160, 161–3, 165–7, 173–4,
      175
    priorities of licensees and, 181
  first,
    acquisition of good security
      by, 167
    obtaining of beneficiaries'
      consents by, 168, 169

Mortgagees—*cont.*
joint,
  presumption of tenancy in common, 137
rights on death of mortgagor, 134, 135
right to possession, 213, 214, 215
sale by, 212, 213
  beneficiaries behind trusts and, 216
  estoppel interests and, 217
  licensee, 216, 217
second,
  obtaining of beneficiaries' consents by, 168

Mortgages, 1, 5, 11, 23, 61
See also Endowment Mortgage *and* Instalment Mortgage.
capital repayment, 1, 8, 49
interest rates and, 8
legal, 144
registered interests and, 157, 158
second, 51, 168
trusts of, 153
unregistered conveyancing and, 165, 166
valuation of beneficial interests and, 52, 53, 54, 55, 56, 60, 61, 69, 70
  fluctuations in interest rates, 55, 60, 70
  tax relief on interest, 55

Occupation Rents, 2, 14, 71, 72, 86, 89
Official Receiver, 195
See also Trustee in Bankruptcy.
Overreaching, 18, 167, 170–5
Owner-Occupation, 1, 3, 4, 5
See also Building Societies —encouragement of owner-occupation.
conveyancing reform and, 18, 19

Owner-Occupation—*cont.*
distinguished from renting, 11
family law and, 20
government encouragement of, 6, 9, 10, 11
increase in, 34, 80
property adjustment on divorce and, 21
significance of, 11, 12
the 1925 Code and, 18
valuation of beneficial interests, 48

Part Performance, 112, 113, 189, 190
Partnership Property, 154
presumption of tenancy in common, 137
Personal Representatives,
application to sell property, by, 139, 144
bound by an equity, 142, 202
duties of, 130, 134
where estate insolvent, 143, 144
where estate solvent, 142, 143
licensee, of, 142
licensor, of, 140, 141
Planning Controls, 3
Presumption of Advancement, 31, 34
basis of, 33
blood relationships and, 32
children and, 33, 34
modern conditions, and, 35, 44
rebuttable, 32
wives, 33, 34, 35
Primogeniture, 16, 17, 18
Private Acts of Parliament,
breaking settlements, for, 2, 15, 16
Private Renting, 11, 14, 21
building for, 1, 6
decline of, 3, 80
security of tenure, 3
Profit, 99
Public Health Regulation, 3

Receiver,
  appointment of, 211, 212
Registration, 84
  bona fide purchasers,
    proprietary estoppel, 187
  cautions, 83, 158
  charges, 210
  mortgagees, proprietary
    estoppel and, 188
  notices, 83, 158
  overriding interests and, 157,
    159, 161, 162, 175, 181, 182
  part performance and, 188, 189,
    190
  protection of beneficial interests
    by, 28, 157, 158
  purchasers, and, 155, 156, 158
  spouses' occupation rights, 83,
    84, 158, 159, 215
  two-trustee rule and, 174, 175
Rent,
  settlements of income from, 2,
    14, 15
    apportionment amongst
      family, 14
  See also Settlements—partible
    inheritance *and* Strict
    Settlements
  statutory control of, 3, 6
Resulting Trust, 43, 96, 120
  See also Presumption of
    Advancement.
  contributions, 44
    direct/indirect, 37, 38, 39, 43
    financial/non-financial
      distinction, 34
    improvements as, 36, 40, 41
  disputes between spouses, 34,
    35
    principle of equality, 35, 41
  intention, 36, 38, 40
    "actual common," 36, 41, 43
    valuation of shares and, 58
    "imputed common," 36, 37
  "interest consensus," 41, 42
  modern, 34, 35, 36, 44

Resulting Trust—*cont.*
  "money consensus," 41, 42, 43
  origins of, 29, 30
  purchase money, 30, 47
  valuation of shares, 47, 52

Secret Trusts, 51n.
Settlements,
  impartible inheritance. *See*
    Strict Settlements.
  inter vivos, 80
  partible inheritance, 15
    fragmentation of title under,
      16
    freehold or leasehold estate,
      of, 15
    personalty, of, 15
    power of the landed classes and,
      16
Severance. *See* Joint
    Tenancy—severance.
Social Security Law, 22
Solicitors,
  conveyancing monopoly of, 17
  fraudulent dealing with trust
    property, 154
Stamp Duty, 51n.
Statute of Frauds, 30, 31
Strict Settlements, 15, 155, 174
  charges in, as provision for
    family members, 15
  conveyancing difficulties, 15
  devolution through male line,
    15
  interest under,
    overriding, 188
  objectives of, 15
  reform of, 16, 17, 88
  tenancy in common under, 90
  tenant for life, 15, 16, 19, 118,
    119, 187, 188
    protection of occupation of,
      88, 184, 186

Tax,
  land values, 4

Tenancies, 97, 185, 186
  exclusive possession, 101
  licence and, 101
Tenancies at Will, 112
Tenancies in Common, 15, 18, 28
  as means of settling rents, 89
  death of one tenant under, 136
  equitable,
    implied trust, 137
    occupation rents, 71, 72
    occupation rights, 93, 94, 96
  legal estate, of, 17, 90, 136, 137
  occupation rights under, 88, 89,
    93, 94, 95, 96
  presumption of, 137
  receipts for rents and profits,
    89
  reform of, 17, 18
  use in strict settlements, 90
Tenants for Life. *See* Strict
  Settlements—tenant for life.
Testate Succession.
  See Executors, Inheritance,
    Personal Representatives
  bequests, 131
  devises, 131, 132
  legacies, 131, 132
  priority of claims, 131
  procedure, 130
  residuary estate, 131, 132
Testation,
  freedom of, 131, 132
Trustees,
  fiduciary obligations of, 89,
    91
  fraudulent dealings, 153, 154
  giving of good title by, 152
  See also Registration,
    Unregistered Land.
  sole trustee,
    protection of beneficiaries
      where, 157, 158
Trustees for Sale,
  application to sell by, 95
  need to obtain possession order
    95

Trustees in Bankruptcy, 195,
  211
  application to sell home, 197,
    198, 199, 201, 202
  bankrupts' contracts and, 199,
    200
  contractual licensees, and, 199,
    200, 204
  duties of, 196, 204, 205
  equitable licences and, 203
  estoppel and, 204
  land charges and, 83, 84
Trusts. *See* Beneficial Interest,
    Constructive Trusts, Express
    Trusts *and* Resulting Trusts.
  breach of, 84
  doctrine of notice and, 153, 157
  protection of beneficiaries, 18
  protection of purchasers, 18,
    152–5
  tenancy in common behind, 18
  valuation of shares,
    deposit, 48
    mortgage instalments, 48
Trusts for Sale, 90, 91
  bankruptcy and, 67, 197, 198
  beneficiary,
    bankruptcy of, 204
  beneficiaries' rights,
    election of, 92
    to object to sale, 94
    to occupy property under, 62,
      72
  Courts' discretion over, 62, 63
    family home and, 63, 64, 65,
      66, 68
  doctrine of conversion, 92
  duty of trustees to consult
    beneficiaries, 95
  estoppel to prevent sale under,
    67
  express requirement of
    beneficiaries' consent to
    sell under, 152, 155
  interests of children and, 66,
    68

Trusts for Sale—*cont.*
  intestacy, on, 92
  life interest under,
    protection of occupation by,
      88
  occupation under, 93, 96
  postponement of sale, 91,
    94
  purpose test, 63, 64, 66,
    67
  registrability of interests
    behind, 174
  statutory,
    consultation of beneficiaries,
      156
    importance of, 62, 91
  two trustee rule and, 155, 156

Unconscionability, 42, 43, 44, 45,
  46
  estoppel and, 111
Unjust Enrichment, 113, 114,
  183
Unregistered Land, 159
  bona fide purchasers,

Unregistered Land—*cont.*
  bona fide purchasers—*cont.*
    beneficial interests behind
      trusts and, 167, 168, 170,
      181
    doctrine of notice, 181
    personal/proprietary rights
      distinction, 181
    proprietary estoppel and, 187
  charges, 210
  Class F land charges, 83, 164,
    165
  difficulties of acquiring a good
    title, 167
  doctrine of notice, 165, 166, 167
  enquiries as to occupation, 165
  lis pendens, 164
  two trustee rule,
    fraud and, 172, 173
    protection of purchasers, 170
      good faith requirement,
        172
      "money or money's worth"
        requirement, 171
Use, 29, 30, 32